"Ireland's social and economic transformation in the second half of the twentieth century has been dramatic, exemplified by the fact that the population has almost doubled and we are now one of the wealthiest countries in Europe. *The Mandarin, the Musician and the Mage* makes a compelling case that the origins of this transformation lie in a Second Irish Revival that occurred in the late 1950s and 1960s and which had three remarkable men at its core: T.K. Whitaker, Sean Ó Riada and Thomas Kinsella."

– Kieran McGowan, Former Managing Director IDA Ireland and Chairman CRH plc

"The most interesting books are often written on the cusp of different disciplines. As Managing Director of Ireland's biggest Advertising Agency in the last quarter of the twentieth century John Fanning enjoyed a front row seat during Ireland's economic transformation and here he combines his business experience with literary and cultural insights to provide an original perspective on the country's extraordinary journey during the last sixty years."

– Declan Kiberd

The Mandarin, the Musician and the Mage

Reimagining Ireland

Volume 110

Edited by Dr Eamon Maher,
Technological University Dublin – Tallaght Campus

PETER LANG
Oxford • Bern • Berlin • Bruxelles • New York • Wien

The Mandarin, the Musician and the Mage

T. K. Whitaker, Seán Ó Riada, Thomas Kinsella and the Lessons of Ireland's Mid-Twentieth-Century Revival

John Fanning

PETER LANG
Oxford • Bern • Berlin • Bruxelles • New York • Wien

Bibliographic information published by Die Deutsche Nationalbibliothek. Die Deutsche Nationalbibliothek lists this publication in the Deutsche Nationalbibliografie; detailed bibliographic data is available on the Internet at http://dnb.d-nb.de.

A catalogue record for this book is available from the British Library.

Library of Congress Cataloging-in-Publication Data

Names: Fanning, John, 1944– author.
Title: The mandarin, the musician and the mage : T.K. Whitaker, Sean Ó Riada, Thomas Kinsella and the lessons of Ireland's mid-twentieth century revival / John Fanning.
Description: Oxford ; New York : Peter Lang, [2022] | Series: Reimagining Ireland, 1662-9094 ; vol no. 110 | Includes bibliographical references and index.
Identifiers: LCCN 2022003942 (print) | LCCN 2022003943 (ebook) | ISBN 9781800795990 (paperback) | ISBN 9781800796003 (ebook) | ISBN 9781800796010 (epub)
Subjects: LCSH: Ireland—History—1922- | Ireland—Civilization—20th century. | Ireland—Economic conditions—1949- | Ireland—Social conditions—20th century. | Whitaker, T. K., 1916-2017—Influence. | Ó Riada, Seán—Influence. | Kinsella, Thomas—Influence. | Ireland—Statistics. | Social indicators—Ireland. | Irish literature—20th century—History and criticism. | Music—Ireland—20th century—History and criticism.
Classification: LCC DA963 .F357 2022 (print) | LCC DA963 (ebook) | DDC 941.7082—dc23/eng/20220328
LC record available at https://lccn.loc.gov/2022003942
LC ebook record available at https://lccn.loc.gov/2022003943

Cover image: *After the long walk – Poolbeg Light*. By John Doherty.
Cover design by Peter Lang Ltd.

ISSN 1662-9094
ISBN 978-1-80079-599-0 (print)
ISBN 978-1-80079-600-3 (ePDF)
ISBN 978-1-80079-601-0 (ePub)

© Peter Lang Group AG 2022

Published by Peter Lang Ltd, International Academic Publishers, Oxford, United Kingdom
oxford@peterlang.com, www.peterlang.com

John Fanning has asserted his right under the Copyright, Designs and Patents Act, 1988, to be identified as Author of this Work.

All rights reserved.
All parts of this publication are protected by copyright.
Any utilisation outside the strict limits of the copyright law,
without the permission of the publisher, is forbidden and liable to prosecution.
This applies in particular to reproductions, translations, microfilming,
and storage and processing in electronic retrieval systems.

This publication has been peer reviewed.

In memory of Kaye Fanning 1940–2020

Contents

List of Tables ... ix

Acknowledgements ... xi

Introduction ... 1

PART I The Contribution of Whitaker, Ó Riada and Kinsella to the Second Revival of the Mid-Twentieth Century ... 9

CHAPTER 1
How Three Young Irishmen Shouted 'Stop' in the 1950s ... 11

CHAPTER 2
T. K. Whitaker and the Second Revival ... 43

CHAPTER 3
Seán Ó Riada: Musical Regeneration ... 63

CHAPTER 4
Thomas Kinsella: The Poetic Muse ... 89

PART II Ireland 1956–2020: From Emigrants' to Immigrants' Remittances ... 123

CHAPTER 5
Ireland 1960–2020: Statistical Analysis of the Transformation ... 125

PART III The World in the 2020s and How Ireland Might
           Respond   147

CHAPTER 6
The Sceptics: Globalisation, Contents and Discontents   149

CHAPTER 7
The World from the Perspective of the 2020s   183

CHAPTER 8
Possible Lessons from the Mandarin, the Musician and the Mage
for a New Revival   207

Bibliography   237

Index   251

List of Tables

Table 1.	Population (Millions) 1841–2021	128
Table 2.	Life Expectancy at Birth 1950–2017	129
Table 3.	Women in the Labour Force (21st century)	130
Table 4.	Net Migration 2009–2021	130
Table 5.	Percentage of Adult Population Completing Third-Level Education 1960–2019	131
Table 6.	Constant GDP 1920–2020	132
Table 7.	Perception of EU Responsiveness to Interests of Members	137
Table 8.	Trust in the EU by Member States	138
Table 9.	Importance of Religion/Faith to Personal Identity	139
Table 10.	Changing Mores	140
Table 11.	Births Outside Marriage	140
Table 12.	Pride in Country	141

Acknowledgements

The genesis of this book was work carried out for a PhD, which was awarded from the School of English, Drama and Film in University College Dublin in November 2009. I would therefore firstly express my gratitude to my supervisor, Dr Catríona Clutterbuck, who was given the unenviable, some might say impossible, task of introducing a modicum of academic rigour to someone thoroughly absorbed, some might say contaminated, in the rough and rowdy ways of the advertising business for the previous forty years. I was also fortunate to have the support of other members of the College of Arts and Celtic Studies staff: Lucy Collins, P. J. Mathews and Frank McGuinness. I would also like to acknowledge the support I received from colleagues in the Smurfit Business School, Damien McLoughlin and Maeve Guthrie. I am particularly grateful to Laoighseach Ní Choistealbha for her patience, dedication and footnoting and formatting skills, and to the library staff in the UCD James Joyce Library, who were incredibly helpful in tracking down awkward source material. Particular thanks are due to Eamon Maher, the Editor of the Re-Imagining Ireland series, and Tony Mason, commissioning editor at Peter Lang, who skilfully guided me through the publishing process. I also benefitted from a personal technical support team: Margaret Gilsenan, Sean Mulkerrin, Martha Fanning and David Fanning. Finally, I have dedicated this book to my late wife Kaye, who was there for the book's long gestation but who sadly died before it came to fruition.

Introduction

This book is based on the premise that a Second Irish Revival took place during the period 1956–1966, that it shared many of the characteristics of the much commented on Celtic Revival from the late nineteenth to the early twentieth century, and that a critical element of the new revival was an active opening out to the rest of the world following three decades of withdrawal.

The Second Revival is examined through the lives of three men whose careers and personal lives crossed during these years. T. K. Whitaker was the architect of the economic plan that provided the main impetus to the economic growth which began in the 1960s. Seán Ó Riada's significant musical output transformed Irish traditional music, provided the country with some much-needed self-confidence and inspired numerous musical groups to export Irish music to every corner of the world. Thomas Kinsella ploughed a lonelier furrow, but his translations of ancient Irish literature performed a similar, albeit lower key, role to Ó Riada's.

Over sixty years ago, in 1956, a particularly draconian budget was introduced in an attempt to correct a severe imbalance in Ireland's finances. In the proceeding decades hundreds of thousands had fled the country, and a much commented on book from that period, *The Vanishing Irish*, predicted that Ireland was haemorrhaging people so fast that the country was in grave danger of imminent extinction:

> Nothing in recent centuries is so puzzling or so challenging as the strange phenomenon being enacted before our eyes: the fading away of the once great and populous nation of Ireland. If the past century's rate of decline continues for anther century, the Irish will virtually disappear as a nation.[1]

---

1   John A. O'Brien, *The Vanishing Irish: The Enigma of the Modern World* (London: W. H. Allen, 1954), 7.

But from the early 1950s groups of concerned citizens had been engaged in debate and discussion about alternative directions for the still newly independent state, directions which would secure its economic future and provide a more flourishing environment for its people. Among them were three men whose lives were curiously interconnected but worked in very different fields.

T. K. Whitaker had just been appointed the youngest ever Secretary of the Department of Finance at the age of thirty-nine. Seán Ó Riada and Thomas Kinsella, two promising young men in their twenties at the beginning of their artistic careers; best friends living in what used to be called 'digs' in a run-down capital city where signs of a nascent artistic revival was faintly visible. There was no possibility that their respective ambitions, music in the case of Ó Riada and poetry for Kinsella, could provide them with a living, so both were employed by the state, Ó Riada in the music department of RTÉ and Kinsella in the Department of Finance. The connection referred to above was that Kinsella was Whitaker's Private Secretary in that Department.

Although they worked in different disciplines and their careers took very different turns, the three men shared a number of important characteristics which had a profound influence on their subsequent careers. They were all notably self-confident at a time when self-confidence in Ireland was in short supply. They were intellectually gifted at a time when independent thinking was regarded with suspicion, and at a time when Ireland was emerging from a period of self-imposed hibernation from the rest of the world, and they were all determined to learn from the best of what the rest of the world had to offer in their chosen fields. Moreover, their deep knowledge of and intense attraction to the Irish language, history and cultural heritage meant that the experience they gained from the outside world was always mediated through a very strong Irish lens. It will be argued that the integration of an international with a national focus was critical to their work and would, be a critical factor in the transformation of the country from the mid-1950s to the early years of the twenty-first century and is of continuing, relevance as we confront an uncertain post-Great Recession post-COVID-19 world.

The Celtic Revival of the late nineteenth and early twentieth century has been analysed in depth in terms of its literary impact, but Mathews's influential examination of the period presents a much more rounded perspective, showing how it was a time of economic as well as cultural development.[2] It will be shown that, although the economic developments of the years 1956–1966 have been widely commented on, the parallel cultural output and intense questioning of existing orthodoxies have not been connected to date, and that when viewed together they justify the 'revival' appellation. The opening up of Ireland to the outside world, which was a key feature of the second revival, needs to be understood in the wider context of what is now referred to as 'globalisation'. It will be argued that the three men featured as exemplifying the second revival were all indebted to important global ideas and influences for their own careers, but that a critical factor in their success in widely different disciplines was an ability to filter these outside influences through a thorough knowledge and understanding of Irish history, heritage and culture.

Finally, as we prepare to cope with the formidable challenges facing small countries in the world of the 2020s, consideration will be given to whether the experiences and example of the three men might have some relevance for Ireland in the immediate future.

The book is divided into three parts. Part I will examine the contribution of Whitaker, Ó Riada and Kinsella to the second revival of the mid-twentieth century. Part II will describe the transformation of the country in the sixty-five years from 1956 to 2021 and Part III will consider whether we now need to consider the possibility of a new revival.

---

[2] P. J. Mathews, *Revival: The Abbey Theatre, Sinn Féin, the Gaelic League and the Co-Operative Movement* (Cork: Cork University Press/Field Day Publications, 2003).

Part I: The Contribution of Whitaker, Ó Riada and Kinsella to the Second Revival of the Mid-Twentieth Century

At a Conference in 2008 to mark the fiftieth anniversary of the publication of *Economic Development*, Frances Ruane noted:

> What was exceptional in the mid-1950s was that a group of civil servants and carefully selected others put into the public domain their considered view of the real problems that faced the Irish economy and identified the changes they thought were required.[3]

The economy responded almost immediately to the Plan, and the average annual growth in GDP during the 1960s was over 4 per cent, easily the highest of any decade since independence. Whitaker always emphasised the importance of psychology to economic development, and the first green shoots of economic growth were soon followed by greater cultural self-confidence, exemplified by the extraordinary reaction to Seán Ó Riada's theme music for the film *Mise Éire*. In the words of Thomas Kinsella, the music managed to 'startle the heart of a whole people,'[4] and throughout the 1960s there was a renewed interest in traditional Irish music, culminating in the 'most eagerly awaited gig in the history of Irish music',[5] *Ó Riada sa Gaiety*, in 1969. Meanwhile in the literary field Thomas Kinsella was engaged in a parallel exercise of cultural retrieval and transformation. His publishing career had begun in the early 1950s when, at the request of Liam Miller, who was bringing Irish publishing back to life with the Dolmen Press, he had undertaken the translation of a number of Old Irish poems, and this was to lead to his fifteen-year-long engagement with a new translation of Ireland's *Iliad*, *The Táin*. This restoration of what he referred to as 'part of the bedrock of our imagination'

---

[3] Frances Ruane, 'Resonances from Economic Development for Current Economic Policy-Making', Paper given at IPA Conference: *Economic Development 50 Years On*. Dublin Castle, November 2008, 2.

[4] Thomas Kinsella, *Fifteen Dead* (Dublin: Dolmen Press/Oxford University Press, 1979), 29.

[5] Philip King, Interview with the author, 1 April 2007.

was begun in the mid-1950s and completed in 1969, the year of the Gaiety concert, in an elegantly produced edition with specially commissioned illustrations by Louis le Brocquy.

Part I will describe how Whitaker carefully orchestrated the publication of his economic planning documents and will outline the highlights of his long public service career. It will also outline the highlights of Ó Riada's tragically short career but make the point that his influence since then has been out of all proportion to his musical output because of the wide range of subsequent music groups, from Horslips to Altan, from U2 to Riverdance, that drew much of their inspiration from his compositions.

Kinsella's contribution to the second revival will also be documented, and it will be argued here that his early translations and excavation of ancient Irish texts were a preparation for an as yet under-recognised, yet crucial, element of his contribution to national revival: the remarkable fifteen-year Jungian exploration of his immediate family history and the mythic origins of Ireland leading to his self-defining line; 'and I always remembered who and what I am'.[6] It will be shown that Kinsella's Jungian period was facilitated by his exposure to American poets such as Ezra Pound, William Carlos Williams and Robert Lowell, which was heightened in the mid-1960s when he began to divide his time between Ireland and the US. Similar connections between local and global will be traced in the careers of the other two men.

Whitaker's interest in the success of French economic planning in the 1950s influenced his own economic thinking, and Ó Riada's early involvement with jazz was a factor in the way his traditional music ensemble Ceoltóirí Chualann presented solo players who remained soloists while also playing together.

---

6   Thomas Kinsella, *Collected Poems* (Winston-Salem: Wake Forest University Press, 2006), 263.

Part II: Ireland 1956–2020: From Emigrants' to Immigrants' Remittances

The second Part of the book will compare Ireland in 1956 and 2020 using a range of statistics and survey research data under a number of headings: demographic, economic, educational, religious observance, life satisfaction and well-being, attitudes to identity, the EU and globalisation. The results will show a transformed society, the most dramatic manifestation being the recent announcement by the CSO that the population had passed 5 million for the first time in 170 years and was now almost double the number in the mid-1950s.

However, the opening up of Ireland to the world has always attracted critics. The criticisms, from outright opposition to the strategy of attracting overseas investment to the contention that economic success has resulted in the loss of a distinctive national identity will be assessed, but it will be argued that although they make many telling points, especially in relation to the continuing high levels of inequality, they don't give enough credit for the undoubted improvements created by economic growth. The point will also be made that too many of their criticisms focus on issues which could be considered to be the inevitable consequences of modernity.

Globalisation lies at the heart of this dilemma, and Part II will also examine the extensive literature of globalisation in the 1980s and 1990s and conclude that in spite of the problems it poses for small countries the wisest course of action is to accept its reality while being mindful of the threats it can pose:

> Globalisation could in a very short time wipe out the ecological and cultural diversity that took millions of years of human and biological effort to produce; countries need to develop sufficiently strong cultural and environmental filters so that they can interact with the electronic herd (international capital markets), without being so overwhelmed by it so that it turns their culture into a global mush and their environment into a global mash.[7]

---

7 Thomas L. Friedman, *The Lexus and the Olive Tree* (London: Harper Collins, 1999), 221.

A case will be made for the fact that Ireland did indeed manage to develop 'strong cultural and environmental filters'. It will be argued that globalisation enhances rather than diminishes the role of the nation state, and that the careers and achievements of Whitaker, Ó Riada and Kinsella show how these 'filters' can be put in place.

Part III: The World in the 2020s and How Ireland Might Respond

The transformation of Ireland from 1956 to 2020 is now in danger of being undermined by the world economic crisis that began with the financial market crash in 2008, continued through the years of austerity and which is now compounded by the effects of the COVID-19 pandemic. The fall-out from the resulting economic uncertainty has created additional tensions from the undermining of faith in democracy to increasing inequality created by lightly regulated capitalism and to unease resulting from our constant surveillance by ungovernable all-powerful tech corporations. Looming over all this is our growing awareness of the possibility of planetary extinction and a world war between America and China, which some believe has already begun.

It will be argued that against this backdrop Ireland fared comparatively well. Although one of the worst hit by the 2008 recession and resulting austerity, the Irish economy recovered surprisingly quickly and managed to do so with its citizens' faith in democracy more or less intact. However, as a small open economy, we are never immune to global forces, and if we were to absorb the lessons of previous revivals, we would encourage another round of debate and discussion on how to navigate in the uncertain world that lies ahead.

In keeping with the spirit of the three men at the heart of this book, I've suggested three themes for this debate: *fiosracht*, representing intellectual curiosity; *meitheal*, representing community spirit and active citizenship; and *dinnseanchas*, representing knowledge of local history and traditions.

Under *Fiosracht* I will discuss the lack of long-term strategic thinking and discussion of alternative visions and futures which has often been noted as characterising Irish policy-making. Under the *Meitheal* heading I will discuss the need to ensure a strong commitment to democratic values and practices which are being undermined in the modern world and which require continual re-energising. In this context, I will suggest that we may have much to learn from the philosophy of civic republicanism in combatting the current democratic deficit. Our own sense of self and our place in the world is also under threat from the constant bombardment of global media and digital platforms, and we need to continually renew our *Dinnseanchas* credentials, cultivating the lure and lore of our cultural traditions and heritage. Kinsella's line 'and I always remembered who and what I was', is a continual presence throughout this book, emphasising one of the critical lessons from the three protagonists: success in a competitive global world is enhanced by strong local roots.

PART I

The Contribution of Whitaker, Ó Riada and Kinsella to the
Second Revival of the Mid-Twentieth Century

CHAPTER I

How Three Young Irishmen Shouted 'Stop' in the 1950s

Introduction: The State of the Nation in 1956

As we reach the coming of age of the twenty-first century, Ireland is one of the wealthiest countries on the planet and appears relatively comfortable and confident as a nation. The contrast with the Ireland of sixty years ago could not be more marked. Then a people utterly lacking in self-confidence were deserting a failed society in droves. The 1950s was the lowest point in four successive decades of economic failure, a decade in which three out of every four people born between 1931 and 1941 emigrated. Even more damaging was the fact that not all of the emigration was involuntary; many emigrated not out of necessity, that is, for lack of a job, but to escape a sense of bleak despair about Ireland's future.

In spite of the generous protection afforded by a high tariff wall around the newly independent country, native entrepreneurs had failed to emerge in sufficient numbers, and the political and professional establishment at the time offered little leadership. In fact, their attitude to the scourge of emigration bordered on the cynically complacent. The report of the Commission on Emigration, which in spite of the urgency of the problem managed to deliberate for six years, from 1948 to 1954, contained the following conclusion: 'High emigration, granted a population excess, releases social tensions which would otherwise explode, and makes possible a stability of manners and customs which would otherwise be the subject of radical change.'[1] However harsh this may appear, it was positively benign compared to the statement attributed to

1 Joseph J. Lee, *Ireland 1912–1985: Politics and Society* (Cambridge: Cambridge

the Minister for Industry and Commerce, Patrick McGilligan, in 1927: 'It is not the function of Government to provide work for everyone, people may have to die in this country and die through starvation.'[2]

If the 1950s represented the lowest point for Ireland in the twentieth century, 1956 was the lowest point in that decade, and budget day, 14 May, was the lowest point of that year. The budget details announced by Minister of Finance Gerard Sweetman included massive tax hikes for cigarettes, petrol, betting, dances, matches and table waters. I remember listening to the radio at home at the time, and even as a child I sensed the air of foreboding. The wonders of bottled water hadn't reached our house, and possibly our shores, so I asked my mother what 'table waters' meant. 'It means no more lemonade for you', she shot back in uncharacteristically sharp tones. I kept my trap shut for the rest of the day.

The standard economic indices were all in place in Ireland at the time, and data on unemployment, inflation, imports, exports and GNP growth rates were readily available, but a striking feature of many of the commentaries on the period is the emphasis on the psychological trauma involved – an area where measurement is not so readily available. Nevertheless, there are frequent references to mental as well as physical deprivation, and a recurring theme is the nagging suspicion that the struggle for independence which had absorbed so much of the energies and lives of a previous generation had been in vain, which in turn led to the unmentionable fear that the Irish weren't up to it, unable to provide a decent standard of living for themselves and to compete with the rest of the world:

> ... the years 1955–56 had plumbed the depths of hopelessness. One of the recurring balance-of-payments crises was overcome but only at the cost of stagnation, high unemployment, and emigration. The mood of despondency was palpable. Something had to be done or the achievement of national independence would prove to have been a futility. Various attempts were made to shine a beam forward in this dark night of the soul.[3]

University Press, 1989), 381.

2   Patrick McGilligan, Quoted in Paul Sweeney, *The Celtic Tiger: Ireland's Continuing Economic Miracle*. 2nd edn (Oxford: Oak Tree Press, 1999), 31.

3   Thomas Kenneth Whitaker, *Protectionism or Free Trade: The Final Battle* (Dublin: IPA Publications, 2006), 8.

John Banville, who was aged eleven in 1956, remembers hearing the grim news of redundancies in Pierce's Foundry in Wexford:

> The weekly exodus of redundant workers from Pierce's Foundry was echoed on a national scale in the waves of emigrants leaving for England and America. I recall very clearly a blustery spring in Rosslare Harbour where I had gone to see off a relative who was going for a holiday in England. There they were, the crowds of awkward lost young men with their cardboard suitcases heading for the building sites of places with cruel-sounding names: Hackney, Wolverhampton, Liverpool, the Bronx. Many years later at the very end of the Sixties, when I was living in London, I would see them again, these same men, grown older and harder, but still awkward, still lost, playing mournful two-man games of hurling in Hyde Park on summer Sunday mornings.[4]

Years later Thomas Kinsella, who was working in the Department of Finance at the time, also captured the mood in a poem, appropriately titled '1956':

> A couple of hundred yards around the corner
> in a moon-flooded office in Merrion Street
> my Finance files dreamed
> propped at the ledge
> my desk moved
> infinitesimally
> Over the entire country
> over market and harbour in silvery light
> A small herd of friends
> stared back from the Mailboat
> a mongrel dog lapped
> in a deserted town square. (*CP* 198)[5]

Professor Joe Lee's influential history of twentieth-century Ireland is even more damning: 'The source of the bleakness must be sought more in the inertia of the indigenes than in the niggardliness of nature.'[6] Limerick

---

4 John Banville, 'The Island of de Valera and O'Faolain', *The Irish Review* 17/18 Winter (1995), 143.
5 Thomas Kinsella, *Collected Poems: 1956–2001* (Manchester: Carcanet Press, 1979), 20.
6 Lee, *Ireland 1912–1985*, 523.

poet Desmond O'Grady, writing about the 1950s, most accurately caught the mood of the time:

> The voice on the radio – remote, unmelodic – gives news of events
> And things that are happening – urban expansion rural improvements
> Revolutions and riots, social reforms and new intellectual movements
> In lands with more future than this one presents.
>
> In the lanes and the archways the children are few, the lovers fewer still
> And those who are left have plans and intentions of joining the rest
> On emigrant tickets. In the streets there is no one but old men and widows cursed
> With sorry separation and a broken will.[7]

It was a sad end to the national ideal of a self-contained, self-sufficient, predominantly rural enclave memorably articulated in the famous St Patrick's Day radio broadcast by the then Taoiseach, Eamon de Valera, which, as Clair Wills has noted, attracted a high level of popular support: 'His dream reflected a widespread belief that the integrity of Irish existence should be defended against the commercial, industrial and cosmopolitan life of modern society.'[8] By the mid-1950s that dream had been shattered by harsh economic reality, as Diarmaid Ferriter has rightly observed: 'Economic malaise was cutting away Irish confidence like a cancer.'[9]

There have been some recent attempts to present the post-independence decades in a more favourable light. For example, Brian Fallon argues that the late twentieth-century demonisation of the period was unfair: 'The accepted picture of a culturally chauvinistic statelet shutting its doors and windows on international currents, turns out, in several respects to be almost the reverse of the truth.' But although Fallon makes a spirited defence of the cultural output of the period, he is eventually forced to concede that

---

7   Desmond O'Grady, *The Headgear of the Tribe* (Oldcastle: Gallery Press, 1979), 20.
8   Clair Wills, *That Neutral Isle: A Critical History of Ireland during the Second World War* (London: Faber & Faber, 2007), 28.
9   Diarmaid Ferriter, *The Transformation of Ireland 1900–2000* (London: Profile Books, 2004), 463.

> undoubtedly there is a specific intellectual malaise underlying this milieu, a sense of frustration which was partly the outcome of disappointed and perhaps exaggerated hopes for what independence might achieve, partly an exasperation created by censorship, by economic failure and lack of opportunity, and by native muddle and an inbred oddity and eccentricity which seemed to be woven into the texture of Irish life.[10]

Joe Cleary attempts to redress the balance between demonising the pre-1960s and valorising the later part of the century: 'Contemporary Ireland in short may have escaped the crises of the autarkic capitalism of "de Valera's Ireland" but the new neo-liberal version it has embraced has its own structural crises in abundance.'[11] This book will be discussing those 'structural crises' later, but a point that should be made here is that whatever the real or imagined faults of contemporary Ireland they cannot be used to absolve the failures of the earlier period. Elmer Andrews, in his introduction to a series of essays on contemporary Irish poetry, summarises these failures:

> Ireland emerged in the 1950s blinking in the daylight to find that its post-war image of itself looked conspicuously out of place in the modern world. The traditional ideology of cultural nationalism, which enshrined the idea of a self-sufficient Catholic rural society dedicated to the re-unification of the island was seriously challenged by the pressures of modern life.[12]

Patrick Kavanagh, in his long poem *Lough Derg*, was more succinct when he wrote, 'All Ireland ... froze for want of Europe.'[13]

However, the truism that the darkest hour comes just before a new dawn was proven again in this mid-1950s crisis, and as often happens in Ireland, the harbinger of that dawn came from the sporting arena. Two months after that fateful budget, news filtered through to a beleaguered nation that a young Dubliner, Ronnie Delany, had won a gold medal at the

---

10 Brian Fallon, *An Age of Innocence: Irish Culture, 1930–1960* (Dublin: Gill & Macmillan, 1998), 11.
11 Joe Cleary, *Outrageous Fortune: Capital and Culture in Modern Ireland* (Dublin: Field Day Publications, 2007), 12.
12 Elmer Andrews, ed., *Contemporary Irish Poetry: A Collection of Critical Essays* (London: Palgrave Macmillan, 1992), 2.
13 Patrick Kavanagh, *Collected Poetry* (London: Allen Lane, 2004), 103.

Melbourne Olympics. It provided the present author with a vivid memory from that year. The news was announced to us in school by a hard-nosed Christian Brother. His pride in Delany's victory didn't surprise us given his ferocious patriotism, but the tears in his eyes as he explained that the 1500 metres was the single most important event in the whole of the Olympics made a deep impression on a somewhat startled group of twelve-year-olds. It was a harbinger of things to come. It signalled that we could compete after all on an international stage, and the three young intellectuals whose example is at the heart of this book – T. K. Whitaker, Seán Ó Riada and Thomas Kinsella – were determined to do just that.

The Economy Assumes Centre Stage

The mid-1950s Irish political and administrative establishment had lived with a protectionist strategy of self-sufficiency for so long that it was difficult for them to countenance any radical change. Economic development had never featured prominently in the traditional ideology of cultural nationalism; on the contrary, economics was treated with suspicion, and there were two somewhat contradictory assumptions about economic development:

1. Irish economic development had been deliberately subordinated to the interests of the wider British economic strategy for the last two hundred years, and therefore independence would enable us to solve most of our economic problems.
2. The Irish were a more spiritually minded people than the British, less obsessed with material goods and more interested in living life in preparation for the hereafter.

The first of these assumptions was a basic tenet of Irish nationalism:

> According to nationalist interpretation national sovereignty was a condition for economic development – and it was always claimed that British legislation blocked

Irish industrialisation in the 17th and 18th centuries, that Grattan's parliament created industrial growth in the late 18th century and that this was again stymied by the Act of Union throughout the 19th century.[14]

Ireland wasn't unique in this assumption or in this respect. Throughout the twentieth century, as many previously colonised nations gained independence, the initial euphoria was often followed by disenchantment, uncertainty and doubt – and in some cases violence. There were some signs of these tensions in the first decades of post-independence Ireland, but leading politicians managed to steer a steady course, keeping the fledgling democracy on the rails. The protectionist policy of self-sufficiency was designed to demonstrate how an independent Ireland freed at long last from a dependent relationship within the much larger British economy could flourish on its own. The budgetary crisis of 1956 was to prove the final undoing of this thinking.

The second assumption dated from the mid-to-late nineteenth century, when nation construction was at its height and smaller countries dominated by bigger neighbours tended to position themselves as the antithesis of the values and ambitions of that bigger power. So if Britain was practical, rational, materialistic and hard-headed, Ireland was emotional, artistic, spiritual and other-worldly:

> ... through many centuries Ireland was pressed into service as a foil to set off English virtues, as a laboratory in which to conduct experiments, and as a fantasy land in which to meet fairies and monsters ... during the 19th century the image of Ireland as non-English was at its height, if John Bull was industrious and reliable, Paddy was held to be indolent and contrary, if the English were adult and manly, the Irish must be childish and feminine.[15]

A fairly obvious corollary of these stereotypes is that the values attributed to the English were very business-like, while those attributed to the Irish were decidedly not. Kerby Miller, in his wide-ranging study of Irish emigration in the nineteenth century, has tried to present a more

---

14 Lars Mjøset, *The Irish Economy in a Contemporary Institutional Perspective* (Dublin: NESC Report, 1992), 238.
15 Declan Kiberd, *Inventing Ireland* (London: Jonathan Cape, 1995), 1.

reasoned analysis of the Irish lack of commercial success by suggesting that it was due to a combination of the ethos of the Catholic Church, the Irish language and, somewhat bizarrely, the Irish weather. Miller makes the case that Irish Catholicism's worldview was the exact opposite of Weber's Protestant ethic; it was 'hierarchical, communal, familial, and traditional – each quality diminishing the individual's importance in relation to society as a whole – and severely limited the scope for self-regeneration through reason'.[16] He goes on to blame the semantic structure of the Irish language for reinforcing a culture of dependence and passivity, and argues that the unpredictability of the weather made any form of planning, an essential pre-requisite for business, an impossibility. He concludes that 'their outlook on life remained basically passive, fatalistic and non-responsible'.[17]

It is generally assumed that the architects of the Celtic Revival at the end of the nineteenth century sought to make a virtue out of the assumed attributes of Irish identity, and in doing so pointed out the defects of the opposite British worldview:

> Archaic, peasant but spiritual Ireland versus modern, urban and materialist Britain became an article of faith among the literary revivalists – the Irish countryman would never fall victim to the utilitarian materialism which the unfortunate Englishman [was prone to] because his racial memory, imagination, even his very landscape, were saturated with the ethos of an alternative and ancient world.[18]

W. B. Yeats was the most articulate exponent of this vision: 'At this stage his imagined Ireland was destined to do spiritual warfare against an unholy trinity of British materialism, middle class mass culture and orthodox Christianity that rendered the modern world ugly and accordingly in desperate need of a cleansing renewal.'[19] This anti-materialist, anti-modern

---

16   Kerby A. Miller, *Emigrants and Exiles: Ireland and the Irish Exodus to North America* (Oxford: Oxford University Press, 1985), 114.
17   Ibid., 132.
18   George J. Watson, *Irish Identity and the Irish Literary Revival* (Washington, DC: The Catholic University Press of America, 1979), 97.
19   Joe Cleary and Claire Connolly, eds, *The Cambridge Companion to Modern Irish Culture* (Cambridge: Cambridge University Press, 2005), 12.

vision was cemented into the rubric of the newly independent state by an extraordinary and unlikely alliance between Yeats's pre-independence ideas and those of the two dominant leaders of the post-independence new state: Éamon de Valera and John Charles McQuaid.

For somewhat different reasons, de Valera and McQuaid wanted to clearly distinguish Ireland from Britain. Both were committed to a rural rather than an urban ethos, the former because his support base was strongest among small farmers, the latter because the wealthier farm households were the main supply line for future clerics. In their different ways, both were anti-materialistic, and it could be argued that both were more committed to a strongly devotional-based form of Irish Catholicism than to a more orthodox Christianity. Behind suitably ascetic exteriors both men were intensely ambitious and were conscious of the scale of their respective visions for the new state, as seen here in de Valera's opinion of 'the Irish genius':

> The Irish genius has always stressed spiritual and intellectual rather than material values. It is these characteristics that fit the Irish people in a special manner for the task, now a vital one, of helping western civilisation. The great material progress of recent times, coming in a world where false philosophy already reigns, has distorted men's sense of proportion.[20]

The fact that this ambitious vision for the country comes from the political rather than the religious leader is indicative of the lack of sympathy for a business culture that prevailed during the early decades following independence. Bhreathnach-Lynch summarised the official positioning of the newly independent country:

> In the decades of Free State government Ireland's overwhelming desire to envision itself as uniquely different from its erstwhile ruler, Great Britain, led to the construction of a national identity: the new nation was to be viewed as a pure unitary race, rural based, Irish-speaking and Roman Catholic.[21]

20 Michele Dowling, 'The Ireland that I would have: De Valera and the Creation of an Irish National Image', *History Ireland* 2/5 (Summer 1997), 39.
21 Síghle Bhreathnach-Lynch, *Ireland's Art, Ireland's History: Representing History 1845 to Present* (Omaha: Creighton University Press, 2007), 73.

But not everyone was convinced, particularly with the notion of a lack of material values. Commenting on the period, Lee argued that there was no evidence that the Irish were less material than anyone else: 'If their values be deemed spiritual then spirituality must be defined as covetousness tempered only by sloth.'[22] Miller is even more damning: 'The notion of "Holy Ireland" was merely a rhetorical cloak woven of medieval dogmas and Victorian pieties masking a petty bourgeois society whose vaunted stability and sacralised family farm both mandated and depended on constant emigration by the disinherited and dispossessed.'[23] Liam de Paor has stated bluntly that the 'official' vision was always flawed, 'both as a perception of what is essentially Irish about Ireland and as an objective of political action', and goes on to pronounce it dead by the late 1950s:

> The vision came to grief politically in Ireland largely on the simple failure to provide employment and on the consequent scandal of mass emigration. Sean Lemass who succeeded de Valera in 1959 told us to forget the Poor Old Woman lamenting over her fourth green field and look forward to the bright future offered by the modern world.[24]

P. J. Mathews, in his re-interpretation of the first revival, takes the years 1899–1905 as his central focus.[25] In suggesting that a second revival took place in the middle of the twentieth century, the present study concentrates on the years 1958–1963, following Terence Brown's identification of the transformative changes in Irish society kick-started in 1958 by the publication of Whitaker's *Economic Development*:

> In the collective memory 1958–1963 is seen as the period when a new kind of Ireland began to come to life. Most associate the success of those years with a renewed national self-confidence that continues to sustain the country even in its present vicissitudes.[26]

---

22   Lee, *Ireland 1912–1985*, 522.
23   Miller, *Emigrants and Exiles*, 103.
24   Liam de Paor, 'Ireland's Identities', *The Crane Bag* 3/1 (The Question of Tradition: 1979), 23–24.
25   Mathews, *Revival*.
26   Terence Brown, *Ireland: A Social and Cultural History 1922–2002* (New York: Harper Perennial, 2004), 229.

The Genesis and Ideology of the Second Revival

If the publication of *Economic Development* in 1958 represented the start of the second revival, it was immediately followed by a number of important changes in Irish life which facilitated the thinking that is an essential component in any such new beginning. In 1959, the transfer of power from de Valera to Lemass marked a significant change in ideology. Although a veteran of the War of Independence, Lemass was a pragmatist and a moderniser; it was under his auspices that Whitaker's initiative was launched, and were it not for his support, it is difficult to imagine this development would have happened at all. It was under his leadership that a group of able, ambitious and energetic younger men were promoted to positions of power in the ruling party. The three most prominent, Charles Haughey, Donogh O'Malley and George Colley were to prove controversial figures; they were eager for change and were more comfortable with the world of business and commerce than their predecessors. In 1960, the election of John F. Kennedy to the White House was to prove a massive boost to Irish self-confidence. It wasn't just that the first direct descendent of Irish Catholic immigrants had been elected to the most powerful political position in the world; Kennedy also brought style, swagger and sophistication to the Presidency. In 1961 the launch of Teilifís Éireann represented a further loosening up of Irish society. The initial overseas programming opened a window to the outside world, while home-produced programmes like the *Late Late Show* facilitated a more open relationship with, and between, the Irish themselves. In 1962, Vatican II was established by another innovative world leader and its recommendations were to have far-reaching implications for the deeply conservative Irish Church. That year was also marked by the publication of the *Dolmen Miscellany of New Irish Writing*, which featured work by a wide range of new writers including John McGahern, John Montague, Richard Murphy, Pearse Hutchinson, Brian Moore and Thomas Kinsella. In his recent collection of interviews with Dennis O'Driscoll, Seamus Heaney recalls the impact this publication made on him at the time:

> I got my hands on a copy of the *Miscellany* very early on. It was a marvellous thing to behold-and to hold – the paper so heavy, the printing so obviously letterpress, the sense of respect and achievement endorsed in the actual fabric of the volume. It marked a moment – it changed the game; it secured the ground. The work it carried told readers and young writers that cultural and artistic maturity had arrived in the land for good.[27]

A breakthrough in Irish traditional music came in 1959 with the launch of the film *Mise Éire*, accompanied by a dramatic music score by Seán Ó Riada; 'one man in particular responded to the challenge presented to Irish music by the twentieth century. His name was Seán Ó Riada. He was a man for all seasons; a composer classically trained in the art music of Europe who immersed himself in the oral music tradition of Ireland.'[28] There were also important developments in Irish theatre, in particular the first productions of Tom Murphy's *Whistle in the Dark* (1961) and Brian Friel's *Philadelphia, Here I Come!* (1964). It can be argued that both these plays followed the Whitaker/Lemass initiative, in that they broke new ground in Irish theatre by confronting some of the darker realities of Irish life and identified Ireland as 'a claustrophobically closed society with people as estranged from their environment as the most alienated of industrialised city-dwellers'.[29]

But the events of the late 1950s and early 1960s took place against a backdrop of debate, discussion and increasing intellectual curiosity that had been simmering since the early 1950s, often taking a lead from articles in a number of influential periodicals like the long-established *Studies* and the more recent *Administration*.

If the political and administrative establishment had lived with the protectionist strategy of self-sufficiency for so long that it was difficult for them to countenance radical change, even before the budget crisis of 1956, a number of younger civil servants and academics had come to the

---

27   Dennis O'Driscoll, *Stepping Stones: Interviews with Seamus Heaney* (London: Faber & Faber, 2008), 51–52.
28   Nuala O'Connor, *Bringing it All Back Home: The Influence of Irish Music.* (London: BBC Books, 1991), 91.
29   Nicholas Grene, *The Politics of Irish Drama* (Cambridge: Cambridge University Press, 1999), 212.

conclusion that new thinking was required. The leading members of this group were the civil servants Ken Whitaker and Tom Barrington, the UCD economists Patrick Lynch and Garret FitzGerald and two young UCD legal graduates, Donal Barrington (Tom's younger brother) and Paddy Kilroy. The civil servants had to be cautious, but the two periodicals mentioned above, *Studies* and *Administration*, provided ideal cover for the dissemination of their ideas because of the impeccable credentials of these publications. *Studies* was a critical and literary magazine in continuous publication since 1912 by the Irish Jesuits, while *Administration* was a journal dealing with Irish public sector issues, in continuous publication since 1952 by the Institute of Public Administration. Whitaker and Lynch were interested in French economic planning, which had attracted widespread comment in the 1950s because the more interventionist approach associated with traditional French dirigisme appeared to have been successful. Bryan Fanning, reviewing the role of Irish literary journals, argues that:

> *Studies* championed and prepared the ground for T. K. Whitaker's *Economic Development*. It gave a platform to Patrick Lynch to argue for Keynesian planning and offered reassurances about growing state activism. *Studies* published a number of seminal articles advocating an economic development role for the state.[30]

Lynch's 1953 article in *Studies*, 'The Economist and Public Policy', was an important contribution to the debate, arguing against the views of F. A. Hayek, the author of the virulently anti-planning manifesto *The Road to Serfdom*, Lynch's argument was that government intervention was the only remedy for Ireland's economic woes.[31]

The role of the journal *Administration* was even more interesting. The magazine began in the early 1950s as an outlet for concerned civil servants and academics. Barrington became editor without being named as such, and the first three issues carried a secrecy notice to the effect that 'no public reference to its existence could be made'. Fanning also quotes a

---

30   Bryan Fanning, *The Quest for Modern Ireland: The Battle for Ideas 1912–1986* (Newbridge: Irish Academic Press, 2008), 138.
31   Patrick Lynch, 'The Economist and Public Policy', *Studies: An Irish Quarterly Review* 42/167 (Autumn 1953), 241–274.

subsequent account of the founding of *Administration* as a time of 'studied disenchantment that had been distilled into a spirit of biting cynicism'.[32]

The closely knit interconnections between the new generation of emerging leaders in the civil service, academia, business and the professions is shown by the fact that one of the main instigators behind the formation of an influential discussion group, Tuairim, was a rising young barrister: Donal Barrington. Tuairim, the Gaelic for 'opinion', played an important role in the second revival, and was described in 1954 as 'an association of people who are interested in ideas and are not afraid of discussing them'.[33] The notion that people would be 'afraid' of discussing ideas may seem quaint now, but in 1950s Ireland ideas were assumed to be the preserve of the Catholic Church and the ruling political parties. But by the mid-1950s there was a feeling that social changes were on the way, as even the all-powerful Church was showing signs of weakness:

> In October 1955 over 21,000 soccer supporters defied John Charles McQuaid's instruction not to attend a soccer match between Yugoslavia and Ireland. Many were incensed at McQuaid's perceived bullying of the Football Association of Ireland and there was a feeling that he had overstepped the mark.[34]

Tom Garvin has suggested that the power of the Church had already been undermined by the 'Mother and Child' controversy earlier in the same decade:

> The Mother and Child affair in 1951 was a major cultural event which altered permanently many Irish people's quiet acceptance of the overweening political claims of the Catholic Church.[35]

Before concentrating on the central practical and exemplary roles of Whitaker, Ó Riada and Kinsella in the second revival, it is necessary to

---

32 Fanning, *The Quest for Modern Ireland*, 194.
33 Donal Barrington, Interview with author, 9 April 2009.
34 Ferriter, *The Transformation of Ireland*, 519
35 Tom Garvin, *Preventing the Future: Why Ireland was Poor for so Long* (Dublin: Gill & Macmillan, 2004), 92.

set the scene for their input with a brief outline of three separate developments which played a critical part in shaping that revival:

1. The role of Tuairim as the driving intellectual force of the second revival.
2. A new 'self-help' movement, similar in nature to some of the initiatives of the first revival, exemplified by the role of the Semi-State Bodies.
3. A series of initiatives in the new academic discipline of business studies designed to compensate for the lack of an indigenous business culture.

Tuairim: An Intellectual Driving Force of the Second Revival

With the exception of Ferriter (2004) and Garvin (2004), most histories of twentieth-century Ireland ignore Tuairim. A possible reason for this omission is the difficulty of categorising the organisation. Ferriter describes it as follows: 'a research group composed of younger academics and researchers looking for solutions to Irish social, economic and political problems'.[36] Garvin refers to it as 'a nascent Irish movement of liberal opinion'[37] and O'Sullivan, in his study of the Irish educational system, refers to Tuairim as

> a forum to facilitate the study and discussion of Irish affairs by young people. It sought to achieve its objectives by organising meetings and conferences, commissioning research projects and publishing the work of members and groups of members.[38]

In an interview with the present author, one of the two founding members, Donal Barrington (the other was a prominent solicitor and businessman,

---

36 Ferriter, *The Transformation of Ireland*, 25.
37 Garvin, *Preventing the Future*, 150.
38 Denis O'Sullivan, *Cultural Politics and Irish Education since the 1950s* (Dublin: IPA Publications, 2005), 257.

Paddy Kilroy), described Tuairim as a cross between the Young Irelanders and the long-established left-wing think tank in London, the Fabian Society. Although the term 'think tank' wasn't in common usage in the 1950s, it is probably the most accurate description of the movement, which was founded in 1954, and which provided much of the intellectual underpinning of the second revival. The founder members were from a legal student background in UCD. Barrington explained that their parents would have held very strong opinions on Irish social, economic and political issues dating from the Civil War period. Barrington's generation, acutely conscious of the failure of the new state and its increasing inability to provide for its citizens, wanted change and regarded the older generation as too set in their ways to provide the necessary impetus. This explains Tuairim's restrictive age conditions; membership was confined to those aged between twenty-one and forty. Anyone over forty couldn't join, and anyone who reached forty had to leave. Ken Whitaker became ineligible by 1956 although he was, in Barrington's words, 'a hero to us all'.[39]

In his major study of Tuairim's influence on intellectual debate and policy formation in Ireland, Tomás Finn describes the movement's main objective as wanting to shift public debate in Ireland from Civil War issues to the more immediate problems facing the country and in the process escape from a culture defined by 'nationalism, authoritarianism, anti-intellectualism and personalism'.[40] A number of respondents who were interviewed by the present author confirmed the sense of exhilaration of the time, due to a belief that change was possible and that they viewed themselves as a self-confident elite, 'imbued with idealism and a determination to ensure that Ireland would be a success'.[41] This was fuelled by the ambitious programme of Tuairim events, which encompassed monthly meetings, study weekends, research groups, the publication of articles in newspapers and periodicals, the establishment of branches around the country (including one for emigrants in London), and a lecturer scheme which provided a list of experts on different subjects who could be contacted

39 Donal Barrington, Interview with author, 9 April 2009.
40 Tomás Finn, *The Influence of Tuairim on Intellectual Debate and Policy Formation in Ireland 1954–1975*. PhD dissertation, NUI Galway December 2008, p. 71
41 Professor Anthony Cunningham, Interview with author, 10 February 2009.

by other organisations to speak at meetings. The extent of Tuairim's ambition was shown in their logo: two young faces with that of the woman's superimposed on the man's, representing a society looking to the future or, in Barrington's words, 'pioneering for a new world'.[42] The logo was designed by the well-known artist, Gary Trimble.

One of Tuairim's leading members, Garret FitzGerald, while confirming the sense of excitement surrounding the movement, also confirmed the prevailing gloom of the time and regarded Irish society in general as completely lacking self-confidence, exempting himself because of his more cosmopolitan upbringing: 'My father was English and half the books in the house were in French.'[43] He himself was to become one of the most powerful advocates of EEC membership. Nevertheless, in spite of FitzGerald's caution about confidence levels in the 1950s, the prospect of meeting ambitious young men and women in research groups and study weekends must have raised the spirits, and two of the interviewees for this research spontaneously mentioned that they had met their wives through membership of Tuairim.

Although the movement lasted from 1954 to 1974 it is probably no coincidence that its most active period occurred during the years of the second revival, from 1958 to 1963. According to Finn, 'the society was at its most active during the late fifties and early sixties; a period when new policies emerged in relation to Northern Ireland, the economy and education.'[44] Accurate records were never kept, but Barrington estimates that during the early 1960s there were between 1,000 and 2,000 members of Tuairim. Although the poor state of the Irish economy was a major concern, Tuairim covered a broad range of issues. Northern Ireland was high on the agenda, and Barrington's pamphlet *Uniting Ireland*, published in 1958, sold 10,000 copies. In it, he argued that a lasting settlement could only be brought about with the consent of the majority of the population: a view eventually accepted in the 1998 Good Friday Agreement, but unusual during the 1950s. Tuairim's attitude to the North could be summed

---

42 Donal Barrington, Interview with author, 9 April 2009.
43 Garret FitzGerald, Interview with author, 9 September 2009.
44 Finn, *Tuairim*, 383.

up by the title of a debate sponsored by the Republic society in 1970: 'Is Passionate Moderation Still Possible?'

Education was another regularly featured topic, and there were frequent debates and papers on controversial issues like the move of UCD to Belfield and the proposed merger of UCD and Trinity. Tuairim was also concerned with Oireachtas reform and in particular with political institutions that would attract greater participation from citizens, which as we will see is a key concern of the 'third revival' later to be proposed by this thesis.

Tuairim's complete independence from the Catholic Church, unusual in 1950s Ireland, and from any of the political parties, was one of its defining characteristics and a critical factor in its success. The new generation wanted to free themselves from a culture defined by nationalism, authoritarianism, anti-intellectualism and personalism, and Tuairim provided a safe haven. The media were also interested in a more open society, and were more than willing to grant generous coverage to the society's publications and debates. Not everyone was supportive, and the powerful and authoritarian Archbishop of Dublin, John Charles McQuaid, was sufficiently worried to appoint a spy to infiltrate meetings.

By the early 1970s the success of the second revival meant that many of the original aims of the society had been achieved, and in the words of Donal Barrington, 'it slowly just petered out'.[45] Finn acknowledges the difficulty of assessing the precise nature of Tuairim's contribution to Irish life, but comes to the following conclusion:

> Tuairim contributed to a wide variety of debates that shaped the nature of modern Ireland. The society facilitated the emergence of new policies in relation to Northern Ireland, the economy, education and Europe. In relation to Northern Ireland Tuairim's influence was reflected in the extent to which the terms of the debate changed and a new understanding of Unionism emerged during this period. With respect to the economy, education and censorship, Tuairim's views increased awareness of the need for planning, increased investment and new government legislation.[46]

A Tuairim pamphlet (1959) published shortly after Whitaker's *Economic Development* heaped praise on the new strategy while pouring scorn on

---

45   Donal Barrington, Interview with author, 9 April 2009.
46   Finn, *Tuairim*, 383.

what it referred to as the 'Sinn Féin Myth': the assumption that Irish political independence implied economic independence. The paper went on to argue that the 'myth' could only survive if Irish people were prepared to accept a permanently lower standard of living:

> The problem exists because there has been a desire to reconcile an imperial standard of living with a republican income – rightly or wrongly the Irish people demand the standard of living to which they might be entitled if all of Ireland were still part of the United Kingdom.[47]

As this was not considered an option, the only realistic alternative was a more open economy and an acceptance of Ireland's interdependence with the rest of the world. A later publication (1965) by David Thornley called for an end to the 'clichés of nationalist amateur sociology', the delusion that we could cling to an ideal of being somehow free from materialist impulses while wanting to embrace modernity:

> We are shown a country which has somehow managed to combine uniquely a revolution in its attitudes to growth and productivity with the preservation of the simple, unsophisticated and familial virtues of a rural and deeply Catholic community. This is nonsense.[48]

In the early 1960s Tuairim ventured into more dangerous territory when it criticised what was, in effect, the export of deprived young people once they left institutions like orphanages, industrial schools and correction houses. The London branch went so far as to question the treatment meted out to inmates of these institutions. The prescience of the contribution was only fully endorsed following the revelations of the Ryan Commission in 2009.

Notwithstanding Finn's difficulty, alluded to earlier, in assessing the precise nature of Tuairim's contribution, there is little doubt that by opening up so many contentious areas for debate it helped to create an atmosphere that was more conducive to change in a society that had resisted change for so long.

47   Ibid., 122.
48   Ibid., 73.

Semi-State Bodies: An Irish Solution to an Irish Problem

In the 1950s large sectors of the economy were under state ownership in most European countries. Many industries were nationalised mainly as a result of left-wing governments wanting to control what the European Left used to refer to as the commanding heights of the economy. This was also the case in Ireland, but the reason was nothing to do with left-wing politics, as Garret FitzGerald has pointed out:

> Some of them [state-sponsored bodies] are designed to fill gaps left by private enterprise in the industrial or financial sectors, or in the field of communications, while others are designed to encourage and promote the expansion of the private sector by assisting private firms to find capital for expansion, to gain footholds in foreign markets, or otherwise to develop their business.[49]

Thus, although Ireland has never had a socialist-dominated government, large parts of the economy were effectively nationalised. But this was more to do with deficiencies in the private sector than any attempt by the state to absorb an excessive share of available capital. Garret FitzGerald (1961) has calculated that in 1957 these enterprises absorbed 23 per cent of total gross fixed investment compared with a European average of between 9 per cent and 5 per cent.[50] Although most of the senior appointments were former civil servants, these organisations were given a considerable degree of autonomy. Many of the Irish development agencies were the first of their kind in the world, and although the experience they built up over the years was to prove of huge benefit to the country, the original decision to establish them owed more to desperation than to prescience.

The main developmental and promotional bodies were established in the 1950s to act as promoter, cheerleader, advisor and general confidant to their respective industry sectors. Bord Fáilte, established in 1939, was one of the first national tourist agencies. Córas Tráchtála Teoranta (CTT), established in 1959, was one of the first national export development agencies

---

49   Garret FitzGerald, *State-Sponsored Bodies* (Dublin: IPA Publications, 1961), 2.
50   Ibid., 8.

and the Industrial Development Authority (IDA), which was established in 1951, was one of the first national promotional agencies specifically charged with the attraction of overseas investment. The IDA was at the time also responsible for the development of indigenous industry.

Ambitious civil servants were seconded from government departments to staff these organisations, and during the late 1950s and 1960s some of the most entrepreneurially minded Irish civil servants were running them: Tim O'Driscoll at Bord Fáilte, Michael Killeen in the IDA and Tom Garvey in CTT. Although technically civil servants, these men acted like private entrepreneurs in terms of their work ethic and flair for innovation. Brendan O'Regan, a legendary example of this breed, ran the Shannon Development Corporation, set up the first Industrial Export Processing Zone and invented the concept of the duty-free airport. Kieran McGowan, who became Chief Executive of the IDA in 1990, recalls visiting Taiwan in the 1980s, when the IDA was beginning to target the Far East as a source of overseas investment, and being struck by the number of Taiwanese who kept asking 'How is Brendan O'Regan?'[51] O'Regan had been a major influence on the Taiwanese, who had by then successfully imitated the Irish initiative of airport industrial zones. O'Regan's example was also followed by his staff in Shannon, one of whom first came up with the idea of mixing coffee, cream and Irish Whiskey. The need to create some sense of momentum in the stricken economy was such that they were given enormous leeway and that generation of public servants responded to the challenge. Bord Fáilte didn't just advertise Ireland overseas; they initiated a series of development programmes in Ireland with the domestic industry to raise standards and created the imaginative 'Tidy Towns' competition to encourage greater awareness among the population as a whole of their power to contribute to the success of Irish tourism.

Under Michael Killeen's leadership IDA executives were encouraged to travel at all hours of the day and night, leaving no stone unturned, in their quest for overseas investment. That culture still survives, and a good example of the lengths to which the IDA will go to close a sale is the story of how in the late 1980s they fought off stiff competition from Scotland,

---

51   Kieran McGowan, Interview with author, 9 September 2009.

Wales and Austria to ensure that Intel chose Ireland as their European base for microchip manufacture. A key issue in the negotiations was the need to convince Intel that Ireland had sufficient experienced engineers qualified to produce microchips. The IDA commissioned a formal report from an international management consultancy to locate Irish engineers working abroad with the relevant experience:

> Within five weeks, over 300 Irish engineers, mainly in the US, had been identified and individually contacted; each of them had between three and seven years experience in the production of volume semi-conductors. The formal report handed to Intel had the positive finding that 80% of the expatriate engineers would return to Ireland if given a good career opportunity with a quality company. This report was crucial in satisfying Intel that Ireland could satisfactorily host an advanced microchip plant.[52]

The promotional agencies established in the 1940s and 1950s were among the first of their kind in the world. The executives who ran them were on their own; there was no blueprint and no roadmap, and there were no experts, consultants or academics who were able to draw on case histories of previous experience. They had to dig deep into their own experience and develop an Irish response to the problems they confronted.

A clear parallel to the innovative ethos of the mid-twentieth-century Irish state-sponsored bodies was the self-help nature of an earlier 'revival' at the end of the previous century. P. J. Mathews has made the point that this 'revival' is too often seen only as a literary phenomenon, 'a purely mystical affair characterised by a preoccupation with a backward looking Celtic spirituality and a nostalgia for Gaelic Ireland and an obsessive anti-modern tradition'.[53] He argues that it was a much more hard-headed enterprise which was dedicated to the establishment of a separate Irish nation, but which was conscious that material advances were essential if that nation was to be successful. Like the executives in the semi-state bodies in the mid-twentieth century, many of the earlier revivalists were modernisers whose initiatives and innovations were exactly that, however much they may have appeared otherwise:

52 Ray MacSharry and Padraic White, *The Making of the Celtic Tiger: The Inside Story of Ireland's Boom Economy* (Cork: Mercier Press, 2000), 217.
53 Mathews, *Revival*, back cover.

> Many of the 'rediscovered traditions', while appearing to be well established practices reaching back into the immemorial past, were at best loosely based on earlier customs and at worst of recent origin ...[54]

Two semi-state bodies in particular offer interesting insights into the rationale of the state-sponsored bodies and the period of innovation and creativity that marked their heyday in the late 1950s and 1960s. These were the two who strayed the furthest from their government origins: Bord na Móna and the Irish Sugar Company, both of which entered highly competitive mass consumer markets. Bord na Móna, under the leadership of the tough-minded ex-Republican activist C. S. (Todd) Andrews, had been established in the aftermath of the Second World War to develop Ireland's peat resources, and is now one of the largest producers of peat in the world, employing 1,800 people. In the 1960s, it developed a domestic fuel, peat briquettes, which rapidly developed a strong consumer franchise in Irish households. It also developed a range of horticultural products under the Shamrock brand name which are also widely used by Irish gardeners and exported to the British market.

The Irish Sugar Company has had a more chequered history. A privately owned sugar company was set up in Carlow in 1927 but was about to collapse in 1933 when the government stepped in to save the enterprise by establishing the Irish Sugar Company to run its affairs and expand production to other centres in Ireland. In the late 1950s, under the dynamic leadership of Lt Colonel M. J. (Mickey Joe) Costello, it diversified into the convenience food market in an effort to find an outlet for Irish vegetable growers. Using licensed technology from Unilever it launched a range of soups and Accelerated Freeze-Dried vegetables in the UK market under the Erin brand name. The venture had mixed results, but the name survived and the brand is now in private ownership, as is the original sugar business, which was privatised in 1991 under Greencore plc.

During the 1990s, when the hegemony of free market fundamentalism was at its height, there were repeated calls for the privatisation of any state body engaged in commercial activity. The most celebrated example was Bord Telecom, which was launched on the stock market with great

54 Ibid., 27–28.

fanfare at the end of that decade in 1999 under a new name, fashionably kitted out in lower case as eircom. The expected initial share price surge was short-lived, leaving hundreds of thousands of small investors all over the country disillusioned with stock market investments. There were no further public stock offerings, and when the financial crisis struck eight years later the main government initiative to rescue the economy was a new semi-state body, NAMA. Reports of the demise of the semi-state body appear to have been exaggerated.

Business Education: Compensating for a Lack of Business Culture

The second revival arose out of the failures of the first decades after independence, which reached a nadir in 1956. There was a growing belief that the old ideas and policies had failed, and that new thinking was required. An important aspect of openness to new ideas was to discover what was happening in the outside world. There was a feeling in Ireland at the time of being imprisoned in a version of Plato's Cave, cut off from the outside by censorship and rule by old men. However, new technology in the form of more accessible air travel and new broadcast media allowed more light to shine through. The number of school leavers embarking on some form of third-level education expanded rapidly during the late 1950s and early 1960s, and this was accompanied by a mass exodus of students to work in England during the summer months to pay for their college fees (free third-level education wasn't introduced until 1995). It was in the canning factories of Hereford and the frozen pea factories of Cleethorpes and Great Yarmouth that a generation of Irish third-level students met their British contemporaries for the first time and came to what was for them the astonishing conclusion that these others were pretty much the same as themselves. The reason for their astonishment was that because of the inferiority complex that was 'general all over Ireland' at the time, they had assumed that their British counterparts would be intellectually and culturally superior. A few years later, when many of the same students emigrated to London and beyond, they were again surprised. In the words of one senior Irish businessman:

> I arrived over in London in the 60s thinking that people from Oxford, Cambridge and the LSE would be the high-powered ones and then realised that you were as good if not better than any of them.[55]

If a dawning realisation of their own worth was the first component in moulding a new generation, a determination to contribute to the building of a successful economy was the second. When they started to travel, even if it was only to the canning and frozen food factories of Britain, these students seized on anything new with a single question on their minds: 'how would that work in Ireland?' This was particularly evident in the young business academics whose eyes were opened by American business schools, but respondents interviewed for this book recalled similar experiences, and although they didn't specifically use the word 'patriotism' they were all conscious of being engaged in some kind of nation-building exercise. They wanted to grow whatever businesses they were involved with for their own sake, but they were also conscious that they were helping to solve a national problem. Most of these respondents commented on the collegiality of the business community at the time and specifically mentioned the Irish Management Institute (IMI) as a focal point not so much for what would now be referred to as 'networking' but as a forum for discussing national issues.

Michael Dargan was one of the early business pioneers who moved from the civil service to the semi-state sector, joining Aer Lingus in 1947. He came from Ballivor in Co. Meath, where his father was a farmer and a butcher, the nearest to a business background that most Irish people would have had at the time. He spent some time in the US with Aer Lingus in the 1940s and came to the conclusion that there was a level of professional competency in American business that was almost completely lacking in Ireland, and that there was a growing corpus of knowledge about the management of business organisations which Irish business needed to access.

---

55 Lochlann Quinn, Interview with author, 22 November 2006.

He joined the American Management Association and the Conference Board of America 'and was introduced to a stream of data on how management worked and how managers' performance could be improved – a treasury of seminars, books, analysis and research unavailable in Ireland'.[56] The Ireland that Dargan returned to in the early 1950s was beginning to stretch itself out of the lethargy of the previous decades and, as we have seen earlier, there were faint stirrings of resistance to the prevailing orthodoxy. Dargan gathered a group of like-minded businessmen around him for regular meetings in the Grafton St offices of Domas, a Dublin advertising agency, and wrote to others seeking support for more organised professional business education. They decided to form a management organisation and canvassed hard prior to the launch:

> The inaugural meeting was an outstanding success. At 3.00pm on Tuesday the 9th of December 1952 over 600 businessmen, eager to see this new management organisation launched, crowded into the Gresham's mirrored, elegant Aberdeen Room, a popular venue for dinners and society balls.[57]

This was the start of the Irish Management Institute, an organisation which was to play an influential role not only in providing a high standard of professional management education but in creating an ethos of collegiality and a sense of mission, particularly in the early years, when a tight-knit group of specialists was hired in the early 1960s. The first few years of the IMI consisted of ad hoc meetings, seminars and guest lectures from overseas experts who either happened to be in Dublin or could be persuaded to visit. In 1956 a committee was established to devise a programme of organised courses, and the first two-week course was held in 1957.

America was the spiritual home of management education at the time (to some extent it still is), and the IMI kept a close watch on developments there. But Europe played an important financial role: when Ivor Kenny

---

56 Tom Cox, *The Making of Managers: A History of the IMI 1952–2002* (Oxford: Oak Tree Press, 2002), 5.
57 Frank Bradley, Interview with author, 28 January 2009.

became Chief Executive in 1964, he was sent on a two-month mission to the US to visit business schools in eleven cities all funded by a European grant.

At the same time the universities were becoming more interested in business as a possible subject, although there was considerable scepticism in the academy about the credentials of the fledgling discipline. Once again, the American card was to prove decisive. A young lecturer in Political Geography in UCD, M. J. McCormick, began giving some management classes in the Commerce department and secured a European Productivity Agency grant to travel to the States for four months to study the potential of a Master of Business Administration degree. He compiled a report on behalf of eighteen European countries, recommending the advantages of the new field of business education, but according to a business lecturer, Tony Cunningham, who eventually became a Professor in UCD, McCormick faced opposition every step of the way in his attempt to introduce the MBA in UCD.[58] He succeeded in 1964 and UCD became one of the first, if not the first university in Europe to offer an MBA. According to Bradley[59] it was only allowed to go ahead on the grounds that 'it'll go nowhere quickly'. Cunningham remembers his own appointment to the new Department of Business Studies, as the third staff member, with the then Registrar sarcastically remarking: 'that department, they're breeding like rabbits'.[60]

An interesting example of the extraordinary collegiality of the time was the emergence of a dining club-cum-discussion group in the early 1960s called the 'Murphies'. The name was chosen because of the initial meetings in the late 1950s in a city centre room in Henry Street. These initial meetings evolved into formal dinner meetings which were held in the then Irish Intercontinental Hotel in Ballsbridge, and it was felt that booking a private room in a hotel under the 'Murphies' name wouldn't attract undue attention. The founders of the club were Michael Dargan, Chief Executive of Aer Lingus and Colm Barnes, the Chief Executive of Glenabbey, a leading private company at the time. A private letter from

---

58 Tony Cunningham, Interview with author, 10 February 2009.
59 Bradley, Interview with author, 28 January 2009.
60 Cunningham, Interview with author, 10 February 2009.

Colm Barnes to the author of an unpublished history of the 'Murphies' explains the thinking behind the idea:

> It was Michael Dargan's idea that we should create an informal forum of people who were involved in the economy and in politics. The hope was that members could discuss issues of the day with a fair degree of candour. We sought a cross-section of people drawn from the public and private sector, along with a lawyer or two. It was found convenient to meet after office hours about 6.30 and have dinner together. In this respect it was a dining club but the emphasis was on discussion.[61]

Attendees at the first dinner included Dargan and Barnes, along with Guy Jackson (Guinness), Ian Morrison (Bank of Ireland), Michael Rigby-Jones (Irish Ropes), Douglas Gageby (*Irish Times*), Paddy O'Keefe (Irish Farm Centre) and Donal Roche (Roadstone). Tadhg Ó Cearbhaill, a senior civil servant, joined in the mid-1960s, followed by Ken Whitaker. Further evidence of the closely knit nature of the different elements of Irish society at the time was the following comment from the 'unofficial' history of the club:

> An experiment was tried in the 1960s to expand the membership to include literary figures and on the initiative of Ken Whitaker and Tom Hardiman respectively, the poet, Thomas Kinsella and James Plunkett Kelly, the novelist, were invited to join but neither persisted. Folklore suggests that they found themselves ill at ease (some say intimidated), in the largely business environment of the discussions at the dinners.[62]

This book has argued that a radical upgrading of Irish management education and professionalism took place in Ireland during the second revival, exemplified by the creation of the IMI, the introduction of third-level business education, with particular emphasis on the role of UCD, and the increasing recognition of the importance of developing a professional business culture in the country among the political and administrative elite through the commercial freedom allowed to the state-sponsored bodies and participation in informal dining clubs like the 'Murphies'. The seeds of some successful business enterprises such as Smurfits, Cement

---

61   Seán Cromien, *History of the Murphies*. Unpublished correspondence (2005), 3.
62   Cromien, *History of the Murphies*, 4.

Roadstone Holdings (CRH), Kerry Group, Glen Dimplex and Glanbia were sown at the time, but the size of the Irish market meant that the most successful businesses created more employment abroad than in the home market. This has meant that Ireland remained dependent on overseas investment, a position which continues to this day. Writing in 1989, Joe Lee's assessment of the business community was harsh:

> A variety of factors have contributed to the poor performance of native Irish business, but sheer intellectual inadequacy counts among the basic weaknesses. A first-class business mind would be a joy to behold. There were too few of them in Ireland.[63]

This generalised condemnation doesn't take account of the distinction between the entrepreneur and the professional business manager. Until very recently Ireland was characterised by a low level of entrepreneurial activity, but it could also be argued that the success of the IDA in attracting overseas businesses was partly dependent on a plentiful supply of professional business managers, a supply that was in turn dependent on the business education initiatives begun during the second revival.

The Mandarin, the Musician and the Mage in the mid-1950s

Brian Fallon's attempt to rehabilitate the literary and artistic reputation of the 1930s, 1940s and 1950s may be a little exaggerated, as I have argued above, but in one respect he was right. If 1956 was Ireland's darkest hour it was around the same time that the seeds of the later economic and artistic successes were sown:

> The 50s were in every way a watershed, in which an entire epoch ended and the modern one emerged … by the 1960s most of the battles had already been fought so that stubbornly, bloodily and over a long period, the walls and bastions of conservatism had been steadily mined from underneath, so that in the end they collapsed with a suddenness which surprised most people.[64]

63   Lee, *Ireland 1912–1985*, 577.
64   Fallon, *The Age of Innocence*, 257.

T. K. Whitaker, Seán Ó Riada and Thomas Kinsella were three of the most prominent participants in the mining of the 'bastions of conservatism'. The second revival in Ireland unleashed a sense of intellectual freedom, creative opportunity and national potential which was characterised by the three men at the heart of this story.

In the fateful year of 1956, T. K. (Ken) Whitaker had just been appointed Secretary of the Department of Finance, traditionally the most powerful position in the Irish civil service. He was just thirty-nine, an unprecedented age for such a senior position in an administrative and political establishment still dominated by veterans of the struggle for independence. He did have considerable experience, having worked in the service since coming first place in Ireland in the 1934 civil service competition for Clerical Officer.

Whitaker's private secretary Thomas Kinsella was also a Christian Brothers-educated boy who gained a scholarship, first to university, and a few months later to the civil service. He started at University College Dublin but when the civil service scholarship came through, he abandoned his studies and accepted. A combination of lack of interest in his chosen subject, science, and a working-class preference for a secure and pensionable position swayed him, but he was already beginning to write poetry and, as Ken Whitaker has noted, somewhat wryly, it was not uncommon in the civil service at the time for people to dabble in literature.[65] Kinsella subsequently signed up in UCD for an evening degree in German but never completed it. He became friendly with Liam Miller, who was interested in publishing poetry and Kinsella's first volume, the modestly titled *Poems*, was published in the same eventful year of 1956.

Kinsella moved out of the family home in 1951 to a small attic flat in Baggot Street, an interesting choice given that it was Paddy Kavanagh's old stomping ground and the nearby presence of the eccentric Parsons bookshop gave it a vaguely artistic aura. Kinsella became part of a literary and arty set that hung around the coffee shops and bars in the immediate vicinity of UCD in Earlsfort Terrace and rambled over the Wicklow hills at weekends as members of An Óige, the Irish youth hosteller's association.

---

65   Thomas Kenneth Whitaker, Interview with author, 28 May 2007.

Two of the most notable members of this artistic coterie were the glamorous Eleanor Walsh, whom Kinsella married in 1955, and the exotic John Reidy, who had just graduated with a degree in music from University College Cork, and who arrived unannounced at Kinsella's Baggot St flat, having been introduced to the budding poet in the UCD students' restaurant in 86 St Stephen's Green. He stayed for a week before Kinsella managed to persuade him to acquire a place of his own. He was a born showman who would wholeheartedly enter into the spirit of the different roles he enacted: English gentleman, Irish Gaeltacht scholar, inarticulate drunken Latvian sailor. Most of the time he cultivated a foppish style: curly brimmed hat, embroidered waistcoat, cane and a carefully nurtured and trimmed moustache. He drove a second-hand Jaguar and brought colour to an impoverished time. He later morphed into Seán Ó Riada – the role he was to play for the rest of his life. T. K. Whitaker, Thomas Kinsella and Seán Ó Riada shared three characteristics which were unusual at the time. They were exceptionally self-confident at a time when an inferiority complex hung like a huge nimbus cloud over the country. Secondly, they were prepared to challenge existing conventions in their chosen fields. And finally, they were deeply knowledgeable of and passionately committed to Irish language and culture.

CHAPTER 2

T. K. Whitaker and the Second Revival

Whitaker's Reputation Today

In a nation noted for its often mean-minded begrudgery and healthy scepticism of established heroes, Ken Whitaker is the exception who commands universal respect. He was voted the 'Greatest Living Irish Person' in 2002, and his ninetieth birthday in 2006 was celebrated by a Presidential party at Áras an Uachtaráin. The man himself commented modestly: 'The problem with living so long is that you'll either be canonised or found out.'[1] Far from being 'found out', there has been an extraordinary level of agreement among economists, historians and political commentators on the seminal importance of Whitaker's contribution to the change in Ireland's economic fortunes in the latter part of the twentieth century:

> The dawn that slowly broke over this dismal night was heralded not by some dramatically sudden development nor by some charismatic public figure, but by an expert working in the relative obscurity of civil service.[2]

---

1 Thomas Kenneth Whitaker, *Retrospect 2006–1916* (Dublin: IPA Publications, 2006), 34.
2 John A. Murphy, *Ireland in the Twentieth Century* (Dublin: Gill & Macmillan, 1975), 142–144.

> *Economic Development* – is now generally recognised to have played a key role in re-directing government thinking and in preparing the way for the economic policies of the 1960s.[3]

> The man who really changed things was Ken Whitaker, I don't think there is any other official who has a remotely comparable impact upon Irish history in the second half of the 20th century.[4]

The change for which Whitaker has been given so much credit was the reversal of the protectionist economic policies of the preceding decades in favour of the opening up of the Irish economy to the global economy. Following the collapse of the Berlin Wall in 1989, the notion that national economies could be protected from the global economy and from the growing volume of capital market flows which knew no boundaries was completely discredited. But thirty years earlier, in a nervous nation sorely lacking in self-confidence, it took a high level of political will to abandon the comfort of high tariff walls. There were of course more pressing reasons for Whitaker's initiative, namely the fact that the previous policies had obviously failed and there were moves afoot to establish free trade areas in Europe. But the decisions instigated by Whitaker in the mid-to-late 1950s ensured that Ireland was better placed than other countries to benefit from the worldwide explosion of economic growth in the 1990s.

Whitaker's Commitment to the Nation

The most detailed source of information on the career of T. K. Whitaker is contained in two of his own publications from the Institute of Public Administration (IPA): *Interests* (1983) and *Retrospect 2006–1916* (2006). He was born in Rostrevor, Co. Down in 1916. His father worked in a

---

3   Brendan Walsh, 'Economic Growth and Development: 1945–70', in Joseph J. Lee, ed., *Ireland 1945–70* (Dublin: Gill & Macmillan, 1979), 30.
4   Ronan Fanning, Article in *The University Observer* (8 February 2005), 3.

linen factory in Newry and the family moved to Drogheda in 1922 when his father switched jobs to work in the well-known Greenmount & Boyne linen factory in the town. His mother was from Co. Clare and it was through a combination of her interest in Irish culture and a number of inspirational teachers in the Christian Brothers school in Drogheda that he developed a life-long love of the Irish language and literature. His mother was very ambitious for her son, and in Whitaker's own words he was always well turned out, 'like a little Lord Fauntleroy'.[5] Needless to say, this resulted in a few scrapes with the other boys at school, but he was tall and physically strong and well able to take care of himself. He was also extremely bright and was awarded first place in Ireland in no less than four civil service exams. His early self-confidence – 'Yes, I was good at school – I suppose I did come more or less at the top of the class in most things'[6] – combined with his academic achievements and rapid promotion in the civil service was ideal preparation for the formidable tasks that lay ahead. During his early years in the civil service, he studied at night and obtained a Master's degree in Economic Science from the University of London.

Whitaker was a man of wide-ranging political and cultural interests. As a Northern Irishman he had an abiding interest in the problems created by partition and the border, and just as he played a leading role in breaking the economic logjam created by the insular protectionist policies of the first decades of the new Irish state, he played a similar role in the first attempts to develop a dialogue between the administrations on both sides of the border by brokering the famous Lemass-O'Neill meeting in January 1965 at Stormont. This meeting was unable to prevent the terrible toll of death and destruction that followed, but it was a historic occasion and may well be seen as the start of a process that culminated in the historic handshake between Ian Paisley and Bertie Ahern in 2007. Whitaker maintained an interest in the North all his life and set out his position on the 'national question' in a paper written in 1981:

> The viewpoint presented here is that of a peaceful and patient Irishman, born in the North but for a long-time resident in the South, who hoped that the people of

---

[5] Thomas Kenneth Whitaker, Interview with author, 6 November 2007.
[6] Ibid.

Northern Ireland will one day freely decide to join the people of the Republic in a new Irish constitutional framework and who meanwhile wishes the door to be kept open to such an eventuality.[7]

He goes on to make the point that unity can only come about if the majority of the population of the North are in favour, and notes that 'the wording of Article 3 of our Constitution is unfortunate in this respect'.[8] This was of course removed as part of the Good-Friday Agreement in 1998.

Whitaker maintained a strong commitment to the Irish language all his life, believing it to be a critical part of our identity. However, like his attitude to the North, he was a cautious moderate in this regard, and warned the language movement not to overstate the case or overly antagonise those who are less committed:

> The assumption that the aim is to make Irish the everyday language of everyone in Ireland sharpens the antagonism of those who see no point in preserving Irish, alienates the sympathy of those who cherish Irish but value the possession of English and discourages even idealists who recognise such an extreme aim to be unattainable.[9]

He was convinced that our sense of national independence is strengthened by the Irish language and that it expresses our deepest thoughts and feelings more naturally than any other language:

> The Irish language is a most precious heritage, the thing that most signifies and maintains our continuity as a distinctive people, the key to a treasure trove of poetry and prose epics, folklore and song, which has expressed the imagination and feeling, the wisdom and humour, all the varied responses of generations of Irish people to life and its vicissitudes, from the early centuries down, indeed, to our own day.[10]

Whitaker was extremely knowledgeable about the 'treasure trove of poetry and prose epics', and through his education and family background, was steeped in the literature and music from the earliest historic times to the end of the Elizabethan Age, when the old Gaelic order in

---

7   Thomas Kenneth Whitaker, *Interests* (Dublin: IPA Publications, 1983), 202.
8   Ibid., 202.
9   Ibid., 228.
10 Ibid., 239.

Ireland collapsed and Irish began to be replaced by English as the language of literature.

Whitaker's New Thinking on Irish Economic Policy

When Whitaker joined the civil service in the mid-1930s, the first Fianna Fail government under the leadership of Éamon de Valera had just come into power on a strongly protectionist economic platform. From the vantage point of the twenty-first century this appears to be a strange policy for a small European country to adopt, but it was far from unusual in the 1930s as national governments sought shelter from the fall-out of the Great Crash of 1929. There were, however, additional, more deeply rooted psychological reasons for adopting a stand-alone economic policy in Ireland. The new state was just over a decade in existence, memories of the bitter struggle for independence were still firmly etched in the minds and hearts of the entire population, particularly the ruling political elite, and it had been a key nationalistic article of faith, especially since the Famine, that the major cause of Ireland's economic under-performance was British control of economic policy and the subjection of Ireland's economy to the long-term strategic goals of the UK. Given the close geographic proximity to such a powerful country, there was widespread agreement that Ireland needed to pursue a policy of economic self-sufficiency.

This strategy flew in the face of one of the most basic tenets of economics: Ricardo's Theory of Comparative Advantage, which states that countries should concentrate on producing what they can at a lower comparative cost than other countries. The 1930s witnessed a partial retreat from this philosophy. In fact, one of the most famous economists of the twentieth century, John Maynard Keynes, addressing a meeting in Dublin in the 1930s, stated that he understood why the Irish government had adopted a protectionist strategy. But regardless of outside endorsements, from however eminent a source, it was a strategy perfectly in tune with the mind-set of the new government, who were imbued with the widely held Irish republican belief that Ireland's economic woes were due largely to being tied to British economic interests and that the economy would thrive if Ireland were free to pursue an independent economic strategy. The resulting policy of economic autarky led to the establishment of a range of indigenous businesses which created a level of employment but which were only viable behind a high protective tariff wall. Cormac Ó Gráda's history of the Irish economy since the 1920s concludes that

> [...] the Irish economy performed poorly in the 1920s, 30s, 40s and most of the 50s – tariff protection aimed at reviving Irish manufacturing, produced instead a stagnant inefficient and largely inward-looking industrial sector – as a result the South's labour force was no bigger in the late 50s than it had been at the dawn of the state.[11]

When T. K. Whitaker succeeded the long-serving J. J. McElligott as Secretary of the Department of Finance in the mid-1950s at the age of thirty-nine, he was faced with a grim economic landscape. He had already concluded that an alternative strategy was urgently needed. Although of quiet, suitably mandarin demeanour, Whitaker was a forceful personality who, unusually for an Irish public servant, was willing to express his views in public. By the time of his appointment, he had already published a technical financial book, *Financing by Credit Creation* (1947), which was, in his own words, 'an unusual event for a civil servant'.[12] He was also a frequent speaker at academic seminars. At the time of his promotion to the most senior position in the civil service he gave a paper to the Statistical and Social Inquiry Society which specifically criticised the policy of protective tariffs. Garret FitzGerald has described this paper as 'remarkable' not just for its criticism of long-established government policy but because 'most novel of all, its author was a civil servant emerging voluntarily from the security of anonymity into the public forum'.[13] This paper could be regarded as the genesis of the paper on economic planning which advocated a new economic strategy: abandoning protectionism, welcoming

---

11   Cormac Ó Gráda, *A Rocky Road: The Irish Economy since the 1920s* (Manchester: Manchester University Press, 1997), 1.
12   Thomas Kenneth Whitaker, Interview with author, 6 November 2007.
13   Garret FitzGerald, 'Grey, White and Blue: A Review of Three Recent Economic Publications', in Basil Chubb and Patrick Lynch, eds, *Economic Development and Planning* (Dublin: IPA Publications, 1969), 121.

foreign investment into the country and beginning the planning for active participation in a free trade world.

The Meticulous Planning of the Economic Plan

On the afternoon of 11 November 1958, members of the Dáil received copies of a white paper, *The First Programme for Economic Expansion*. It was based on an exhaustive and often painful examination of the performance of the Irish economy since the foundation of the state in 1922. Later that afternoon there was a modest celebration in the Department of Finance for the dedicated group of civil servants Whitaker had assembled two years earlier for the task of preparing the report. Whitaker had known for some time that something had to be done to reverse the country's economic fortunes. His appointment as Secretary of the Department in 1956 gave him the power to act.

Ivor Kenny (1987) has described the preparation of the new development plan.[14] Whitaker gathered together a group of the brightest and the best to compile the data that would be required, and in the process created a unique *esprit de corps* as his selected band worked extra-curricular hours, conscious that they were engaged in work of the utmost importance:

> There was a great esprit de corps, this was exhilarating and comforting. Finance was a small Department and there was a kind of monastic austerity about it. Everyone was prepared to work far beyond the normal hours and there was the feeling of being part of a particularly responsible elite.[15]

The preparation involved three stages: Whitaker's initial research, the recruitment of the special staff and then the drafting and editing of the final report. The main conclusions were that national output needed to be increased and more of it used for productive purposes like factories and

14   Ivor Kenny, *In Good Company: Conversations with Irish Leaders* (Dublin: Gill & Macmillan, 1987), 284.
15   Kenny, *In Good Company*, 288.

plants and that savings should be encouraged by lower taxes. Whitaker played the civil service adroitly to ensure their natural caution and conservatism would be overcome. Some of the original thinking was published in journals like *Administration* and in internal civil service memoranda. One of these, appropriately labelled 'The Whitaker Memorandum', outlined five reasons for embarking on the project: the prevailing mood of despondency, the need for coherence, the prospect of increased unemployment, the balance-of-payments problem and, more prosaically, the need to prepare for a World Bank meeting.

Although always worded with impeccable politeness, in the time-honoured civil service tradition, Whitaker pulled no punches in his determination to achieve his objectives, and in a memorandum entitled *The Irish Economy 1957* he stated bluntly:

> Indeed, if we expect to fail it would be better to make an immediate move towards re-incorporation in the United Kingdom rather than to wait until our economic decadence became even more apparent.[16]

The civil service culture doesn't allow for direct confrontation or complete disagreement with superiors or political masters, but because its members will usually outlast these masters they can afford to wait in the long grass and delay, disrupt and obfuscate at every available opportunity until they have achieved their objective. This often happens after the official announcement of whatever it is they disapprove of, so that it can then be subjected to the proverbial 'death by a thousand cuts'. Whitaker was alert to this possibility and a series of recently released internal correspondences show how ably he dealt with any obstruction to his determination to change the basic policies of agricultural self-sufficiency and industrial protectionism. The correspondences were called 'semi-official', which was a term inherited from the British civil service tradition and used to supplement discussion by telephone, face-to-face or in committee, of undecided issues. This exchange was intended, at least by Whitaker, to

---

16 Ronan Fanning, 'The Genesis of Economic Development', in J. C. B. McCarthy, ed., *Planning Ireland's Future: The Legacy of T. K. Whitaker* (Dublin: Glendale Press: 1990), 97.

be seen by other senior officials and politicians who would have a role to play and to some extent they take the form of an extended debate with the onlookers left to decide the outcome. Whitaker's main antagonist was the Secretary of the Department of Industry and Commerce, the formidable mandarin James Charles Brendan (J. C. B.) McCarthy. They disagreed on the likely effects of free trade, with McCarthy desperately trying to prevent any move in that direction by arguing that the unemployment consequences would be too high. The form of address between the two men also adopted the British tradition of dispensing with Christian names, which lends a slightly comic touch to the proceedings to twenty-first-century ears used to the familiar adoption of Christian names even among people who have never met:

> Dear Whitaker, There is one statement in that letter which surprises us here, namely that the, 15% rule would mean that very few of our industries – and those the strongest – would have to eliminate tariffs in less than twenty years. I'm afraid this is not a generalisation we could accept ...[17]

> Dear McCarthy, I have, of course, seen your statistical statement but still consider my generalisation fair ...[18]

The published correspondence ends on a slightly peevish note:

> Dear Whitaker, Thanks for your letter of 7th January, though it grieves me to note that our exchange of correspondence seems to have done nothing to bring the discussion down to earth ...[19]

> Dear McCarthy, I suppose I'm entitled to the last word in our correspondence about the Reasons for Reducing Protection. I am sorry it must be that I cannot accept the second paragraph of your letter of the 9th of January as being a fair or reasonable summary of the views expressed in my previous letters ...[20]

---

17 Thomas Kenneth Whitaker, *Protection or Free Trade: The Final Battle* (Dublin: IPA Publications, 2006), 24.
18 Ibid., 33.
19 Ibid., 93.
20 Ibid., 94.

Whitaker won the debate. Tariffs were lowered unilaterally in the early 1960s, and although the original intention of joining the European Free Trade Association was dropped, a Free Trade Agreement was concluded with Britain in 1965 and after tortuous negotiations the Irish Republic finally joined the EEC in 1973. Although some inefficient indigenous industries failed as a result of free trade, thus justifying McCarthy's fears, these losses were more than compensated for by the increased efficiency of the rest of the indigenous sector and the attraction of overseas industries, resulting in an immediate increase in economic growth in the early 1960s, vindicating Whitaker's confidence.

The footwear sector provides a good example of the advantages and disadvantages of the protectionist policy. Between 1929 and 1931 before the high tariff walls were erected, indigenous footwear accounted for only 13 per cent of total sales. By the late 1930s the position had completely reversed, with imports down to 13 per cent and domestic firms accounting for 87 per cent of the market. Following the reduction of tariff barriers and the adoption of full free trade the indigenous share of the market fell steadily to its present level of 10 per cent. However, not all of the businesses established under protectionist tariff wall failed in the more competitive climate of the 1960s onwards. Smurfit's cardboard packaging business, which began life in Clonskeagh in 1935, is probably the most spectacular success.

The most tangible outcome of the debates and discussion about Ireland's future that took place in the 1950s was the abandonment of the protectionist policies of the three preceding decades and the adoption of a more outward-looking attitude to the rest of the world. But there was also an intangible psychological outcome. FitzGerald has shown how Whitaker was always conscious of this issue:

> The psychological value of the programme would lie in the hope it would offer of a more orderly and successful approach to the tackling of national problems – ... and in its targets which could ... harness the enthusiasm of the young and buttress the faith of the active members of the community.[21]

---

21   Garret FitzGerald, *Planning in Ireland* (Dublin: IPA Publications, 1968), 24.

Ireland's Economic Progress since the 1950s

Whitaker himself has divided our economic history since the late 1950s into three phases: the first recovery period (1958–1969), a setback period (1970–1986) and a second recovery period (1987–2000).[22] The following is a brief outline of these three phases.

The First Recovery Period (1958–1969)

Cormac Ó Gráda's influential history of the Irish economy since the 1920s states that 'in the late 1950s something changed and Ireland entered a sustained economic growth – there is no consensus as to why this happened – some claim it was the publication in 1958 of *Economic Development* ... and the ensuing *Programme for Economic Expansion* which augured a new era.'[23] O'Grada's conclusion that there was 'no consensus' about why the economic recovery of the late 1950s occurred is probably due to the fact that a variety of circumstances were involved, including a buoyancy in world trade at the time and a tide of liberalism associated with the 1960s which lifted hopes around the world. There is considerable support among historians and economists, however, for the argument that the publication of Whitaker's plan provided the critical psychological kick-start for the first period of sustained economic growth in Ireland since the foundation of the state. This new psychological mood in the country was aided and abetted by the launch of Teilifís Éireann in 1961, the succession of the pragmatic business-orientated Seán Lemass as Taoiseach and the decline in the authority of the Catholic Church. The first fruits of the policy of actively seeking overseas investment also played a crucial role. O'Gráda argues that the transformation of the economy between the late 1950s and early 1970s 'may be largely attributed to the arrival of

---

22 Thomas Kenneth Whitaker, 'We Have Come a Long Way; We Still Have a Long Way to Go', *Irish Times* (8 December 2001), 10.
23 Ó Gráda, *A Rocky Road*, 114.

multi-nationals',[24] and by 1973 overseas firms accounted for almost a third of a manufacturing employment. The average growth in Gross Domestic Product (GDP) each year during the 1960s was over 4 per cent, making it easily the most successful economic decade since independence.

The Setback Period (1970–1986)

Although Whitaker himself refers to these sixteen years as 'setback' years, this seems a harsh judgement. The world economy began to experience difficulties as a result of the quadrupling of the price of oil in 1973, but Irish growth rates again averaged over 4 per cent during the decade. Unfortunately, government reaction to the oil crises was, in Whitaker's own words, 'perverse'; in a newspaper article published in 2001 he went on to conclude that

> the crowning mistake was the 1977 (Fianna Fáil Election) manifesto which aimed at spending our way to full employment in a few years by even bigger borrowing ... The second oil crisis of 1979 put further pressure on the Irish economy, which was again compounded by official ineptitude in handling the problem. Growth slowed to a trickle in the early 1980s, which saw three General Elections in quick succession – the resulting political instability resulted in complete stasis until politicians were forced to take a firmer grip by putting the nation's finances on a sound footing.[25]

The Second Recovery Period (1987–2007)

The economy stuttered for a while in the wake of the corrective action taken to reduce our dependence on overseas borrowing, but from 1995 onwards a combination of factors produced an unprecedented economic boom which ultimately transformed the country demographically and psychologically, as well as economically. The reasons behind the dramatic economic growth from the mid-1990s to 2007 are the subject of some

---

24 Ibid., 114.
25 Whitaker, 'We Have Come a Long Way', 10.

dispute, but the extent of the transformation is accepted by all. Even the authoritative *Economist* magazine, historically dubious about Ireland's economic performance and policies, ran a cover story in 1997 under the title 'Europe's Shining Light', which concluded that 'Ireland's performance is so dazzling – one of the most remarkable economic transformations in recent times, from "basket case" to emerald tiger in ten years'.[26] The main factors behind this success are generally recognised to be the attraction of significant overseas investment as a result of determined state action and a favourable tax regime, a fortuitously timed devaluation of the punt (the then currency) and a well-educated and resourceful workforce, many of whom were under-employed and which also included a stock of highly qualified emigrants willing to return home and a sustained period of industrial peace resulting from social partnership agreements between trades unions, business and agricultural interests. The main disputes regarding this latest period of very high rates of economic growth are between those who argue for a convergence theory; that is, the Irish economy was merely catching up with the rest of developed Europe, and those who maintain that the country was the beneficiary of a long economic boom in the US and Ireland's attractiveness as a location for the Single European market for US business: 'While the convergence models are the automatic outcome of textbook economic theory they may not be the most appropriate for Ireland.'[27]

The results of the survey of leading businessmen carried out for the original thesis in 2008/9, on which this book is based, would tend to support the argument that the economic boom of the 1990s was primarily the outcome of favourable circumstances in the US in the early part of that decade. The US economy was booming, the financial services sector was becoming a major driving force in the world economy and was in the process becoming a global business, and there were a number of mainly fortuitous factors playing in Ireland's favour: Irish people spoke English; the country operated as a subset of London, one of the three financial time

---

26 Front cover, *The Economist*, 17 May 1997.
27 Frank Barry, *The Celtic Tiger: Delayed Convergence or Regional Boom. ESRI Quarterly Commentary* (Summer 2002).

zone centres, and a key number of third-generation Irish people were assuming leadership roles in US business who were more 'at home abroad' in Ireland than elsewhere. Almost all of the interviewees mentioned 'luck' as a significant factor in the economic boom of the 1990s. One respondent asked rhetorically: 'Why is Spain the biggest investor in South America? Why is France the biggest investor in North Africa? Why is Germany the biggest investor in Eastern Europe? Because they are all more at home than anyone else in these locations – the way the Americans are in Ireland!' But although luck played a part, we cannot ignore Louis Pasteur's dictum that 'fortune favours the prepared mind'.[28] Ireland had prepared well: in the IDA the country had a well-oiled machine for dealing with overseas investment, and the state had invested heavily in education and telecommunications.

In spite of the problems encountered in the late 1970s and early 1980s the economic record since the 1960s has been impressive and has certainly justified the change in strategy initiated by Whitaker in the late 1950s. By positioning Ireland as a location for overseas investment, facilitating that investment with a variety of grants and tax breaks, and aggressively chasing after targeted industry sectors in the 1960s, when no other country was competing in this way, Ireland developed an invaluable level of expertise, which it was able to put to good use when intensified globalisation in the latter part of the twentieth century came into play – a development which meant that a much wider variety of businesses began to think in global terms and that the competition for mobile investment would become much more intense.

The progress of the Irish economy from the Great Recession in 2008, the years of austerity that followed and the rapid recovery from 2013 up to the 2020s in spite of the disruptive effects of Brexit and COVID-19 will be examined in Part III of this book.

A key premise of this book is that a country's economic performance cannot be isolated from the prevailing culture of that country. This is a debate that has attracted increasing attention in recent years as the search for explanations of different economic growth rates between different countries and regions has become more intense. Not everyone agrees with this

---

28   Lochlann Quinn, Interview with author, 22 November 2006.

premise. The more muscular advocates of unfettered free markets believe that the only factor impeding high rates of economic growth is the lack of absolute commitment to deregulation, privatisation and the other attributes of unfettered free markets. It is necessary now to take a close look at this debate in relation to Ireland, by way of concluding this section on Whitaker and paving the way for our understanding of the contribution of the other two major second revival figures treated in this book, Seán Ó Riada and Thomas Kinsella.

Cultural Explanations for Economic Change

Raymond Williams has described 'culture' as one of the two or three most difficult words in the English language, because it has come to be used for important concepts in several distinct intellectual disciplines and in several distinct and incompatible systems of thought. I'm using the term 'culture' in the anthropological sense, in the way Geertz means when he annotates it as 'thick description', or in other words, descriptions of the entire way of life of a people, 'its values, practices, symbols, institutions and human relationships'.[29]

Two of the most famous historical texts on the subject, de Tocqueville's *Democracy in America* (1835–1840) and Max Weber's *The Protestant Ethic and the Spirit of Capitalism* (1930), put the prevailing culture at the centre of their analysis of economic growth in their respective continents. De Tocqueville concluded that the strongly embedded democratic culture in America was a key to economic growth, and Weber records that Europe began to prosper after the Reformation. It is still generally accepted that there is a strong correlation between religion and economic development, as Kay noted in his study of the way markets work: 'The correlation between religion and economic development is inescapable but the nature of the correlation is controversial.'[30] The Protestant ethic was important for the

---

29 Clifford Geertz, *The Interpretation of Culture* (London: Fontana Press, 1993), 27.
30 John Kay, *How Markets Work* (London: Penguin Books, 2003), 39.

growth of capitalism mainly because the individualistic ethos it inspired was more compatible with business development and growth than the more collectivist ethos of Catholicism; the fact that Protestantism challenged the status quo also aligned it more closely with the business mindset. An American historian, Kerby Miller, has, as we have seen, made a similar case from the opposite direction by arguing that part of the reason for Ireland's poor economic performance is the Catholic religion: 'The traditional Irish Catholic worldview devalues individual action, ambition and the assumption of personal responsibility.'[31]

However, for most of the twentieth century, cultural explanations were rarely mentioned in discussions about economic development and growth:

> As far as most economists were concerned the topic faded into the background. From time-to-time economists did and still do allude to culture but usually *en passant* or as a supplementary explanation that is proclaimed rather than demonstrated. A handful have gone to the other extreme and fiercely demanded that all cultural explanation should be rejected ...[32]

Now, in what has been described as the intellectual *volte face* of the 1990s, cultural explanations in economics have come back into fashion. This is partly due to academic interest in the so-called 'Asian values' which have been put forward as an explanation for the spectacular emergence of the Japanese economy in the 1980s, followed by that of South Korea in the 1990s and more recently those of India and China. Although all of these economies are to a greater or lesser extent integrated into the new world economy, they do not conform to the dominant Anglo-American capitalist model, and specifically Asian values are regarded as one of the reasons for their success. Similarly, the very lack of economic growth in many Middle Eastern countries is often attributed to Muslim values.

The weight of economic opinion is now running strongly in favour of cultural explanations for all kinds of societal change:

31   Kerby A. Miller, 'Emigration, Capitalism and Ideology in Post-Famine Ireland', in Richard Kearney, ed., *Migrations: The Irish at Home and Abroad* (Dublin: Wolfhound Press, 1990), 93.
32   Michael J. Mazarr, *Global Trends 2005: An Owner's Manual for the Next Decade* (London: Macmillan, 1999), 65.

> If one is searching for the foundational issues on which the engines of history fashion their trends, culture must surely rank among them. Culture plays an important role in shaping the everyday thoughts, beliefs, commitments and decisions of all human beings. Some cultures will equip their people for success over the next decade better than others. Culture therefore ranks as a critical tectonic plate of history, no less so than resource, supplies or the condition of the environment.[33]

However, cultural explanations in economics came back in fashion in the final quarter of the twentieth century because of interest in the so-called Asian values, which resulted in three key changes in the national psyche:

1. the gradual lifting of the inferiority complex that had clouded over the country.
2. an opening out to the world after decades of isolation and censorship.
3. a more accommodating attitude towards business and finance, especially among opinion formers.

The all-pervasive sense of a society in the grip of a giant inferiority complex has been widely noted. In Cathal Black's film *Korea* (1995), based on a John McGahern short story of the same name, there is a scene where the people of a rural village West of the Shannon await the installation of electricity in 1952 and a local declares that 'rural electrification is more than an amenity – it is a revolution that will sweep away the inferiority complexes'.[34] Garret FitzGerald, recalling Ireland in the late 1950s, made a similar point when he argued that one of the main benefits of our application for membership of the European Economic Community in the 1960s was the psychological impact on the population in wiping away the last vestiges of a post-colonial inferiority complex that had dogged the country since independence. It is one of the most remarkable aspects of Whitaker's achievement that although he was a civil servant by profession and an economist by trade – two careers which put a premium on rational thinking and seek to minimise emotional complications – he was always

---

33 Mazarr, *Global Trends*, 65.
34 Cathal Black, *Korea*, 1995.

acutely aware of the role of the psyche and the need for a sea change in the psychological make-up of Irish society if the economic targets set in the *First Programme for Economic Expansion* were to be achieved: 'Behind its sober prose *Economic Development* extended an invitation to Irish society to embark on a search for self-knowledge and not to flinch from the findings.'[35]

It would have been clear to Whitaker from the early stages of the planning process that he was about to overthrow the economic policies that had reigned supreme since 1932 and to some extent since 1922. In doing so, he was not just treading on the received economic wisdom of the established order, he was also in the process of discarding treasured nationalist shibboleths. By recommending that the protectionist policies of high tariff barriers be abandoned in favour of the opening up of the country to free trade and to the welcoming of foreign investment, he and his supporters were not only admitting that the 'ourselves alone' policies had not worked; they were also reversing the anti-materialist ethos of the new state. This ethos was located not only in the fact that Ireland was economically backward during the time, but in the fact that economic backwardness was regarded as a good thing. Acceptance, however tacit, of the desirability of economic growth with the objective of greater wealth meant jettisoning the Arcadian idyll famously articulated in de Valera's radio broadcast in 1943:

> The Ireland which we have dreamed of would be a home to a people who have valued material wealth only as a basis for right living, of a people who were satisfied with frugal things of the spirit, a land whose countryside would be bright with cosy homesteads, whose fields and villages would be joyous with the sounds of industry, with the romping of sturdy children, the laughter of comely maidens, whose firesides would be forums for the wisdom of old age. It would in a word be the home of people living the life that God desires that men should live.[36]

It is important to remember that this vision of an Ireland that was to be in the vanguard of a stand against the 'filthy modern tide' was by no means a

---

35 Joseph J. Lee, 'Society and Culture', in Frank Litton, ed., *Unequal Achievement: The Irish Experience 1957–1982* (Dublin: IPA Publications, 1982), 2.
36 Maurice Moynihan, *Éamon De Valera: Speeches and Statements, 1917–1973* (Dublin: Gill & Macmillan, 1980), 466.

Fianna Fáil monopoly. Five years later the first coalition Taoiseach, John A. Costello, similarly inveighed against the 'dark forces of materialism'.

Another aspect of the proposed plan was that it contained no reference to the issue of national sovereignty, which until then had been the main official objective of the new state. As Professor Ronan Fanning commented, 'what *Economic Development* did was to bring to an end the ruthless subordination of economic imperatives to the more compelling imperatives of Irish nationalism'.[37]

Whitaker was under no illusions about the enormity of the task, and that it would not be achieved merely by changing economic policies; he sensed all along that it wasn't just the economy that had become run down; the whole national psyche was in a similar state, and it was impossible to fix one without the other. This explains the unusual language he employed in his analysis. We still don't expect civil servants to use expressions like 'dark night of the soul' whilst on official duty.

Throughout his reports and memoranda there are constant references to the psychological damage to the population caused by the failure of the economy to provide an adequate standard of living, and to the all too prevalent mood of despondency about the country's future. Officials in Whitaker's position usually assume that economic policies alone will make a difference; he, in contrast, was always aware of how much the public mood contributed to the success or failure of these same policies.

---

37   Fanning, 'The Genesis of Economic Development Essay', 82.

CHAPTER 3

Seán Ó Riada: Musical Regeneration

Seán Ó Riada is the second major exemplar to be examined in relation to the revival that began in Ireland in the mid-to-late 1950s. Like Whitaker and Kinsella, he was a bright, self-confident Christian Brothers boy with a deep knowledge of and commitment to Irish history and culture, in particular to its musical tradition. Before examining Ó Riada's work and influence it is apposite to briefly comment on the special place of music in Irish life and culture.

Music: 'The Whole Nation Seems to Have a Turn That Way'

The history of Ireland contains prominent examples of intrepid visitors who travel from mainland Britain to witness for themselves the barbarity of the natives, and from the twelfth century onwards Irish society was portrayed by them, according to Leerssen, as a 'pool of the blackest ignorance, barbarity and superstition'.[1] The twelfth-century Welsh historian Giraldus Cambrensis reported in the late 1180s that 'this people then is one of forest dwellers and inhospitable, a people living off beasts and like beasts, a people that as yet adheres to the most primitive way of pastoral living'.[2] The philosopher David Hume blamed it all on the fact that the Romans never graced the country with their presence:

---

1   Joep Leerssen, *Mere Irish and Fíor-Ghael: Studies in the Idea of Irish Nationality, Its Development and Literary Expression Prior to the Nineteenth Century* (Cork: Cork University Press, 1996), 35.
2   Giraldus Cambrensis, quoted in Ibid., 35.

> The Irish from the beginning of time had been buried in the most profound barbarism and ignorance and as they were never conquered, or even invaded by the Romans, from whom all the western world derived its civility, they continued still in the most rude state of society and were distinguished only by those vices, to which human nature, not tamed by education nor restrained by laws, is forever subject ...[3]

However, Irish music was deemed an exception, and even Cambrensis was able to distinguish between the barbarity of the people and the subtlety of their music, which he described in his *Topographia Hibernica* as 'incomparably more skilful than any other nation I have ever seen', before adding:

> the perfection of their art seems to lie in their concealing it, as if it were the better for being hidden – an art revealed brings shame. Hence it happens that the very things that bring unspeakable delight to the minds of those who bring a fine perception and who can penetrate carefully to the secrets of the art, bore, rather than delight, those who have no such perception – who look without seeing and hear without being able to understand.[4]

He was not alone. An eighteenth-century traveller, Wiliam Chetwood, made a similar point: 'The Irish Musick has something particularly sweet and melancholy and the whole nation seems to have a turn that way.'[5]

But it wasn't just the case of overseas visitors recognising music as the one positive feature of Irish life; indigenous commentators were also acutely aware of the strength of the Irish music tradition. A survey of Irish minstrelsy in 1831 concluded 'that this country from an early period was famous for the cultivation of the kindred arts of poetry and music, stands universally admitted'.[6] A decade later the founder of the Young Ireland movement, Thomas Davis, confirms the importance of music in Irish society:

---

3   David Hume, quoted in Robert O'Driscoll, 'Foundations of the Literary and Musical Revival', in Cyril J. Byrne and Margaret Harry, eds, *Talamh an Éisc: Canadian and Irish Essays* (Halifax: Nimbus Publications, 1986), 52.
4   Kinsella, *Collected Poems 1956–2001*, 253.
5   Leerssen, *Mere Gael*, 68.
6   Marie Frances McCarthy, *Passing it On: Music and Irish Culture* (Cork: Cork University Press, 1999), 29.

> Music is the first facility of the Irish, and scarcely anything has such power for good over them – the use of this facility and this power, publicly and constantly to keep up their spirits, refine their tastes, warm their courage, increase their union and renew their zeal is the duty of every patriot.[7]

Music played an important role in mobilising support for the various phases of nationalism which sought to revitalise and legitimise an authentic Gaelic culture between the eighteenth and twentieth centuries, and in this role, its lineage can be traced back to ancient times:

> Sources indicate that music played a powerful role in pre-Christian Irish society; it was perceived as having magical effects and the power to control and shape behaviour, it had its origins in the 'other' world with the music of the fairies which was said to be of exceptional beauty and to have particular powers – the fairies sometimes conferred the gift of music on human beings ...[8]

In his seminal address 'The Necessity for De-Anglicising Ireland', Douglas Hyde, the founder of the Gaelic League, also recognised the central role of music in Irish culture: 'If Ireland loses her music she loses what is after her Gaelic language and literature her most characteristic possession.'[9] The emphasis on the importance of music continued into the new Irish Free State, and one of the first Ministers for Education, Tom Derrig, once again made an elaborate case for traditional music being at the core of Irish identity:

> That set of values which makes the Irish mind different looks out at us clearly from our old music, its idiom having in some subtle way the idiom of the Irish mind, its rhythms, its intervals, its speeds, its builds have not been chosen arbitrarily, but they are what they are because they are the musical expression, the musical equivalent of Irish thought and its modes ...[10]

---

7   Thomas Davies, quoted in Harry White, *The Keeper's Recital: Music and Cultural History in Ireland 1770–1970* (Cork: Cork University Press, 1998), 53.
8   McCarthy, *Passing it On*, 40.
9   Douglas Hyde, quoted in ibid., 73.
10 Gerry Smyth, *Noisy Island: A Short History of Irish Popular Music* (Cork: Cork University Press, 2005), 140.

We should bear in mind, however, that music is universally regarded as an important expression of culture: 'Music is in a sense a summatory activity for the expression of values, a means whereby the heart of the psychology of a culture is exposed.'[11] Music is one of the most accessible of all the arts and is therefore present in some shape or form in all societies. It has played a critical role in the establishment of national identity in countries as diverse as Poland, where Chopin's work performed this function, to Afghanistan, where 'music was a vital arm and not just a reflection of state cultural policy'.[12] Traditional musician Seamus Tansey makes a strong case for the special position of music in Irish culture, suggesting it derives from 'the wind, the rain, the flowing river that shapes the minds and passions of our ancient forefathers inspiring them to harness together all the sounds of animals, minerals, birds and insects so as it moulded itself into a melody of Ireland's soul'.[13] We have already seen that the Irish music tradition has been widely noted by a variety of overseas visitors throughout the ages and today Fáilte Ireland, the state organisation responsible for overseas tourism, categorises music as one of Ireland's main tourist attractions.

There is also the recognition of the Irish musical tradition across the world. The traditional music of Ireland was the only cultural baggage that impoverished emigrants took with them in the nineteenth century, and it made a significant impact on the development of American popular music. A young Bob Dylan, listening to the singing of The Clancy Brothers and Tommy Makem in the café bars of New York in the early 1960s, was struck by the similarity of their airs and traditions to his own music roots in the Midwest which had been strongly influenced by the railroad-building Irish emigrants. His anti-war protest song from that period, 'With God on their Side', was deliberately based on a well-known Irish air. A final argument

---

11 McCarthy, *Passing it On*, 17.
12 Martin Stokes, ed., *Ethnicity, Identity and Music* (Oxford: Berg Publishers, 1997), 11.
13 Scott Reiz, 'Tradition and Imagery: Irish Traditional Music and the Celtic Phenomenon', in Martin Stokes and Philip V. Bohlman, eds, Celtic *Music: Music at the Global Fringe* (Lanham, MD: Scarecrow Press, 2003), 163.

for the particular significance of traditional music in Irish culture is the fact that it is still orally transmitted:

> Ireland is unique in the Western world in still retaining a vigorous orally transmitted tradition of music – Ireland has two developed musical forms, folk music and sean-nós; the latter as complex and sophisticated as classical or European art music ...[14]

It may be possible to throw some further light on Ireland's musical tradition by considering Professor Michael Porter's 'Competitive Advantage of Nations' thesis, which seeks to explain why some countries are more successful than others in different areas of activity. He was referring to business and commerce, but it could also be argued that his idea can be used to explain aspects of cultural development – in any case, music is now a big business in its own right and therefore fits his contention. Porter believes that 'ultimately nations succeed in particular industries [activities] because their home environment is the most dynamic and the most challenging and stimulates and prods firms [musicians] to upgrade and widen their advantages over time'.[15] He puts forward four main determinants of national advantage:

1. Factor conditions: the inputs necessary to compete, for example, natural resources, capital and infrastructure.
2. Demand conditions: the nature of home demand for the product or service.
3. Related and supporting industries: the presence or absence of supplier industries.
4. Structure and rivalry: level and amount of competition within the industry.

Porter explains how the theory works for a variety of different businesses in different countries. For example, the Dutch have traditionally been above average purchasers of flowers to decorate their homes and

---

14   O'Connor, *Bringing It All Back Home*, 9.
15   Michael E. Porter, *The Competitive Advantage of Nations* (London: Macmillan, 1990), 71.

give to friends, so the industry in Holland developed very sophisticated methods of cultivation and preservation, as the climate is not ideal; hence the country is the world leader in cut flower exports in spite of a cold, grey climate. Porter also analyses the successful Italian shoe industry, arguing that its success is a direct result of the above-average propensity of the Italians for buying shoes. Applying this analysis to the music business in Ireland, we can see that Ireland probably scores quite highly for the four main determinants of competitive advantage. In terms of natural resources, the fact that it has been the accepted custom in Ireland for a long time that everyone should have at least one song to perform in company enables whatever talent there is to emerge and develops an interest in such performance among the whole population.

This in turn enhances domestic demand, and because consumers are highly sophisticated and demand is high, standards among musicians and groups are also high, which in turn means that anyone who makes it to the top in Ireland has come through an intensely competitive process which makes them more likely to succeed abroad. The number of groups competing for attention in the Irish market also facilitates a sophisticated infrastructure of recording studios, session musicians and management.

In spite of such a well-recognised tradition for musical excellence, by the 1950s the native art form had, like so many other aspects of Irish life, fallen into a deep malaise. That malaise had its roots in the nineteenth century, a time when Irish society was characterised by what Thomas Kinsella conceptualised as 'The Divided Mind'.[16] As the nation changed over from one language to another an entire cultural tradition was lost for the majority of the population in the process. The most popular music at the time in Ireland was the eponymous *Moore's Melodies*. A recent biographer of Thomas Moore, Kelly, has made the point that 'Irishness in Moore's era was a concept in flux',[17] and White has pointed out that his haunting and often beautifully written melodies 'repeatedly drew an association between the inherent nature of Irish melody and the historical conditions of

---

16 Thomas Kinsella, *Prose Occasions 1951–2006* (Manchester: Carcanet, 2009), 31.
17 Ronan Kelly, *Bard of Erin: The Life of Thomas Moore* (Dublin: Penguin Ireland, 2008), 71.

oppression, lament and betrayal which he believed to be its source'.[18] The melodies 'formed the secular hymn book of Irish nationalism', but they too often weaved a fine line between genuine sentiment and mawkish sentimentality, and 'they could never quite shake off the aura of the drawing room'.[19] Thomas Kinsella has also been particularly dismissive of Moore and his influence: 'He initiated the imagery of harp, heartbreak and vague patriotism that still passes for Irish in England and America – commonplace ideas with verbal ingenuity and charm – always a marketable combination.'[20] In Moore's defence it has been pointed out that he was appealing to a particular audience:

> The aim of the melodies was not to appeal to the passions of the angry multitudes but rather to the rich and educated who can afford to have their national zeal a little stimulated without exciting much dread of the excesses into which it might hurry them ...[21]

Although Moore has been out of fashion with Irish musical audiences for over half a century, he has recently been the subject of more favourable coverage: 'Despite the superficially frivolous aural impression, Moore's musical box contained more incendiary material – Irish audiences could hear claims to a national identity distinctly, if softly, voiced in his songs, his work then indicated the close but always ambivalent connection between nationalism, poetry and music.'[22]

The development of the ancient Irish traditional music heritage was not helped by the rise of a new Catholic middle class who, in their efforts to assume the mantle of the Anglo-Irish Protestant ascendancy they were replacing, were anxious to follow the ascendency's lead in matters of taste. There was confusion and uncertainty in musical development in Ireland from the late nineteenth century until the middle of the twentieth century

---

18   White, *The Keeper's Recital*, 45.
19   Ibid., 51.
20   Thomas Kinsella, *The Dual Tradition: An Essay on Poetry and Politics in Ireland* (Manchester: Carcanet, 1995), 48.
21   McCarthy, *Passing it On*, 40.
22   Lillis Ó Laoire, 'Irish Music', in Joe Cleary, ed., *The Cambridge Companion to Modern Irish Culture* (Cambridge: Cambridge University Press, 2005), 271.

between two different, often opposing traditions: a Gaelic tradition rooted in the past, rejecting harmony, and the formal classical European tradition.

In the immediate aftermath of the establishment of the Free State, the newly formed Raidió Éireann needed to have a more formal Irish musical repertoire and Seamus Clandillon, the first head of Broadcasting, conceived the idea of the céilidh band. This consisted of eight or nine musicians playing traditional Irish airs together with a mixture of instruments common to the big band 'swing' sound from America. But it was always an essentially hybrid sound with a jigging fairground beat based on a basic three-four time signature. It was capable of arousing a certain kind of atavistic response even in a society suspicious of excess, the emotionally intense and the erotic, as evidenced in Brian Friel's play *Dancing at Lughnasa* by the wild dance of the Mundy sisters when Raidió Éireann reaches the village of Ballybeg. But by the 1950s, the céilidh band had become an object of derision, particularly among the young, who succumbed *en masse* to the exotic attractions of Radio Luxembourg. Traditional music at the time was held in low esteem: 'Many regarded it as part of the "bogman" inheritance they wished to leave behind, while the minority who valued it did so by and large in terms which were not conducive to the long-term health of the music itself.'[23]

In 1959, Thomas Kinsella and John Reidy (the Ó Riada name-change came later) and their two young families arranged to go on holiday together to Ballyferriter in West Kerry. Reidy had travelled down a week early and when Kinsella arrived he was in a state of great excitement; he had found great singers and music in Kruger Kavanagh's pub in Dunquin, among them a sean-nós singer, Jerry Flaherty. Kinsella takes up the story:

> A voice from a dark corner near the fireplace began to sing. The song was *Casadh an tSugáin* and the singer Jerry Flaherty. I had heard the sean-nós, or old style before, without being attracted by the raw Oriental tonalities or the nasalized, strangulated delivery. For whatever reasons the effect was different now. Nothing intervened between the song and its expression. The singer managed many different things, but the result was to focus attention on the song, not on the performance or the quality of the voice. It was a special voice, adapted (like a reptile or an insect) to its

---

23   Smyth, *Noisy Island*, 21.

function. Mere beauty of tone would have distracted, attracting attention for its own sake. And the singer's act of communication was thoroughly completed by his audience. They sat erect and listened, lifted their glasses and drank, and murmured phrases of appreciation.[24]

That holiday was to have a profound influence on John Reidy. The sounds in the pub in Dunquin resonated with the traditional musical tradition of his childhood in Bruff, Co. Limerick, and he was inspired to dig deep into the roots of the traditional airs and graces of Irish music, an exercise that would ultimately 'startle the heart of a whole people'.[25] The singer, Jerry Flaherty, was drowned later the same year fishing for mackerel. He is commemorated in Kinsella's poignant and deeply felt elegy 'The Shoals Returning':

> He sings at the back of the shop:
> Slit eyes above high cheeks,
> Jaws drawn back
> Teeth bared to the voice.
> In the exercise of his gift
> His throat constricts. (CP 69)

Seán Ó Riada and the Transformation of Irish Music: Background

'It is not often that a single person, however gifted, can alter the character of a nation's culture. Ó Riada managed to do this, to a degree as was now [so] obvious that the personal nature of his achievement can be forgotten ...'[26] Surprisingly, given his influence and the fact that he died over fifty years ago, there has, as yet, been no biography of Seán Ó Riada. However,

---

24 Thomas Kinsella, *Fifteen Dead*, 67.
25 Ibid., 29.
26 Thomas Kinsella, 'Introduction', in Thomas Kinsella and Tomás Ó Canainn, eds, *Our Musical Heritage* (Dublin: Dolmen Press, 1982), 9.

biographical details are included in Kinsella & Ó Canainn[27] and Harris & Freyer.[28]

The Irish musical tradition was regarded with some contempt in the 1950s, especially by the urban population, who sneeringly referred to it as 'diddly eye' music. Ó Riada set out to change all that and rescue the Irish musical tradition from the mediocrity into which it had become emasculated by the céilidh band.

Seán Ó Riada was born in Cork city in 1931. The family moved shortly after that to Limerick, where he started to learn music. He himself recalled: 'Both my father and my mother were traditional fiddlers and we often had local musicians in our house.' As a young boy he studied the violin and the piano, and under the tutelage of a Dutch professor he studied music theory, counterpoint and harmony. He attended the Christian Brothers in Adare, but the family moved back to Cork, where he completed his secondary education. In 1948 he gained a scholarship to University College Cork (UCC), where he initially enrolled as a classics student but later switched to music and graduated with Honours in 1952. UCC was a cosmopolitan place in the late 1940s: a number of foreign students flocked there after the Second World War and Ó Riada plunged into a wide course of reading and talking which was oriented towards the ancient and modern cultures of Europe. As a student he earned pocket money by playing the piano with local jazz bands. In his teens and throughout his twenties he was known as John Reidy and his family were always known as the Reidys. Even as a teenager in Cork in the late 1940s he was a flamboyant, self-confident character with a taste for the beau monde: 'He saw himself as a cosmopolitan man, he smoked Gauloises, he affected all those things that we all affected when we were young and radical and read *Being and Nothingness* and all that.'[29] He moved to Dublin in 1953 and worked as assistant director of music for Ráidió Éireann. He quickly became established in Dublin's intellectual and artistic life, and formed a close friendship with Thomas

---

27   Ibid.
28   Bernard Harris and Grattan Freyer, eds, *The Achievement of Seán Ó Riada* (Ballina: The Irish Humanities Centre and Keohanes Ltd Ballina, 1981).
29   Philip King, Interview with author, 20 February 2007.

Kinsella, staying for a week in his Baggot St flat. He continued to cut an impressive dash, as film-maker George Morrison commented:

> At my first meeting with him I was much struck by three aspects of his personality: his very quick intelligence, his sensitivity, and the ingenuous disguise of an almost foppish Edwardian style of dress particularly manifested in a curly-brimmed hat, a cane, an embroidered waistcoat and a carefully nurtured and trimmed moustache.[30]

He soon became bored with his job in Ráidió Éireann, which was mainly administrative, and moved to Paris in 1955, where he began composing music and gave some recitals. But he returned to Dublin two years later and was appointed musical director of the Abbey Theatre. In 1958 the Abbey staged *Song of the Anvil*, by Bryan McMahon, which required a musical accompaniment, and it was this requirement that sparked Ó Riada's interest in the idea of the ensemble-playing of Irish music. It was to prove a fateful and fruitful spark whose flames are still burning brightly, but it required another ingredient before the fire could be properly lit. As we saw earlier, the missing link was supplied by the sean-nós singing of Jerry Flaherty in Dunquin while on holiday with the Kinsellas in 1959, where he

> heard something in the language, in the cadence of the language and in I suppose the onomatopoeic quality of the Irish language, in the sean-nós songs and in the airs attendant to them; he also heard a vernacular music which was the music of the ordinary people ...[31]

The Birth of Ceoltóirí Chualann

Ó Riada began to recruit musicians, initially for his Abbey Theatre assignment, and was introduced to accordionist Eamonn de Buitléir, through

---

30   George Morrison, 'Film Making', in Bernard Harris and Grattan Freyer, eds, *The Achievement of Seán Ó Riada* (Ballina: The Irish Humanities Centre and Keohanes Ltd Ballina, 1981), 64.
31   Philip King, Interview with author, 20 February 2007.

whom he met the piper Paddy Moloney, who was eventually to become the leader of the Chieftains. Others followed: whistle player Sean Potts, fiddler Martin Fay, accordion player Sonny Brogan and flautist Vincent Broderick. They became the nucleus of the group that began to rehearse in Ó Riada's house in Galloping Green and would eventually evolve into Ceoltóirí Chualann.

His approach bears an uncanny resemblance to that of Whitaker's for an equally radical task: the gathering together of a specially chosen group of young men to create change. From the beginning he 'established over them an almost hypnotic sway, and drew from them solo and ensemble performances that astonished even themselves'.[32] The influence of this group was felt immediately and widely, and transformed the world of traditional Irish music for good. His main material was the substantial body of traditional songs and dance tunes which had only survived in their purest form in remote parts of the country, hence the importance of his encounter with Jerry Flaherty. But to re-invent the sound he first had to re-invent the instruments. He went on to formulate his own idea of the ideal combination of musicians and instruments.

A key objective was to provide as much variation as possible in the solo instruments: the uilleann pipes, the flute and the tin whistle would make up the wind section, fiddles and accordions to fill out passages where the whole band were playing and a bodhrán but no drums. He wanted to include the harp, whose history went back to pre-Christian times, but because the traditional harp was almost impossible to find he introduced the harpsichord. The Ceoltóirí Chualann was the first group which presented solo players who remained soloists yet also played together in a completely different way. Ó Riada was utterly clear about the precise sound he wanted, and could be dogmatic and dictatorial about how exactly he wanted it. He disliked the accordion as a solo instrument and made his views known in a way that caused some offence:

> The player doesn't make the notes, they are already there, he only has to press a button. Unfortunately, this instrument, designed by foreigners for the use of peasants, with neither the time, application or inclination for a worthier instrument is gaining

---

32 Philip King, Interview with author, 20 February 2007.

Seán Ó Riada: Musical Regeneration

> vast popularity throughout the country, the reason is the laziness which afflicts this country at the moment ...[33]

It is interesting to note here that the last line, although it would not be spoken in this way by Whitaker or Kinsella, is indicative of how impatient all three were with the paralysis of 1950s Ireland.

Ó Riada's earlier involvement with jazz would also appear to have exerted a significant influence on the way he developed the Ceoltóirí, the degree of variation that occurs during a performance being very similar to how a jazz group performs: ornamentation and variation lie at the heart of all traditional playing and singing. It is through variation, embellishment and ornamentation that the musician expresses his or her technical skill, imaginative powers, mastery of the form and ultimately his or her personality.

But Ó Riada's most revolutionary innovation was his success in changing the whole nature of the way in which traditional Irish music is received:

> Irish traditional music was traditionally played as a solo player, there was a piper, there was a fiddle player, it was usually to put the rhythm under the dancer's, foot, that was its raison d'être, the job of the musician was to put the rhythm under the dancer's foot, this was essentially dance music, the traditional music of Ireland is jigs, reels, polkas but he took an ensemble form, which you could argue is the European art music form, and he took an orally transmitted tradition which was never written down and he blended one with the other ...[34]

Ó Riada transformed dance music into listening music. The ultimate moment of transformation came with the famous Ceoltóirí Chualann concert in the Shelbourne Hotel in 1959. Philip King describes the occasion and the outcome:

> I mean the very first time he played where did he choose to play, the Shelbourne Hotel, he chose the Shelbourne, I mean to bring Irish music into the Shelbourne was deadly, he said no place was too good for this music so we'll bring the mountain to Mohamed, I mean these were boggers, guys down from the country who played

33 Seán Ó Riada, 'Our Musical Heritage', in Thomas Kinsella and Tomás Ó Canainn, eds, *Our Musical Heritage* (Dublin: Funduireacht an Riadigh in association with Dolman Press, 1982), 69.
34 Philip King, Interview with the author, 20 February 2007.

> music that when we think of it was redolent of poverty, depression, deprivation, and they came from the leafy suburbs of Ailesbury Rd, the women wore fur coats and they were all smoking and drinking large ones and after they heard what they heard the people said – that is ours, give it to me, I can be happy with this.³⁵

Having won the hearts of the ladies of Dublin 4, Ó Riada went on to conquer the rest of the country when he was commissioned to write the score for George Morrison's archival film of the 1916 Rising. The soundtrack for *Mise Éire* was the sound that, in Kinsella's memorable phrase 'startled the heart of the whole people'.³⁶ He based the score on the traditional air 'Róisín Dubh'. Kinsella describes this as 'Ireland's great emblematic song of lamentation and pride', and says of Ó Riada that 'he virtually re-created it and wrung from it, in full Mahlerian and Sibelian harmonies every emotional possibility. It is a monument to his talent that the result, while devastating the audience for whom it was produced, remains a fine musical achievement.'³⁷ Even forty years later people who remember little or nothing about the film can vividly recall the impact of the music at the time. Kieran McGowan, one of the senior civil servants and businessman interviewed for this thesis, recalls:

> I was brought up in Ranelagh and had no interest whatsoever in traditional Irish music and still haven't but I will always remember when I first heard *Mise Éire*, the music not the film, it was a goosepimply moment and there was a certain kind of pride that I can't explain.³⁸

The poet John Montague, a friend of Ó Riada's who was also on the faculty of UCC, makes the same point in his autobiography: 'It sent a thrill of astonished pride through the nation to hear one of our oldest tunes, *Róisín Dubh*, surging lavishly out through full orchestra, or in the extremely modern trickle of chords which mourns the execution of rebel leaders of 1916.'³⁹

---

35   Ibid.
36   Kinsella, *Fifteen Dead*, 29.
37   Ibid., 60.
38   Kieran McGowan, Interview with the author, 23 February 2007.
39   John Montague, *The Pear is Ripe: A Memoir* (Dublin: Liberties Press, 2007), 194.

Ó Riada's other lasting legacy came from one of the seminal events of the early 1960s, which was subsequently to have profound implications for Irish society: the Second Vatican Council. One of the new measures introduced by what came to be known as Vatican II was that the Latin Mass was replaced by vernacular languages, so there was a requirement for new church music to replace the traditional music with its plain chant and polyphony. Ó Riada was commissioned by the monks at Glenstal Abbey, and the result is the now famous Ó Riada mass.

A Farewell to English

In 1963, Ó Riada left Dublin and his job in the Abbey, taking his family to live in the Gaeltacht, initially in the Kerry Gaeltacht and then to Cúil Aodha in West Cork. He also took up the post of Lecturer in Irish Music in UCC, but his best work was behind him, as his drinking problem intensified during the last ten years of his life. It could be argued that although the move from Dublin was accompanied by major declarations of intent about the superiority of Irish culture and the Gaeltacht way of life, he had reached an artistic cul-de-sac, and that this move was more of a retreat than an advance. Just before his abandonment of the Pale he gave a series of radio talks on Ráidió Éireann recording his thinking on the history and development of Irish traditional music under the title heading *Our Musical Heritage*. There he articulated ideas on the distinctiveness of the Irish musical tradition which exemplify the kind of recognition of local difference in a global context which this book argues is critical for small nations in a global world. That this recognition is advanced in terms of Ireland's separation from, rather than its connection to, world culture is perhaps symptomatic of Ó Riada's equivocal legacy. In these broadcasts he made the case that distinctiveness was due to the fact that Ireland had remained free from the Greco-Roman intellectual worldview. Ó Riada presents his case in some detail:

> The Renaissance passed us by, the best of our classical poetry was in full flower before it, its effect on Irish poetry was minimal. Traditional Irish art never adopted the Greco-Roman forms spawned by the renaissance which have become the basis of European art, take the European notion of development, a development that moves to a crescendo of tension ending in a crisis the resolution of which produces catharsis, this is the graph of a play by Shakespeare, of a Verdi opera, of a Hollywood film, and it is all quite foreign to traditional Irish art, the simplest picture of traditional Irish art is the ancient symbol of the serpent with the tail in its mouth – in my end is my beginning – a cyclic form – this is more realistic than the European graph because it corresponds more to real life.[40]

Ó Riada here seems to be prefiguring what Richard Kearney would later conceptualise into an account of how the 'Irish Mind' differed from the 'linear centralising logic of the Graeco-Roman culture which dominated most of Western Europe'. Kearney argues that the Irish intellectual tradition represented 'a counter-movement to the mainstream of hegemonic rationalism'.[41] Crosson has noted a similar aspect in Kinsella's poetry: 'A comparable circularity is apparent within Kinsella's work while his recurring use of the ouroboros motif echoes Ó Riada's description of traditional music.'[42]

Ó Riada's theorising became more extreme after he moved to West Cork, and towards the end of his life he became embroiled in a debate with Charles Acton, the music critic of the *Irish Times*. Acton, in the course of a lukewarm review of an Ó Riada concert, had provoked an aggressive response from the musician:

> What have I learned? Very broadly that there are in this small island two nations: the Gaelic, or Irish nation and the Pale. The Irish nation, tiny as it is at the moment, has a long professional, literary and musical tradition. The Pale on the other hand has a tradition of amateurishness.[43]

---

40 Ó Riada, 'Our Musical Heritage', 20.
41 Richard Kearney, *The Irish Mind* (Dublin: Wolfhound Press, 1985), 9.
42 Seán Crossan, 'The Given Note: Traditional Music, Crisis and the Poetry of Seamus Heaney', in Anne Karhio, Seán Crosson and Charles I. Armstrong, eds, *Crisis and Contemporary Poetry* (London: Palgrave Macmillan, 2008), 125.
43 Harris and Freyer, *The Achievement of Seán Ó Riada*, 151.

This seems an unnecessarily harsh assessment and one difficult to sustain, but Acton in a reply wisely chose to ignore it and makes a final plea to the composer not to turn his back on the wider European musical tradition and the wellsprings of his own talent.

Although Ó Riada is now primarily regarded as a composer who revolutionised Irish traditional music, and despite his above protestations, he was always well versed in the mind of Europe and his earlier compositions were in the classical Western tradition. His most highly regarded composition from this period, *Nomos 2*, was based on verses from the Theban plays of Sophocles, and in assessing this work an Irish musical contemporary, Seoirse Bodley, makes the point that

> the recurrent emotional element in much of his work is an underlying pessimism coupled with a sense of ironic despair – *Nomos 2* concerns itself largely with the futility of human existence and the suffering inherent in living, his works show a concern for the development of music, a serious questioning of the purpose of life and a sense of the tragedy of the human condition that belies any impression of him as a lightweight or frivolous person ...[44]

Another contemporary Irish composer, Gerald Victory, makes the point in commenting on Ó Riada that 'Irishmen of sensitivity had realised after the great trauma of the Second World War that the older apparently simple and straightforward aims of Irish culture and nationalism would no longer suffice'.[45]

How then do we account for the fact that in moving to West Cork Ó Riada seemed to be retreating into the opposite direction, away from engagement with world culture? One possible reason for this 'retreat' is that, like his two contemporaries, Whitaker and Kinsella, Ó Riada had complete faith in the validity of Irish traditional culture and the innate capacity of Irish people to compete on any playing field, and sensed that he

---

44   Seoirse Bodley, 'The Original Compositions: An Assessment', in Bernard Harris and Grattan Freyer, eds, *The Achievement of Seán Ó Riada* (Ballina: The Irish Humanities Centre and Keohanes Ltd Ballina, 1981), 30–40.
45   Gerald Victory, 'Ó Riada on Radio', in Bernard Harris and Grattan Freyer, eds, *The Achievement of Seán Ó Riada* (Ballina: The Irish Humanities Centre and Keohanes Ltd Ballina, 1981), 42.

was not going to be a great Irish composer in the Western classical music tradition. In other words, he realised that his contribution to musical culture would be confined to his native tradition. It has been argued here that his knowledge of the European musical tradition and of jazz had a significant influence on his career, and although he may subsequently appear to have disavowed all outside muses, this may have been born more from a sense of frustration than belief. His achievement in reinvigorating the Irish native musical tradition, in other words, still needs to be situated in terms of his engagement with a larger global musical culture.

Seán Ó Riada was taken ill during the Summer of 1971 and was operated on in London, where he died in October at the age of forty. A nurse in the hospital assumed he was in his seventies. Charles Acton made the following point in his obituary: 'As a musician Seán Ó Riada had immense promise to be our first great composer. The width of his activity, his zest for actual life threatened the realisation of this promise, a continued anxiety to many of his friends. As a result, and of his life being so tragically cut short in his prime, this promise cannot now be fulfilled.'[46] Thomas Kinsella echoed the sentiment more succinctly: 'The waste! Abject. Irrecoverable' (CP 145).

Ó Riada's Legacy: Do the Critics Have a Case?

> One man in particular responded to the challenge presented to Irish music by the twentieth century. His name was Seán Ó Riada. He was a man for all seasons: a composer trained in the art music of Europe who immersed himself in the oral music tradition of Ireland. He was exercised all his life by the question of Irish cultural identity, especially but not exclusively concerned with cultural expression through music. The consequences of Ó Riada's work were far-reaching: contemporary, classical, folk and rock musicians of recent years who have chosen to work with Irish idioms, cite him as a creative source in their work: generations of Irish people are indebted to him for restoring to them the nation's music.[47]

46   Charles Acton, 'Obituary for Seán Ó Riada', in Bernard Harris and Grattan Freyer, eds, *The Achievement of Seán Ó Riada* (Ballina: The Irish Humanities Centre and Keohanes Ltd Ballina, 1981), 163.
47   O'Connor, *Bringing It All Back Home*, 91.

Seán Ó Riada: Musical Regeneration

Almost forty years after his death, Seán Ó Riada is still regarded as a 'national treasure' by the Irish traditional music community, the Irish public and above all by Irish poets who continue to revere his memory. However, there are some critics, notably Harry White, who have been critical of Ó Riada's output:

> His work connotes a startling degree of failure and success; at once the only composer to have been wholly received into the cultural matrix of Ireland's preponderantly linguistic sense of itself and at the same time a figure of tragic indirection and unresolved insight ...[48]

Much of White's thesis on Ó Riada is concerned with lamenting the fact that European 'art' music failed to establish a strong foothold in Ireland, and with a belief that, like *Moore's Melodies*, Irish music could never quite shake off the 'aura of the drawing room', because at a deeper cultural level

> the ideological weight of musical preservation and the projection of music as a badge of sectarian culture, second only to language, collectively made the development of an emancipated compositional voice in Irish art music an impossibility – instead the preoccupation with 'folksong' not as a resource but as a substitute for the art tradition hindered the transformation from Gaelic to modern Irish modes of musical expression in the second half of the 19th century ...[49]

White believes that Ó Riada has been seriously over-rated by a complaisant Irish cultural establishment: 'He knew that the predominant perception of an "Irish" art music depended on an undernourished and overworked representation of a corpus of ethnic melody which led again and again to the same hopeless cul-de-sac of arrangement and variation.'[50] If Charles Acton's criticism of Ó Riada was predicated on a waste of a talent that could have led to greater things, White's is more fundamental: that because of the direction pursued by Ó Riada he effectively killed off the possibility of anyone leading on to higher things:

---

48 White, *The Keeper's Recital*, 125.
49 Ibid., 73.
50 Ibid., 126.

> The significance of Ó Riada then is not that he was the 'greatest Irish composer of the twentieth century' but that he silenced it [the possibility of Irish classical composition] too in its address upon the Irish mind, in its stead he advanced the claim not of original composition but of the ethnic repertory itself.[51]

White accepts Ó Riada's talent but believes it was wasted:

> The most interesting voice by far in Irish music, and certainly the most imaginative, was drawn away from the European aesthetic in a crisis of such magnitude – personal, aesthetic, musical and perhaps psychological – that it forced a crisis in turn that was to affect music in Ireland long after his death.[52]

There is undoubtedly some truth in White's thesis that classical music is an underdeveloped art form in Ireland because it became entangled in a 'cultural polarisation between ethnic and colonial ideologies of culture – so that the metaphorical power of music imaginatively eclipsed any real concern with the cultivation of music per se'.[53] It is equally possible that Ó Riada's rejection of the European aesthetic in favour of the pure note of Irish traditional music may have limited his potential. However, it seems unfair to place the entire blame for the lack of significant classical Irish composition at one man's door. Although it hasn't been mentioned as such by his critics, there may also be an unconscious regret that with his knowledge of the Irish traditional and classical European musical traditions he chose to concentrate on the former and never attempted to create an art music based on the traditional musical heritage, following the example of Sibelius in Finland, Chopin in Poland and Grieg in Norway. Instead Ó Riada feared that the Irish tradition was in danger of dying out unless it was re-introduced to the Irish people in a way that was of interest to them. He was also aware of the complexity of the sean-nós tradition and the fact that it was not only different to European art music but closer to oriental music:

---

51 Ibid., 149.
52 Harry White, *The Progress of Music in Ireland* (Dublin: Four Courts Press, 2005), 19.
53 Ibid., 42.

> Irish music doesn't use the same scales as European music, Irish music is modal, western ears are more attuned to harmonic music where notes are sounded together as in chords or harmony singing, Irish music is essentially monophonic, single sound, and depends on a single decorated melody line.[54]

In retrospect, the conclusion that Ó Riada's compositional output was limited is hard to avoid. His classical work is rarely heard nowadays, the *Mise Éire* score is becoming a distant memory and only the 'Ó Riada Mass' is in constant use. But from the point of view of this book, his influence and impact remain hugely significant for a number of reasons. Firstly, there is the crucial role he played during the critical years between the mid-1950s and mid-1960s, when the country swung from despair, disillusionment and despondency to a renewed belief in the future buoyed by an increased self-confidence. To paraphrase Declan Kiberd's line about an earlier cultural revival, he 'made Ireland interesting again to the Irish.'[55] Philip King goes further: 'That part of our ability to be comfortable in identifying with our place, our accent and who we are begins with Ó Riada.' The people who have articulated the influence and impact of Ó Riada best were poets rather than music critics. Kinsella has devoted two entire Peppercanister volumes to the memory of Ó Riada, *A Selected Life* and *Vertical Man*, and a third, *Out of Ireland*, is dominated by the composer. Seamus Heaney has written two significant poems about him: 'In Memoriam' imagines him as 'our' Jacobean prince driving the Ulster Orchestra south, and in 'The Given Note' he recreates Ó Riada's epiphany at Dunquin, where the airs of Irish music are driven in by the wind from the Atlantic. John Montague also wrote in his honour and acknowledged his debt to Ó Riada as an influence for his own most famous work: 'I always saw *The Rough Field* as polyphonic, a long poem with many contrasting voices. And of course it was deeply influenced by my friendship with Seán Ó Riada.'[56] Section VIII of *The Rough Field*, 'Patriotic Suite', is dedicated to Ó Riada, and in a later volume, *A Slow Dance*, Montague

---

54   O'Connor, *Bringing It All Back Home*, 66.
55   Kiberd, *Inventing Ireland*, 3.
56   John Montague, Sleeve notes for *The Rough Field* (Dublin: Claddagh Records, 2003).

ends with a sequence of eight poems under the collective title 'Ó Riada's Farewell':

> Roving, unsatisfied ghost
> Old friend, lean closer
> Lever in your stalls
> But still in this quick
> Of your chosen earth.[57]

Later Montague was to echo some of the ambiguities of Ó Riada's legacy: 'The argument about Seán Ó Riada's central achievement continues. We are all inclined to glamorise those who die young and Seán has come to embody the Irish equivalent of Chopin's legend. That he was musically gifted, in diverse ways, is beyond doubt, but did the diversity deflect the intensity?'[58]

Ó Riada's music continues to reverberate in the work of Irish poets, and a new volume by Gerry Smyth in 2007 contains a typical example:

> This mid-April morning, between oration
> and oration, we hear once more Ó Riada's
> back-stiffening threnody
> familiar, as if it was written yesterday.[59]

The second reason for the significance of Ó Riada is his influence on the subsequent development of Irish music. One of the most enduring and successful of all Irish groups is the Chieftains, who were a direct line of descent from the original Ceoltóirí Chualann and who are still performing all over the world. The hugely influential band Planxty was also indebted to Ó Riada's work, in particular to his fusion of the Irish musical tradition with the improvised jazz ensemble tradition. A wide range of other bands and groups, from Horslips in the 1970s, the Bothy Band in the 1980s, Altan in the 1990s and Matt Molloy's Western Ocean String Quartet in the early twenty-first century, all owe a substantial debt

---

57   John Montague, *New Collected Poem* (Loughcrew: Gallery Press, 2012), 306.
58   Montague, *The Pear is Ripe*, 191.
59   Gerard Smyth, *The Mirror Tent* (Dublin: Dedalus, 2007), 61.

to Ó Riada's innovations. Even *Riverdance*, the most widely visited Irish music event in history, would probably never have happened without the guiding influence of Seán Ó Riada. Both traditional musician and broadcaster Philip King and Bill Whelan, the *Riverdance* composer (2009), have confirmed this to the author.

A recent review of culture in modern Ireland which is highly critical of recent literary output argues that Irish traditional music is our most successful cultural export:

> If Irish culture was once best known to the wider world for its Revivalist poets and dramatists and for its high modernist literary giants, today the only figures of really comparable stature on both the domestic and international stage are popular music icons such as Bono, Van Morrison, Bob Geldof and Sinead O'Connor – Irish musical talent, working domestically in a sustained manner over several decades and in a variety of fields from sean-nós and traditional through classical to punk have created a musical culture capable of tapping into wider global circuits without repudiating a distinctive Irish component.[60]

While the latter argument may be stretching a point, there is no denying the international success of Irish music and Ó Riada's influence on that success. The iconic 1970s group Horslips played a key role in fusing Ó Riada's traditional Irish music with the rock 'n' roll music phenomenon that had captured the imagination of youth over most of the world and had come to epitomise what became known as youth culture. If Ó Riada's Shelbourne Hotel concert in 1959 represented one of the seminal moments in twentieth-century Irish music, the other was a very different one in the Theatre Royal a few years earlier: Bill Haley's introduction of rock 'n' roll to a wildly appreciative audience of a new Irish species – the teenager. Thirteen- to nineteen-year-olds had always existed, but the 'teenager' was different: moody, rebellious and defiantly individual with their own cultural values and worldview, articulated primarily by the new American-inspired music that set them apart from the dominant parental, political and Church influences of the time. A teenager during the late 1950s who subsequently became a leading Irish businessman vividly recalls the event:

60   Joe Cleary, *Outrageous Fortune*, 106–107.

> I remember my mother trying to prevent me going to see Bill Haley but we all went anyway and suddenly there we were dancing in the aisles and jumping round the place – we'd never done anything like it before.[61]

Without Ó Riada's inspired intervention, an entire generation could have abandoned Irish music completely, but Horslips provided a bridge between the two traditions. They were middle class, college educated, worked in advertising and were young men about Dublin in the late 1960s. They were looking for a sound that was Irish but also contemporary: 'It was a matter of holding out for a more integrated culture as opposed to something second hand – which meant forging a new idiom – it was an attempt to create something indigenous and new, but essentially indigenous.'[62] The result is a series of albums from 1972 until they broke up in 1980 which were categorised as 'Celtic Rock', and the Ó Riada influence was clear from the start.

There was also a possible Kinsella influence. They released an album entitled *The Táin* in 1972, and their most celebrated recording was *The Book of Invasions: A Celtic Symphony* (1975). Philip Chevron, who was later to become a member of another influential band, the Pogues, recalls the impact of Horslips: 'Irish music as officially presented didn't speak for me or for thousands like me. But Horslips did and some Horslips fans went away and listened to Seán Ó Riada records.'[63] Jim Lockhart, a member of Horslips, has confirmed Ó Riada's influence on the band, and believes that without him, Horslips's music would never have evolved the way it did. Two members of the group, Barry Devlin and Lockhart himself, were particularly interested in traditional music, but it was the impact and fame achieved by Ó Riada in the 1960s that enabled the evolution of their distinctive fusion into Celtic Rock. At a later date, a similar conversion occurred for Bono, who had rejected everything Irish at school until a teacher introduced him to the music of Seán Ó Riada, 'which despite himself he liked'.[64] Bono now feels that U2 has an indigenous Irish personality: 'I think

---

61 Jerry Liston, Interview with the author, 11 February 2007.
62 Jim Lockhart, Interview with the author, 8 November 2007.
63 Philip Chevron, quoted in O'Connor, *Bringing It All Back Home*, 124.
64 O'Connor, *Bringing it All Back Home*, 130.

there's an Irishness to what U2 do, I'm not quite sure what it is. I think it's something to do with the romantic spirit of the words I write but also of the melodies that Edge makes on the guitar. Now the rock 'n' roll element that comes through Larry would hardly be Irish yet the abandonment in the way he plays the kit is intrinsically Irish.'[65]

Mícheál Ó Súilleabháin, the founder of the Irish World Music Centre at the University of Limerick, who was himself taught by Ó Riada in the late 1960s as a music student in UCC, has commented:

> My own role is one of cultural mediation and in terms of this there are four figures who are cultural bridges. These are: Turlough O'Carolan in the 18th century who was a bridge between Gaelic Ireland and Anglo Ireland at the time; Thomas Moore was another great example, the Catholic who went to Trinity, used Irish melodies but not in an Irish mould. Seán Ó Riada was very much a mediation figure as well, when he took an sean-nós air and put it into an orchestral arrangement, but is also seen holding a goatskin drum and then in a sense rejects the orchestra and starts a band with a bunch of traditional musicians who can't read music. And finally, Tommie Potts who got ensnared or lured into an arena between classical and traditional music ...[66]

Perhaps the last word should go to Joe Cleary, whose recent survey of contemporary Irish literature casts a very cold eye on current standards but is unstinting in his praise for Irish music:

> In the opening decades of the twentieth century the Abbey Theatre may have been the nerve-centre of a literary revival whose stars claimed the attention of the literary capitals of London and Paris. By the closing decades of the same century it was now Windmill Lane Recording Studios that commanded the global limelight; the Abbey Theatre surviving mainly as a museum, a site of pilgrimage for literary tourists in a Dublin now much better known to the world for its rock stars than its writers.[67]

Whether one agrees or not with Cleary's conclusion, I believe that Seán Ó Riada's musical initiative played a critical role in the second revival, a

65 Ibid., 130.
66 Ethel Crowley, 'Finding Myself at the Cultural Crossroads: An Interview with Mícheál Ó Súilleabháin', in Ethel Crowley and Jim MacLoughlin, eds, *Under the Belly of the Tiger: Class, Race, Identity, and Culture in the Global Ireland* (Dublin: Irish Reporter Publications, 1997), 128.
67 Cleary, *Outrageous Fortune*, 107.

role whose influence is still being reflected in Irish culture and whose contribution to national self-confidence, although impossible to measure, is likely to have had a profound effect on the nascent business class which emerged at the same time by reminding them of a tradition of Irish excellence.

The third figure who was at the heart of the second revival was the poet and translator Thomas Kinsella. He was a close friend of Ó Riada's, who himself stayed for a week in Kinsella's small flat in the early 1950s, where they listened to classical music and jazz together:

> I remember the elaborate opulent close of *Der Rosenkavalier* filling the mean little space: the unmade single bed, the dusty electric fire glowing in the grate, spattered with butts, Reidy's narrow unfocussed face intent in the dark like an animal.[68]

In spite of their very different backgrounds and personalities, both artists were to pursue a similar path in re-presenting ancient Irish traditional culture to a twentieth-century audience, and would remain close friends until Ó Riada's death in 1971.

---

68 Kinsella, *Fifteen Dead*, 65.

CHAPTER 4

Thomas Kinsella: The Poetic Muse

Kinsella's contribution to the second revival is less well known than that of Whitaker or Ó Riada, but he was a key figure in the intellectual life of Ireland in the 1950s and 1960s, and was closely associated with both men. The year 1956 was an eventful one for the emerging twenty-eight-year-old Dublin poet. He had married a year earlier and was about to move from his bachelor flat in Baggot Street, shortly to be celebrated in one of his best-known early poems, 'Baggot Street Deserta', to the more suburban environs of Glenageary. His fourth pamphlet poem, *Death of a Queen*, was published in 1956, and it was followed later that year by his first book, *Poems*, in a limited edition of 250 copies. The book was published by Dolmen Press, where Kinsella was a director, having become friendly with Liam Miller, who founded the press, in the early 1950s. Miller believed that anyone involved in the press should have a working knowledge of all the processes, so Kinsella was known to lend a hand in the printing and, indeed, may be one of the few modern poets who physically printed his own work:

> I would play my part in holding the print and inserting the pieces upside-down – it was an old Adana machine that made a noise like a bacon slicer – I set up some of my own early poems.[1]

In an RTÉ TV documentary, *One Fond Embrace*, Kinsella paid tribute to Miller's insistence on the highest artistic and production standards in publishing poetry,[2] and Kinsella continued to pay meticulous attention to

---

[1] O'Driscoll, 'Interview with Thomas Kinsella', *Poetry Ireland* 25 (Spring 1989), 59.
[2] Seán Ó Mordha, *One Fond Embrace* (London: British Broadcasting Corporation, 1991).

the production standards of his own Peppercanister imprint throughout his career.

The young poet was also in the unusual position of being privy to the practical realities of the economic crisis facing the country because of his day job as a civil servant in the Department of Finance. He was appalled by the situation, and in his draft notes for the poem '1956' he wrote: 'In the grim years the whole country was an empty pocket'.[3] He described the large-scale emigration of the time that began on the boat to Holyhead as 'the national journey'.[4] Although he was a dutiful civil servant, remembered by his boss T. K. Whitaker for his 'priestly' attitude to his work, it wasn't his true vocation. He was fascinated by the dedication of the senior civil servants who under Whitaker's direction were beginning the detailed research which would come to fruition two years later with the publication of the *First Programme for Economic Expansion*, but his real interests were literary, and at the time he was immersed in the task of a new translation of the *Táin*. It is worth noting, however, that the working methods of the civil servants did influence his own very precise working methods as a poet:

> I do regard my experience with T. K. Whitaker as having been very helpful: the systematic behaviour that I observed in action. I was his private secretary for a while and I was able to observe this at close quarters. I made my own use of it as best I could and that is how long poems became possible – it was very impressive, alertness, openness, organisation.[5]

Civil servants with literary ambitions were not uncommon in Ireland of the 1950s, and Whitaker refers benignly to the propensity of members of his staff dabbling in the arts as 'common' but regarded it as an 'amiable aberration'.[6]

Kinsella's interest in the ancient manuscripts and stories of Ireland was encouraged first by Miller, who was interested from a publisher's point of

3   Derval Tubridy, *Thomas Kinsella: The Peppercanister Poems* (Dublin: University College Dublin Press, 2001), 98.
4   Andrew Fitzsimons, *The Sea of Disappointment* (Dublin: University College Dublin Press, 2008), 56.
5   O'Driscoll, 'Interview with Thomas Kinsella', 60.
6   Whitaker, Interview with author, 22 February 2007.

view, but also by Whitaker, who was deeply committed to the usage and restoration of the Irish language. It was in fact Whitaker who was ultimately instrumental in securing Kinsella's release from the civil service to become a full-time writer following a visit to his secretary, who was recovering from an illness in hospital. Whitaker noticed the bed strewn with manuscripts and enquired what they were. On being told that these were the beginnings of an attempt to create a modern translation of the *Táin*, he was immediately interested and gave the project every encouragement.

Kinsella's interest in the ancient stories was kindled by his parents and the network of immediate relations who populated the mean streets from Dublin's South inner-city working-class area known as 'The Liberties', westward out to Kilmainham and further out to Chapelizod and Inchicore. It was from this unlikely background that a poet emerged who would in time immortalise these inner-city streets in poetry in the way that an earlier mentor, James Joyce, had done in prose. In order to understand the nature of his artistic impulse as it relates to the central concerns of this book regarding revival, it will be necessary to examine Kinsella's family background.

'Twas down by Anna Liffey'

Kinsella has divulged basic biographical information in interviews, notably with Haffenden[7] and in his own publication *A Dublin Documentary*,[8] but the most detailed biographical details on Kinsella are to be found in Carolyn Rosenberg's Kent State University thesis, *Let Our Gaze Blaze: The Recent Poetry of Thomas Kinsella*. Between 1973 and 1976, Rosenberg interviewed the poet on a number of occasions, but she also conducted separate interviews with the poet's wife, parents, brother, former teacher and neighbourhood friends.[9]

7   John Haffenden, Interview with Thomas Kinsella in *Viewpoint: Poets in Conversation with John Haffenden* (London: Faber & Faber, 1981).
8   Thomas Kinsella, *A Dublin Documentary* (Dublin: O'Brien Press, 2006).
9   Carolyn A. Rosenberg, *Let Our Gaze Blaze: The Recent Poetry of Thomas Kinsella*, unpublished doctoral dissertation: Kent State University Graduate College, 1980.

Thomas Kinsella was born in 1928 in Inchicore, a small village on the outer western fringes of Dublin city. His family lived in an area known as 'The Ranch', between the CIÉ Engineering Works, one of the biggest employers in the area, and the River Liffey, with the Phoenix Park at the other side of the river. A mile or two into the centre of the city was the Guinness Brewery, where his father worked. The family seemed to lead a peripatetic existence, moving from 'The Ranch' during the 1930s closer to town and Kinsella's grandparents, in a succession of house changes from Tyrconnell Street to Phoenix Street to Basin Lane, then Irwin Street, back to Basin Street Upper, before finally, in 1949, moving out of the old inner city to the new working-class suburb of Walkinstown. In the middle of these moves they emigrated to Manchester at the beginning of the Second World War in 1939, but this didn't work out and the family moved back in 1942. There is a suggestion that Thomas lived with aunts and grandparents for some of his childhood, and there is no doubt that his father and mother's relations played a large part in his upbringing:

> My mother's parents, the Casserlys, came from Ballinafid in Co.Westmeath; the Kinsellas from Tinahely in Co. Wicklow. Grandfather Casserly, 'The Boss' was employed by an insurance company as a collector, he was a man about town unreliable on a bicycle. Grandfather Kinsella was a quieter person, long retired from Guinness's when I knew him: deaf, and gentle and bald, a repairer of shoes. The wives of these men were formidable women. They both managed small shops in their houses: one in Basin Lane – the other in Bow Lane.[10]

The grandmothers were obviously an important influence on the young poet and, in what Kinsella has admitted is a composite portrait, they feature in a number of poems from *New Poems 1973*, a volume that represented a significant change in Kinsella's poetic direction as he began a Jungian exploration of family and national history. But the most important influences on his early life were his father and a number of inspirational teachers.

His father was an unusual man of strong character and convictions broadly based in the republican-socialist tradition, which was given little

---

10   Kinsella, *A Dublin Documentary*, 8.

encouragement in 1930s and 1940s Dublin, but which received some sustenance from one of the few militantly left-wing workforces in the city, the CIÉ Engineering Works in Inchicore. John Paul Kinsella is immortalised in the eighth Peppercanister Volume, *The Messenger*. This pamphlet demonstrates Kinsella's commitment to the transmission and contextualisation of the culture of Ireland's recent past in which the personal and public worlds interweave, in a particularly vivid way. As such it rewards sustained attention.

The title and, in particular, the front cover is ample proof of the poet's mordant sense of humour. His father's first job as messenger in the Post Office is described lovingly towards the end of the poem; 'a new messenger boy / stands there in uniform, with shining belt / he is all excitement –' (CP 218) but as *The Messenger* was also the title of a popular religious magazine of the time, the familiar red-and-black cover design of that magazine is wickedly parodied in the cover design of Kinsella's pamphlet, where the religious icons are replaced with Guinness memorabilia. The poem itself shows the poet in complete command of his material, holding the different strands of his father's life in perfect balance as he confidently weaves together his work, political activism, cultural and literary interests and family life.

There is a powerful cinematic quality to the way the life is described, sometimes in flashback, sometimes in fast forward, starting with the feeling of devastation which begins when the funeral and its attendant organisational requirements are complete and the full implications of the departed father never returning sink in, and ending with the poet's customary precision as he describes leaving the graveyard: 'our scattered tribe begins gathering itself / and trudged off onto a gravel path after it / grandchildren colourful and silent' (CP 219). The poem ebbs to and fro in a dazzling series of vignettes and even the risky attempt to describe the moment of his own conception – 'they have tussled in love / they are hidden near the river bank' – is triumphantly carried off by the ironic precision of the concluding line: 'I think this is where I come in' (CP 215). The most memorable vignettes are those which describe his father's political commitment and activities, especially the chilling scene where he angrily clutches the ten-year-old Thomas and drags him out of Mass following anti-socialist comments made by the priest from the pulpit:

> The Oblate Fathers was packed.
> I sat squeezed against a cold pillar.
> A bull voice rang among the arches. –
> He covered my hand with his
> and we started getting out
> in the middle of Mass past everybody.
> Father Collier's top half in the pulpit –
> a black mouth shouting
> Godless Russia after us. (CP 215)

That would have been a defining experience for a ten-year-old today, but in 1930s Ireland with the Church at the height of its powers, basking in the glory of the Eucharistic Congress a few years earlier, it must have made an extraordinary impact.

Kinsella's father would have been in a small minority who espoused socialist views even in the tight-knit working-class enclaves of the inner city, but his strong convictions were nourished by a surprisingly well-stocked library of literary classics: 'Ruskin and Engels and Carlyle: / Shakespeare in tiny print',[11] augmented on a regular basis by a subscription to the Left Book Club which flourished in Britain during the 1930s. In a number of published interviews Kinsella refers to the fact that he grew up surrounded by books: 'My father was a great reader and a very concerned person, he was a member of the Left Book Club and had all the lively books of the thirties, it would be impossible in his company to miss what was going on.'[12] He never comments on how his father's beliefs and behaviour affected his own intellectual and literary development, but it is possible to speculate that it must have contributed to an iconoclastic outlook, a natural scepticism of establishment authority and opinion and a tough-minded self-confidence, all leading to what later has been referred to as 'an almost take-it-or-leave-it aggressiveness unique in Irish poetry'.[13]

The second major influence on Kinsella was his schooling. Although in later life he was critical of many aspects of the Irish educational system there is little doubt that although he came from an underprivileged background

---

[11] Haffenden, Interview with Thomas Kinsella, *Viewpoint*, 101.
[12] Ibid., 101.
[13] Gerard Dawe, *Against Piety: Essays in Irish Poetry* (Derry: Lagan Press, 1995), 114.

he was very fortunate in the two schools he attended: the Model School in Inchicore and the O'Connell's Schools in the north inner city. There was no conscious choice involved in either decision; the former was the local primary school for children in the area, and he was awarded a scholarship to the latter from which he subsequently gained scholarships to both university and the civil service.

The Model School in Inchicore had one of the best reputations in the city and was regarded at the time as having a small degree of independence from the all-powerful Catholic Church authorities, no small feat at a time when the city, especially its education system, was coming under the heavy-handed rule of the Church and its emerging powerful eminence, John Charles McQuaid. McQuaid was a powerful influence on the educational system in the 1930s, and on everything else following his elevation to the post of Archbishop of Dublin in 1940. In an address on education in the late 1930s, McQuaid made his position clear: 'Catholic education of whatever particular age, ancient or modern, in old Cathedral or monastic schools, in this or that more modern system, in this or that country, aims at one essential thing – Catholic living.'[14] But although the system was repressive and narrow in a country with few job opportunities, it managed to attract dedicated teachers, many of whom still retained the idealism of the national struggle for independence and who, at a time when secondary and third level education had to be paid for, worked well beyond the call of duty to ensure that bright but less privileged children were given every opportunity to avail of whatever scholarships were available. It was not unusual for these children to be kept behind after school, and even brought to the teacher's house, for extra tuition to help secure the highest exam results.

In the Model School all subjects were taught through Irish, and this was often a signal of educational ambition because of the greater effort involved in an English-speaking society. It was also a declaration of a more nationalistic outlook. Kinsella's interest in Irish myth and legend was developed here but also fully supported at home by parents who shared these interests.

---

14   John Cooney, *John Charles McQuaid: Ruler of Catholic Ireland* (Dublin: O'Brien Press, 1999), 85.

In Peppercanister 9, *Songs of the Psyche*, regarded by at least one critic as 'the core of the Peppercanister project, epitomising the concerns and methods of Kinsella's poetry',[15] the first poem is an unusually benign reflection on his early schooldays at the Model School. Two teachers are mentioned by name, Miss Carney and Mr Browne, and there is an indication that from an early age young Thomas was intent on becoming a model pupil: 'we are going to start decimals / I am going to know everything' (CP 221).

Rosenberg's interviews with Kinsella reveal that he was part of a bright class in the school, a number of whom could have qualified for scholarships for secondary education, but the prevailing poverty meant that many children were required to earn a living as soon as possible and second level education was not compulsory at the time.[16] Kinsella's resourceful parents were by no means destitute, but they were more keenly interested in education than other families in the neighbourhood, and young Thomas was given every encouragement to pursue his studies.

He was equally fortunate in his secondary school, where he was in a class which was regarded as being exceptionally bright, always a spur to talented children to compete and stretch each other in educational excellence. He was involved with a group of five classmates in the foundation of a magazine, *An Glaoch* (The Call), for which he wrote articles and some verse. This was an adventurous initiative at a time when, as Garvin has suggested in his analysis of the economic failure of the period, the whole idea of an educated society raised all kinds of fears among the clerical and political establishment. In this context the thought of a magazine edited by schoolboys must have raised a few eyebrows.[17]

If Kinsella's primary education was delivered in a mildly nationalistic atmosphere there was no such restraint in O'Connell's Schools, which took great pride in the fact that a significantly greater number of ex-O'Connell students took part in the Easter Rising compared to any other school in the country. The school was run by the Christian Brothers, a teaching order founded by Edmund Ignatius Rice in 1828 to give poorer children the chance

---

15   Peter Denman, 'Significant Element: Songs of the Psyche and Her Vertical Smile', *Irish University Review* 31/1 (Spring / Summer 2001), 95–96.
16   Rosenburg, *Let Our Gaze Blaze*, 83.
17   Garvin, *Preventing the Future*, 125–167.

of a secondary education with fees far lower than the traditional middle-class schools run by the priestly orders. Christian Brothers schools were characterised by a robustly nationalistic ethos, leading the historian F. S. L. Lyons to refer to them as 'nurseries of the new nationalists'.[18] Nowadays, in what we like to consider more enlightened times, the Brothers' reputation has become tarnished by stories of physical and sometimes sexual brutality, and for their narrow-minded nationalistic ethos, but it is also clear that without them many thousands of children in the first half of the twentieth century would never have been able to receive a secondary education.

In some of his interviews Kinsella shares the ambiguous feelings many of his generation have about the Brothers' role. On the one hand he is critical of the narrowly inward-looking nature of the curriculum but on the other he is able to appreciate the idealism that underlay so much of the Christian Brothers' work. Some of this tension comes to the surface in a much-quoted passage from 'Nightwalker':

> Edmund Ignatius Rice founded our Order
> To provide schools that were national in more than name
> Pupils from our schools have played their part
> In the fight for freedom. And you will be called
> In your various ways. To work for the native language.
> To show your love by working for your country
> Today there are past pupils everywhere
> In the Government service. Ministers of State
> Have sat where some of you are sitting now. (CP 82)

By putting the words of this section of the poem into the mouth of a Brother, the poet invites the reader to play the role of pupil and snigger at the tone of pompous earnestness to which teachers are sometimes prone. But if we stop for a moment and think about what is happening in this passage with greater sensitivity, a response Kinsella continually demands from his readers – in other words, if we look at it from the perspective of the speaker rather than that of the audience – then we can begin to accept the justifiable pride here portrayed by the speaker in the achievements of his Order in enabling so many children from less privileged backgrounds to occupy the highest positions in the state. A sensitive reader

---

18   F. S. L. Lyons, *Ireland Since the Famine* (London: Fontana Press, 1973), 89.

of 'Nightwalker', Fitzsimons has suggested that, far from denying the prevailing ethos that the poet was exposed to at O'Connell's, the sometimes bitter tone of the poem is occasioned by his disappointment at the erosion of this ethos in later years:

> The disappointment evoked in 'Nightwalker' is in some measure a result of a falling away of the nationalist ethos instilled at the O'Connell Schools to which Kinsella as a young man subscribed.[19]

Kinsella's criticism of the Christian Brothers themselves was directed at their single-minded pursuit of good exam results and of gaining as many scholarships as possible at the expense of a more broadly based educational experience. Happily, Kinsella's innate self-confidence enabled him to overcome this defect, as he explains how he began to write poetry:

> I wrote my first poem at eighteen out of a slight feeling of curiosity to see whether the thing could actually be done, the system of education under which I laboured for most of my adolescence never suggested to me that the writing of poetry was a human activity, we didn't understand that human beings in the normal course of their lives produced this, it existed in textbooks and was there to be explored.[20]

This self-confidence which he shared with Whitaker and Ó Riada also encouraged him to explore what the rest of the world had to offer. Like the other two men Kinsella combined some of these outside influences with his own interests in Irish language, literature and history to make his contribution to the second revival.

Kinsella's Search for Ideas, Insights and Literary Mentors

In the three decades following independence, Ireland effectively withdrew from the world. This was partly due to exhaustion after the War of

19   Andrew Fitzsimons, 'The Sea of Disappointment: Thomas Kinsella's "Nightwalker" and the New Ireland', *Irish University Review* 36/2 (Autumn/Winter 2006), 344.
20   Rosenberg, *Let Our Gaze Blaze*, 94.

Independence and a debilitating civil war and partly due to the desire to prove that the country could survive on its own merits; but it was too a development very much encouraged by an all-powerful Catholic hierarchy who wanted to prevent any revolutionary ideas that were fermenting around Europe taking hold in their domain. Margaret O'Callaghan has argued that the Catholic Church substituted cosmopolitan liberalism for British imperialism as the enemy that now confronted Ireland after independence.[21] A key weapon in their campaign was the draconian censorship acts which effectively banned some of the most famous texts in world literature. So successful was the ban that one of the few sources of titillation for bold boys in the 1950s was reading the more explicit titles of the banned books which were faithfully, and mischievously, printed in the daily papers. For anyone with more literary aspirations, the ban was the most tangible evidence of a society closed to ideas, prompting Patrick Kavanagh's famous line that 'all Ireland that froze for want of Europe'.[22]

Kinsella, who had been brought up surrounded not only by books but by political ideas which were very incorrect for the time, not only read voraciously but allowed ideas from other writers to infuse his own writing from an early stage. It is therefore not surprising that his poems were so heavily influenced by his wider reading. What is surprising is not so much the extent to which he embraces these influences, but rather the number of times he literally transposes lines from other writers into his own poems. If Whitaker was opposed to protectionism and in favour of free trade in the economic sphere, Kinsella believed the same principles applied in literary matters.

Any analysis of Kinsella's application of 'overseas investment' needs to distinguish between those writers who influenced his style and those who influenced content. His stylistic influences are the better known, and almost all Kinsellian commentators mention his debt to Pound and Carlos Williams. Kinsella himself has acknowledged the debt in a number of interviews, as for instance: 'It was in 1965 when I left the civil service – when I

---

21 Margaret O'Callaghan, 'Language, Nationality and Cultural Identity in the Irish Free State: 1922–1927', *Irish Historical Studies* 24/94 (November 1984), 226–245.
22 Patrick Kavanagh, *Collected Poetry* (London: Allen Lane, 2004), 103.

went to America – that the voice of Williams suddenly took on flesh and made sense.'²³

And again, when he acknowledges that

> I'm certainly grateful to the work of Ezra Pound and William Carlos Williams for having opened up particular lines of style – not by any means for imitation – but revelations of scope and attitude – and in Williams's case a kind of creative relaxation.²⁴

Earlier he had looked across the water, where Auden provided a balance to the overpowering presence of Yeats for all Irish poets in the immediate aftermath of his death in 1939: 'For a while I wrote only imitations of Auden.'²⁵ One of his earliest poems, 'A Lady of Quality', is specifically modelled on Auden and adopts the familiar Auden lilt: 'Among the darkening hearts / Has gone too long on either side / Our trophied love must now decide / Into its separate parts' (CP 7).

One of the most detailed analyses of his early poetry shows it involves extremely intricate experimentation with every possible verse form; Yeats and Auden dominate the first phase of Kinsella's poetic development, characterised by self-contained poems with a beginning, a middle and an end, as offered in his first two major volumes, *Another September* and *Downstream*. The 1968 publication of *Nightwalker* indicated a change of tone, style and content. Here we see the beginnings of a looser structure that would come into full bloom in *Notes from the Land of the Dead*, a more non-linear discursive approach with increasing philosophical undertones, with Pound's *Cantos* providing the model and Williams the rhythms. In place of different well-made individual poems, Kinsella's poetry, following his Poundian conversion, became a continuous rumination on life:

> Critics have commented on the circular process of Kinsella's work, often characterised by allusion and repetition, both within and between volumes, to previous poems as well as the eclectic array of influences the poet draws upon.²⁶

---

23   Ian Flanagan, Interview with Thomas Kinsella, *Metre* 2 (Spring 1997), 114.
24   Haffenden, Interview with Thomas Kinsella, *Viewpoint*, 106.
25   O'Driscoll, 'Interview with Thomas Kinsella'.
26   Crossan, *The Given Note*, 125.

Although Pound and Carlos Williams are generally regarded as the most important influences on Kinsella's style since *Nightwalker and Other Poems*, the poet himself has acknowledged another American, Robert Lowell – in particular the change in Lowell's style that took place between the volumes *Mills of the Kavanaughs* and *Life Studies*.[27]

Dillon Johnston, writing about the American influence on Kinsella, makes the point that the poet changed his mind about 'a culture he once depreciated' following a visit to Harvard in 1963 to consult with scholars about his translation of *The Táin* and declared on his return to Ireland that 'the growth point of contemporary poetry has shifted to America'. Johnston adds a comprehensive but succinct summary of the American influence on the poet:

> Williams became an important influence and Kinsella admired his creative relaxation in the face of complex reality, Lowell taught him not to tighten the unit of each poem but to leave the doors open to a poetic sequence that develops a progressive experience that is shared with the audience. Pound affected him by the deployment of a poetic speaker who was intermediate to levels of consciousness and epochs of history and Roethke demonstrated that the autobiographical could be exploited independently of the confessional.[28]

If the Americans were the dominant influences on Kinsella's style it was a wide and eclectic range of Europeans who most influenced his content. Carl Jung is probably the single most important influence and will be dealt with later, but there were many others including, Mahler, Mann, Montale and Kazantzakis.

Mahler was an important influence on both Kinsella and Ó Riada, and the poet has described his introduction to the composer: 'I heard Mahler there [Kinsella's flat in Baggot St] for the first time. Reidy played *Das Lied von der Erde* again and again.' Mahler had set some of the poems of Hans Bethge's German translations and adaptations of Chinese poetry to music and the philosophy behind them had an obvious fascination for Kinsella's sombre disposition: 'that the beauties of nature renew themselves year after

---

27 Dawe, *Against Piety*, 115.
28 Dillon Johnson, *Irish Poetry after Joyce* (Notre Dame: University of Notre Dame Press, 1985), 104.

year and though man enjoys them for just a brief span and is gone, the earth blossoms again'.[29] In Kinsella's second Peppercanister volume, devoted to the memory of Ó Riada, *Vertical Man*, he inserts his own translations of Bethge: 'Let gloom gather and deject / the soul's gardens / Let joy shrivel up and die / and song with it / for life is a black business / while as for death –'.[30] Mahler is the subject of Peppercanister 10, *Her Vertical Smile*, which includes a heartfelt tribute to the musician from both Kinsella and Ó Riada: 'if only we could wring our talent out / wring it out and wring it dry like that' (CP 240).

In a 2004 interview Kinsella also expressed an early interest in Bach, declaring the importance of his interest in 'music, above all an abiding interest in German music, especially Bach; the manipulation of minute detail, immense quantities of material in radiant order as in the great Masses and Passions, with the skill in miniature, the power in delicacy, as in the cello suites'.[31] Denis Diderot, the eighteenth-century French philosopher, is pressed into harness in *A Technical Supplement*, where drawings from his *Encyclopedia* are used as illustrations and where Kinsella engages in a favourite theme: the impossibility of trying to know everything and the dangerous futility of imposing order on actuality. Mann and Goethe make regular appearances in his oeuvre: 'Death Bed' is based on *Joseph and his Brothers*, and the Baronial Hall scene in *Faust* features in 'The Entire Fabric'. Kinsella, who studied German for a time at night in UCD, was familiar with the work of both writers.

'St Paul's Rocks: 16th February 1832' is based on an entry in Darwin's journal in *The Voyage of the Beagle*; 'The Dispossessed' draws from Renan's *Vie de Jesus*; a line from Cranshaw – 'Ourselves become our own best sacrifice' – appears in 'Phoenix Park'; Villon is thought to be the inspiration behind 'Moralities' and Eliot is an obvious influence on 'Nightwalker'.

Among the Irish influences, Joyce is ever-present, especially in 'Nightwalker', as are Swift in 'Butcher's Dozen', Goldsmith in 'Littlebody', Merriman in 'Open Court' and Eriugena in 'Land of Loss'. But it was

29   Kinsella, *Fifteen Dead*, 65.
30   Ibid., 32.
31   Andrew Fitzsimons, 'Interview with Thomas Kinsella', *Journal of Irish Studies* 19 (2004).

the influence of writers and musicians from other countries which, when grafted onto his own intimacy with the Gaelic literary tradition, was to produce one of the most distinctive Irish poetic voices of the twentieth century. Goodby has noted the irony of the poet who appeared critical of importing overseas investment in 'Nightwalker' making extensive use of overseas poetic capital himself:

> Asserting an Irish identity involves, ironically, the importing of technique and models in a manner analogous to the import of multi-national capital attacked in 'Nightwalker's' most famously splenetic passage.[32]

Thomas Kinsella's Literary Objectives

It is possible to equate Whitaker's objective of reviving the Irish economy and Ó Riada's objective of reviving the ancient airs and melodies of Irish music with Kinsella's recovery of *The Táin* and other 'lost' Irish literature. All three men shared an ambition to 'sweeten Ireland's wrong' in the 1950s and restore some semblance of pride as well as prosperity to a dejected nation. Kinsella's starting point was a preoccupation with what he regarded as a major obstacle that confronted the Irish writer, a problem memorably outlined by Daniel Corkery in *Synge and Anglo-Irish Literature* (1947):

> Everywhere in the mentality of the Irish people are flux and uncertainty. Our national consciousness may be described, in a native phrase, as a quaking sod. It gives no footing. It is not English, nor Irish, nor Anglo-Irish – it does not therefore focus the mind of its own people, teaching him the better to look about him, to understand both himself and his surroundings.[33]

---

32   John Goodby, *Irish Poetry Since 1950* (Manchester: Manchester University Press, 2000), 121.
33   Daniel Corkery, quoted in Thomas Kinsella, *The Dual Tradition*, 87.

In a paper he gave in New York in 1966, Kinsella identified the main cause of the problem:

> The death of a language: it is a calamity. And its effects are at work everywhere in the present, reducing energies of every kind, undermining individual confidence, lessening the quality of thought.[34]

Kinsella may have been echoing Seán de Fréine, whose influential book on the loss of the language, *The Great Silence*, had appeared in 1965. De Fréine had emphasised the sustaining role of language:

> Tradition thus plays a real part in sustaining society and creating a bond between people, catering for their common needs, spiritual, psychological and material.[35]

A year later, in an essay in *Éire-Ireland*, Kinsella provided a more detailed account of the resulting problems facing the Irish writer:

> No matter the preoccupations of an English writer, he will find his forebears in English poetry – an Irish poet will only have a first point of contact – the line begins with Yeats, then back for a hundred years there is total silence – silence is the real condition of Irish literature in the nineteenth century, certainly of poetry, then beyond the nineteenth century there is a real cultural blur – after the dullness of the nineteenth century eighteenth century poetry is suddenly full of life, in the service of real feeling – beyond – the course of Irish poetry stretches back for more than a thousand years, full of riches and variety, poetry as mystery and magic.[36]

He repeatedly returns to the subject in his prose writings. His 1970 publication *Davis, Mangan, Ferguson? Tradition and the Irish Writer*, deals with problems of identity among nineteenth-century Irish poets in the midst of the language change-over, and he returned to the subject on a number of occasions, notably in his introductions to *An Duanaire* (1981) and his anthology *The New Oxford Book of Irish Verse* (1986). In the introduction to the latter, he commented on the nature of the 'dual tradition':

---

34 Ibid., 87.
35 Seán de Fréine, *The Great Silence* (Cork: Mercier Press, 1965), 36.
36 Thomas Kinsella, 'The Irish Writer', *Éire-Ireland* (Summer 1967), 8.

> It should be clear at least that the Irish tradition is a matter of two linguistic entities in dynamic interaction, of two major bodies of poetry asking to be understood together as functions of a shared and painful history. To limit a response to one aspect only, as is often done is … to miss a rare opportunity: that of responding to a notable and venerable literary tradition, the oldest vernacular literature in Western Europe, as it survives a change in vernacular.[37]

His first words in Sean Ó Mordha's TV documentary *One Fond Embrace* were:

> I am an Irish writer and I envy writers from more stable traditions, with no need to keep on investigating their own origins. It's different in Ireland: we have to keep doing that – the Irish tradition is a dual tradition – one-and-a-half millennia of Gaelic and – a large gap.[38]

He returned to the subject in a new publication, *The Dual Tradition* (1995), which was issued as Peppercanister Volume 18:

> Irish literature exists as a dual entity. It was composed in two languages. The changing emphasis between one language and the other reflect changing circumstances through the centuries.[39]

During the thirty-year period from the late 1950s, when he started his major translation of *The Táin*, to the twelfth Peppercanister volume, *St Catherine's Clock* (1987), Kinsella was engaged in a twofold attempt to bridge the 'great divide' and fill the 'gap' he here identifies in the Irish tradition. The first part of the task was physical: the excavation of ancient Irish texts for a modern audience. The second was metaphysical, a Jungian search for roots and origins both on a personal and national level.

---

37 Thomas Kinsella, ed., *The New Oxford Book of Irish Verse* (Oxford: Oxford University Press, 1986), xxvii.
38 Ó Mordha, *One Fond Embrace*.
39 Kinsella, *The Dual Tradition*, 4.

Kinsella's 'Physical' Legacy

Kinsella's initial starting point for his translation work was the recognition that there was a gap in his tradition. Unlike English contemporaries, who could trace their literary inheritance back to Chaucer and beyond that to Beowulf, the Irish writer faces a 'great divide'. In his 1972 essay 'The Divided Mind' for the Thomas Davis Lectures, Kinsella again describes the effect of the divide on the Irish writer:

> I recognise that I stand on the side of a great rift, and can feel the discontinuity in myself. It is a matter of people and places as well as writing – of coming from a broken and uprooted family, of being drawn to those who share my origins and finding that we cannot share our lives.[40]

Kinsella's excavation of the Gaelic literary tradition can be compared with the work of an earlier generation of writers during the first revival, but their goals were somewhat different. The late nineteenth-century writers of the first revival were engaged in a nation-building exercise; a task which was also being undertaken by like-minded intellectuals across Europe. Retrieving national literary epics and patriotic musical compositions were part of these efforts, and the Irish intellectuals of that period were engaged in this task on a number of fronts. First, they had to demonstrate that the nation did have its own unique culture and literary heritage, partly to justify national independence but also to counter accusations of ignorance, indolence and illiteracy from a variety of nineteenth-century British commentators. A second objective was to position Ireland as being as distinctly different to Britain as possible. George Watson, in his study of the leading writers of the period, records:

> The revival's idealisation of the peasant grew naturally from its hatred of progress, modernity, centralisation, commercialisation, and industrialised materialism, all of which were embodied and given definitive shape in England. To the vulgarity of all this could be opposed the values embodied in – or projected on – the Irish

---

40 Thomas Kinsella, 'The Divided Mind', in Seán Lucy, ed., *Irish Poets in English* (Cork: Mercier Press, 1973), 109.

peasant – the power and success of the mighty imperial neighbour became more tolerable when seen as a badge of 'spiritual' incapacity or grossness.[41]

Kinsella's goals in his associated task of cultural retrieval in the second revival were less political and more psychological. By 'bridging the gap' with Ireland's literary heritage, he hoped to restore continuity to the Irish tradition and thereby prevent the stunting of growth in nations and citizens which occurs when they don't have a clear understanding of their past. Kinsella's translation work was undertaken in the early part of his career; it can thus be argued that he was engaged in a Jungian exercise directly on behalf of the nation before his personal search for individuation began.

The early part of Kinsella's writing career was dominated by translations from the Irish: *Faeth Fiadha: The Breastplate of St Patrick* (1953), *The Sons of Usnech* (1954) and *Thirty-Three Triads* (1955) were collected in *Poems and Translations* (1961). His most acclaimed work of translation, the great epic tale *The Táin*, which was published in 1969 in the limited edition accompanied by the magnificent lithographs by Louis le Brocquy, probably represents the supreme achievement of the Dolmen Press. Twelve years later Kinsella completed his contribution to the recovery of Old Irish literature for modern audiences with the publication of *An Duanaire: 1600–1900: Poems of the Dispossessed*. Kinsella's translations are a crucial part of his work, and they contributed to the second revival by reminding a depressed nation of its literary history and achievements.

The Jungian origin of Kinsella's approach would also explain why his translations were more hard-headed than those of his predecessors, and why he was coldly analytical about the merits of some of the original texts involved, especially the most famous, which has been described as 'Ireland's *Iliad*', *The Táin*. Kinsella himself accepted that it was not one of the greatest things in world literature, but that it was critical from an Irish perspective because it foreshadowed themes that would resonate throughout Irish history. His translations are also more realistic than some of the more thematically related work of the first revival. Kearney has noted that

41   George J. Watson, *Irish Identity*, 23.

the experiences of rupture and disinheritance are forever present in his mythic retelling of inner loss. Kinsella refuses the triumphal enthusiasm of the Celtic twilight; his vision of the mythological past is one of homelessness and dispossession evident in his translation of *An Duanaire* and the *Táin*.[42]

It has also been noted that Kinsella's translations are more brutal and bawdy than earlier, more sanitised versions, and this approach is consistent with his quest for the truth, the underlying reality of 'who and what I am':

> *The Táin* is part of our imaginative bedrock and my translation was an act of loyalty to that part of one's past, not necessarily to the quality of that particular work – it's a commitment to tradition, an understanding of them as part of our past, an understanding of our totality.[43]

Critics have argued that Kinsella's translations not only constitute an act of recovery, but are crucial to an understanding of much of his later poetic writings, whose themes are often infused with a deep understanding of Ireland's mythic and real past:

> Such understanding has not been gained lightly, nor through compromise, but won through reaching down into the 'imaginative bedrock' of Irish myth and history. The work of translation has proved no longer a sideline activity but central to Kinsella's achievement. It has enabled him, in a context distinctly Irish and personal, and increasingly with the authority of a major poet, to speak for us all.[44]

Kinsella's 'Metaphysical' Legacy

This part of Kinsella's task was heavily influenced by the work of the analytical psychologist Carl Jung, and in particular his theory of individuation.

---

42 Richard Kearney, 'Myth and Modernity in Irish Poetry', in Elmer Andrews, ed., *Contemporary Irish Poetry* (London: Macmillan, 1992), 47.
43 Haffenden, Interview with Thomas Kinsella, *Viewpoint*, 112.
44 Brian John, 'Imaginative Bedrock: Kinsella's One and the Lebor Gabála Érenn', *Éire-Ireland* 20 (Spring 1985), 132.

Kinsella's most perceptive critics have all commented on the influence of Jung's thinking on the poet's work, although there is some disagreement as to whether it started to emerge with the publication of *Nightwalker and other Poems* (1968) or with the Cuala Press publication of *Notes from the Land of the Dead* (1972). Jackson makes a strong case for the earlier date,[45] but majority opinion would appear to favour the later publication as representing a more radical change in direction in Kinsella's work. There is general agreement that the Jungian influence was very strong in many of the early Peppercanister volumes, at least up to *St Catherine's Clock* (1987). Kinsella freely acknowledges the debt. One of the poems in the seventh Peppercanister volume was called 'C.G. Jung's "First years"', a suitably Jungian title – and in a number of major interviews given by the poet over the years he has been quite open on the subject: 'For me the idea of making use of Jung's ideas is as fascinating as the regional ideas themselves – encountering or dipping into Jung.'[46]

Kinsella's interest in Jung coincided with a decline in his readership and status within the 'standing army of Irish poets', and although there were other reasons for this development, notably the emergence of the Northern poets, there is little doubt that his change of poetic tone and focus, first glimpsed in *Nightwalker* (1968) and confirmed in *Notes From the Land of the Dead* (1973), made much more serious demands on his readers. Dawe, while expressing admiration for Kinsella's ambition ('he asks "big" questions'), acknowledges the difficulties of this change:

> This mysterious unpredictable shift in perception, embodied in Kinsella's freeing of the poetic line, can be troubling to the reader who expects to have the poem's source formally proposed and conclusively reconciled.[47]

Before commenting on the Jungian influence on individual poems, I want to consider in more detail Jung's theory of individuation, which had a particular influence on the poet.

---

45   Thomas Jackson, *The Whole Matter* (Dublin: Lilliput Press, 1995), 61.
46   Flanagan, 'Interview with Thomas Kinsella', 110.
47   Dawe, *Against Piety*, 117.

There are two main reasons why Kinsella was drawn to Jung's work. The first was a belief, shared with the psychoanalyst, that our present predicament cannot be fully understood without a thorough knowledge of our own past. Where Kinsella sees a 'great divide' for the Irish writer between the ancient Gaelic literary tradition and the modern Anglo-Irish tradition, Jung diagnoses an equally 'great divide': the fact that 'our consciousness only constitutes a small part of our total psyche'.[48] Both Kinsella and Jung believe that we need to re-connect with our past in order to be comfortable with our present. Jung developed the concept of individuation to express his idea of successfully integrating knowledge of our psychic past with our present circumstances. He believed that our greatest problem is a lack of awareness of the dark powers that dwell in our psyche but that by understanding these powers we can tame them and make them an organic part of ourselves.

Individuation is central to Jung's psychology, and is regarded as his major contribution to the subject. It is not that easy a concept to summarise, because Jung was a prolific writer and was not always consistent in defining his ideas, but at the core of the theory is the notion of wholeness, of the individual coming to terms with his or her whole personality, both that which is on display to the outer world and the inner demons we all possess. Individuation is a process of 'knowing oneself' in every detail, of understanding how our past has influenced our present and coming to terms with the consequences. It is therefore close to Kinsella's dictum of always being conscious of 'who and what I am' (CP 261). Individuation is achieved when all of the different aspects of our personality are acknowledged, accepted and integrated into one's own idea of oneself.

Jung developed a number of different subsidiary concepts to explain the process of individuation including the collective unconscious, which refers to psychic structures from the archaic heritage of humanity which are common to all: 'The collective unconscious contains the whole spiritual heritage of mankind's evolution born anew in the brain structure of each individual.'[49] Jung believed that the search for individuation begins

---

48 Jolande Jacobi, *The Psychology of C. J. Jung* (New Haven: Yale University Press, 1973), 34.
49 Jacobi, *The Psychology of C. J. Jung*, 34.

in the second part of one's life: 'The primary concerns in the first half of our lives are biological and social; in the second half, spiritual and cultural.'[50] Kinsella began his Jungian quest as he reached middle age in the late 1960s. A central belief of Jung's was that in the psyche of modern man the conscious side has been over-emphasised at the expense of the older unconscious hidden side, but that we spend more time than we think in the unconscious, sleeping and daydreaming, hence the importance he attached to interpreting and understanding dreams:

> I share all my readers' prejudices against dream interpretation as being the quintessence of uncertainty and arbitrariness. But on the other hand, I know that if we meditate on a dream sufficiently long and thoroughly, if we take it about with us and turn it over and over, something almost always comes of it.[51]

Jung developed a technique, referred to as 'active imagination', which helps the subject to descend consciously to the depths of the soul in a seven-stage process, a procedure Kinsella would have identified with because of his awareness of the Celtic *imbas forosnai* ritual. This is 'the process of understanding by which the individual accesses the *anima mundi* and, by corollary, understanding of his own spirit or soul'.[52] Tubridy regards Peppercanister 9, *Songs of the Psyche* (1985), as a version of the *imbas forosnai* which is a form of 'active imagination'.[53]

The second reason for Kinsella's interest in Jung was that both men sensed a vacuum at the heart of modern life. Kinsella repeatedly returns to the theme of living in 'desperate times':

> These are desperate times. – There is
> a poverty of spirit in the wind;
> a shabby richness in braving it. (CP 200)

---

50 Anthony Stevens, *Jung: A Very Short Introduction* (Oxford: Oxford University Press, 1994), 73.
51 Carl Jung, *Modern Man in Search of a Soul* (London: Routledge Classics, 2001), 63.
52 Tubridy, *Thomas Kinsella: The Peppercanister Poems*, 125.
53 Ibid., 125–127.

Jung believed that the reason for this 'poverty of spirit' was that man had moved too far from his origins, having discovered in the Age of Enlightenment that the gods did not exist but were merely projections: 'Thus the gods were disposed of. But the corresponding psychological function was not disposed of, it lapsed into the unconscious.'[54] Jung built on this insight, arguing that the artist has a direct line to the unconscious – an idea that would have had immediate resonance for Kinsella: 'The creative process consists in activating the eternal symbols of mankind which lie dormant in the unconscious and in shaping and elaborating them to produce a finished work of art.'[55]

Rosenberg has revealed that Kinsella's initial awareness of Jung arose somewhat fortuitously when one of his students in Temple University noted a connection between some of the poet's latest work and the ideas of the psychologist.[56] This led him to Jacobi's well-known study, *The Psychology of C. J. Jung* (1942), which he confirmed to the present author was the only book he had ever read on the subject.[57]

Regardless of what Kinsella did or did not read, much of his poetry from the late 1960s to the late 1980s was infused with the ideas and working practices of Carl Jung, in particular his theory of individuation. Kinsella's quest for a comprehensive understanding of 'who and what I am' involved an imaginative re-creation of his childhood, a consideration of the immediate historical background he inherited as well as of Ireland's ancient past, and a more directly psychic exploration of that conjoined background through deliberately setting to work his 'active imagination'.

---

54   Jacobi, *The Psychology of C. J. Jung*, 93.
55   Ibid., 24.
56   Rosenburg, *Let Our Gaze Blaze*, 47.
57   Thomas Kinsella, Interview with author, 15 July 2008.

The Jungian Quest in Kinsella's Childhood, Neighbourhood and Family Poems

Most poets allude at some stage in their work to childhood and family, but Kinsella returned to the subject on a regular basis during most of his Jungian period. There are six poems titled after streets in the Dublin area where Kinsella and his extended family lived: 'Bow Lane', 'The High Road', 'The Liffey Hill', 'Irwin St', 'Phoenix St' and '38 Phoenix St'. The poems also contain references to other well-known streets in the vicinity, Thomas St and Basin Lane. Kinsella, following Jung, delves deep into his childhood and family relationships and these street and place names act as a kind of mantra, their recall and incantation enabling the poet to recover a lost world. But although he writes obsessively about the inner city there is no trace of sentimentality, no attempt to conjure up a romanticised 'Dublin in the rare old times'. The poet's objective is strictly Jungian: to relentlessly and, where necessary, ruthlessly, confront the realities of his immediate family, neighbours and environs in an attempt to come to terms with their influence on his subsequent development and personality.

We have already seen how important the positive influence of Kinsella's grandmothers was, and especially that of his father, but there are hints of more difficult family relationships in these poems, and the poet's mother is conspicuous by her absence except in a later poem, 'Dura Mater'.

This poem opens with a domestic cooking scene where a mother in slippers comes out of the kitchen to address her son: 'Come here to me. Come here to me, my son.' But the outcome, which is not directly stated, is filled with tension as the mother is pictured as having 'ill temper in her eyes'. This is suggested in the next line, not directly attributed to, but seeming to come from, the mother: 'Will you look at him. How do you stick him at all?'[58] Interestingly, the verse containing these quotations was omitted from the 2001 Carcanet edition of Kinsella's *Collected Poems*. The next

---

58 Thomas Kinsella, *Collected Poems 1956–1994* (Oxford: Oxford University Press, 1996), 300–301.

quoted verse below, suggesting a difficult relationship, is included in the Carcarnet edition, however

> the withheld kiss returned
> onto her stone forehead. Dura Mater.
> To take it a seal on her stone will
> In under the screwed lid. (CP 291)

This poem also hints at a difficult relationship with the poet's brother, who makes equally infrequent appearances in the many family poems. The second half of the poem suggests they had met after a funeral – possibly, in view of the subject matter of the poem, their mother's. The relationship couldn't be more awkward: 'He came out, stooping forward / with hands held down before him'.[59] The final section of the poem appears to describe a meeting between the two brothers, possibly to discuss a will or the sharing of the disposal of the contents of a house or share of the proceeds of a sale, which ends abruptly with the poet being promised something he should have received without asking: 'I put the question. Certainly. Of course. / I'm sorry you had to ask. There should be something / next week in the post, or the week after / I'll see to that. And we must keep in touch.'[60] The pointed clipped formality of this conversation is evidence of a severely ruptured relationship. But it wasn't the first time this relationship in all its difficulty had been alluded to: 'I stretched out my hand to you / Brother / The reason for the impulse was unclear: / your behaviour and your work / are incomprehensible to me' (CP 234).

Although the warren of little streets in the Liberties was teeming with people, the young poet appears to have been a solitary, bookish and contemplative child who more often than not preferred his own company. The dominant impression that comes across from the poet's account of his childhood is that of an outsider. From an early age he comes across as someone aware of everything going on around him but also as someone curiously detached from the action. His world is dominated by adults and there is a marked absence of childhood friends of his own age. A number of factors marked him out as a loner. From an early age he was regarded as

---

59   Ibid., 300.
60   Ibid., 301.

Thomas Kinsella: The Poetic Muse

unusually bright like his aunt Bridie: 'the pair of us so alike / everybody agreed / wherever we got the brains' (CP 270). When the other boys at the Model School were shouting and jumping, he 'sat by myself in the shed / and watched the draught / blowing the papers / around the wheels of the bicycles' (CP 222).

When he was at home he obviously spent endless hours alone in an upstairs room reading and rummaging, sometimes to the exasperation of his parents: 'What are you up to in there / always stuck up in that old room' (CP 279). He appears not to have mixed much with the neighbourhood boys: 'I was not a barefaced liar / and never went out with the gets down the street', but he always had a clear sense of his own worth: 'and I always remembered / who and what I am' (CP 277). There is no indication that Kinsella's childhood was unhappy or that he was an unpopular child: Carolyn Rosenberg carried out interviews with some of his teachers and schoolboy contemporaries, who attest to his popularity, but the general conclusion from these interviews is of a self-contained, self-confident child described by one teacher as 'imperturbable'.[61] For example, he never alluded directly to his father's political views, but if he felt they were being challenged he would resolutely defend them. It seems clear that the formative experiences of his childhood stood him in good stead in his Jungian quest in later life, and not only enabled but encouraged his lonely pursuit of his own poetic goals. He would find it easier than most to reject 'the ease of the spurious', and it is easy to see how he was to remain for most of his career at 'the unrewarding outer reaches' testing 'the whole thing' (CP 352).

Kinsella's Jungian Quest into the Influence of History

Modern History in the Poetry of Kinsella

For the first thirty years of the existence of the newly independent state, the years of the poet's youth, adolescence and early manhood, Irish

---

61 Rosenburg, *Let Our Gaze Blaze*, 93.

politics and much of Irish society was dominated by the past, especially the traumatic events between 1916 and 1922. Irish history in the school curriculum of the 1930s, 1940s and 1950s was untainted by any of the 're-visionism' that came later, and was a somewhat simplistic, straightforward narrative of successive 'risings' against British rule characterised by failure due to betrayals, incompetence or slavish attitudes among 'shoneen' sections of the population until the advent of the eventual success of the Easter Rising in 1916. Kinsella's left-wing background would have given him a slightly different slant on this narrative, especially in its later stages, but he would have accepted the broad historical sweep of the main argument. This is obvious from the regular references to historical events in Irish history throughout his work.

In the poem 'His Father's Hands', the speaker's father explains the family's impeccable republican pedigree. The tone is solemn and excessively formal, almost as if he were taking the boy in hand to explain the facts of life:

> Your family, Thomas, met with and helped
> many of the Croppies in hiding from the Yeos
> or on their way home after the defeat
> in south Wexford –
> From hearsay, as far as I can tell
> the Men Folk were either Stone Cutters
> or masons or probably both. (CP 172)

The poem continues its exploration of family history leading the poet to an imagined vision of his ancestors' first landing place: 'first a prow of land / chosen, and webbed with tracks; / then boulders chosen / and sloped together, stabilised in menace' (CP 173). Given the earlier 1798 Rebellion credentials it is hardly surprising that when visiting different parts of the country Kinsella is conscious of the republican '700 years of British rule' mantra. This is particularly evident in the awkwardly titled poem 'Tao and Unfitness at Inistiogue on the River Nore'. His palpable unease when visiting one of the prettiest villages in the country is because it is too 'English' with its 'village green'. He then characterises it as 'sullen' and is unkindly sarcastic about the caretaker of the Protestant church: 'The Protestant church was guarded by a woman / of about forty, a retainer, spastic / and indistinct, who drove us out'. He goes on to reflect on Black and Tan activity in the area and the burning of a 'Big House' in revenge, and dismisses the area as 'a flitting place / for ragged feeling, old angers and rumours' (CP 202–205).

Thirty years later at a wedding in Trinity College he is still 'out of place' in what he regards as a 'protected place'.

Kinsella and the Mythic Origins of Ireland

Jung believed that part of our current malaise or discontent is that modern man has been cut off from his psychic past. It is easy to see how enthusiastically Kinsella embraced this notion, as one of his main preoccupations was the damage resulting from Ireland's disconnection from its entire cultural heritage because of the change of language that took place over a prolonged period between the ends of the seventeenth and nineteenth centuries.

The poet's response was slightly different to Jung's recommendation in that he turned inward and downwards to a reconstruction of the origins and foundations of Ireland rather than a reclaiming of 'the entire psychic heritage of mankind'. His main source materials were the *Lebor Gabála Érenn*, which is usually translated as *The Book of Invasions* and which tells the story of the first peoples of Ireland, and H. D'Arbois de Jubainville's *The Irish Mythological Cycle and Celtic Mythology*. *The Book of Invasions* is essentially a saga describing the successive waves of the earliest settlers in Ireland, and Kinsella relied heavily on it for the mythic origins of Ireland series of poems in *Notes From the Land of the Dead* and *One*. In 'Survivor', Kinsella describes the voyage of Cessair, the legendary granddaughter of Noah, whose people were excluded from the Ark because they were thieves and thus had to escape the flood. Legend suggests that they sailed in 'search of a land without sin / that might go unpunished' (CP 111).

Reputedly two of the three ships in the expedition sank, leaving the remaining vessel with three men and fifty women. Two of the men died from 'sexual overwork' and the third, Fintan, alone remained alive to satisfy the demands of his wife and fifty other women. Exhausted, Fintan fled from the women into a cave, where he weathered the flood and survived successive invasions in various shapes to retell his story. The poem is notable for the beautiful and lyrical depictions of Ireland as seen by the approaching travellers:

> Late afternoon we came in sight
> of promontories beautiful beyond description
> and saw the sea gather in savage currents
> and dash itself against the cliffs –
> Paradise. No serpents. No noxious beasts
> No lions. No toads. No injurious rats
> or dragons or scorpions. Only the she wolf. (CP 111)

Towards the end of the poem there is a line which hints at the source of the newly found land's later expertise and fame for haunting music: 'Sometimes / an otherworldly music sounded on the wind' (CP 112). Oddly enough, around the same time Seamus Heaney made a similar observation: 'On the most Westerly Blasket / in a dry stone hut / he got the air out of the night – / bits of a tune coming in on loud melody'.[62] But the new Eden proves as elusive as the old, and soon the excitement of discovery is overcome by the inevitable famine, disease and pestilence. Thus from the beginning of time in Ireland the Kinsellian formula identified by Fitzsimons, Time = Hope + Disappointment,[63] was present.

'Finistere' presents the story of another invasion, this time by the Milesians, the sons of Mil, who were the invaders who finally succeeded in maintaining a permanent foothold. The narrator this time is Amergin, the first Irish poet who spies the new land: 'from a bald boulder on the cairn top / I spied out the horizon to the northwest / and sensed that minute imperfection again' (CP 8). Once again the landing is difficult: 'grey upheaving slopes of water / sliding under us, collapsing / crawling onward, mountainous', but all ends well as Kinsella skilfully invokes early Irish poetic techniques: 'ill wind end well / mild mother / on wild water pour peace':

> The bad dream ended at last

---

62   Seamus Heaney, *Opened Ground: Poems 1966–1996* (London: Faber & Faber, 1998), 36.
63   Fitzsimons, *Sea of Disappointment*, 8.

> In the morning in a sunny breeze
> bare headlands rose fresh out of the waves.
> We entered a deep bay lying open
> to all the currents of the ocean.
> We were further than anyone had ever been
> And light-headed with exhaustion and relief. (CP 164)

In 'The Oldest Place' Kinsella creates a compendium of successive invasions, from the original voyage of Cessair to the Milesians, repeating the legend that the difficulty of landing through the treacherous seas meant that the island had to be circled three times 'in search of a landing place'. Here we find the most idyllic description of a land of milk and honey:

> We fished and fowled and chopped at the forest,
> cooked and built, ploughed and planted,
> danced and drank, all as before
> but worked inland, and got further
> And there was something in the way the land behaved
> passive, but responding. It grew under our hands.
> We worked it like a dough to our requirements
> yet it surprised us more than once
> with a firm life of its own, as if it
> used us. (CP 165)

The last three lines of this verse remind us of the inevitable problems that always thwart mere mortal men's attempts to re-create Eden. This time the shattering of the dream is particularly savage as the settlers are brought down by a mysterious disease and the narrator is left alone to try to make some sense of the tragedy. The poem ends ambiguously as the narrator sinks down into the land of the dead where he appears to be offered tempting gifts, 'gold and silver things' which turn out to be illusionary.

Kinsella here re-confirms his sense of foreboding about the human condition set out years earlier in *Wormwood* (1968):

> It is certain that maturity and peace are to be sought through ordeal after ordeal and it seems that the search continues until we fail. We reach out after each new beginning, penetrating our context to know ourselves, and our knowledge increases until we recognise again (more profoundly each time) our pain, indignity and triviality (CP 62).

The Result of Kinsella's Search for Individuation

Kinsella's long, painstaking and scrupulously honest excavation of his family background has given his readers a convincing model of how to embark on the search for individuation that leads to 'wholeness' and integration and a coming to terms with uncomfortable aspects of the psyche. Kinsella's detailed depiction of his family and neighbours was more than just a Jungian exercise; it is also an affirmation of his own people's right to a place in the poetic tradition. He has described how strange an activity the writing of poetry was for someone of his background. By defining their lives and locality he not only celebrates them; he engages in a cathartic exercise, clearing a space in his own mind for the journey towards self-actualisation and individuation.

In true Jungian spirit he also confronts his own obstinate personality, recognising that while a stubborn determination to pursue his vision is a necessary component of an artistic vocation, it can lead to difficulties in familial and personal relationships.

To some extent the re-creation of the mythic past of the nation is a parallel exercise: a radical political initiative designed to retrieve the rightful heritage of his wider family, his society, which had been denied access to it by the loss of a language and by a history dominated by colonisation, plantation and a succession of political and societal failures. In the poems examined earlier from *Notes from the Land of the Dead* and *One*, Kinsella imaginatively re-creates the origins of human habitation of the island of Ireland, and by relating the first inhabitants to Noah and his family he connects Ireland directly to the wider story of the human race. Thus, although Kinsella began his Jungian project as a psychological probe into his own psyche with the goal of achieving a more balanced state of wholeness for the individual, the process resulted in a parallel exercise for the nation. In his search for the mythic origins of Ireland, Kinsella retrieves the nation's inheritance and in the process re-balances its history. His translations of ancient Irish texts, including *The Táin*, restored to Irish people what he referred to as the 'bedrock of [their] imagination', thus crossing the 'great divide' and re-balancing its literary history. This was Kinsella's contribution to the second revival.

Conclusions

A key premise of this book is that a second 'revival' took place in the decade between 1956 and 1965, and that the three closely connected individuals whose careers and achievements are outlined above played a leading role. There were many similarities between this revival and the better known, more widely referred to earlier 'revival' in the late nineteenth and early twentieth century:

- a new-found sense of energy, renewal and self-confidence.
- acts of literary retrieval from ancient Gaelic literature for a new generation.
- new artistic work which had a widespread impact.
- business and finance initiatives based on native enterprise and resources.

But there was one critical feature of the second revival that was new: the specific search for ideas, insights and inspiration from overseas, which, when mediated through Irish culture and expertise, would result in cultural and business outputs that were able to make a renewed impact on the world.

The impetus created by the second revival continued to bear fruit for the next half a century. There were one or two poor seasons in the 1970s and 1980s, but these were compensated for by the bumper harvests of the 1990s and the early twenty-first century. In the next section I will examine the extent of the transformation created by the second revival.

In particular, Part II will show that the transformation of the country initiated by the second revival ultimately succeeded not only in ending involuntary emigration but actually attracting immigrants into the country. On a more psychological level it will show that the mood of despondency in the mid-1950s had been replaced by a sense of self-confidence and pride by the twenty-first century. It will examine the criticisms of the more outward-looking economic and social policies adopted during that time, but it will make the case that the adoption of the outward approach was prescient, enabling the country to benefit from the acceleration of globalisation that occurred during the last two decades of the twentieth century.

PART II

Ireland 1956–2020: From Emigrants' to Immigrants' Remittances

CHAPTER 5

Ireland 1960–2020: Statistical Analysis of the Transformation

Introduction

In 1956 'emigrant's *remittances*' were a recorded item in the Balance of Payments of Ireland's National Accounts, a significant reflection of the recent waves of emigrants whose monetary contributions to family members who remained in Ireland represented enough revenue in a poor country to warrant official recognition in the National Accounts. Sixty years later significant sums of money were leaving Ireland to families in Poland, Latvia, Lithuania and further afield following the wave of immigrants that started to arrive in Ireland in the 1990s. This is only one example of the transformation in Irish society since Ken Whitaker, Seán Ó Riada and Thomas Kinsella were embarking on their careers in the 1950s. On his eighty-fifth birthday, Whitaker recalled some of the changes that struck him as particularly significant:

> The enormous improvement I have seen in living standards, bringing them up to those of Britain, France and Germany, can, perhaps be most vividly illustrated by reference to housing and health. As recently as forty years ago, more than half the dwellings in the Republic of Ireland were already over sixty years old and fewer than half of the total number were connected to a public water supply. Now of a 50% higher number, only one third are over sixty years old and a mere 1% without piped water.[1]

---

1   Whitaker, 'We Have Come a Long Way', 10.

Most countries in Europe has witnessed major demographic, economic and sociological changes in the last sixty-five years, but the scale of the changes in Ireland has been particularly dramatic. Most of the literature on the Irish transformation has concentrated on the economic changes and of the latter decades of the twentieth century, albeit with some recognition of the Lemass/Whitaker policy initiatives in the mid-century, which laid the groundwork for the extraordinarily high economic growth rates of the 1990s and early 2000s.

There is increasing recognition that the period of the second revival, 1956–1966, witnessed the main initiatives that created Ireland's economic transformation:

> Policy actions taken from the late 1950's and early 1960's onwards launched the economy on a development path that differed radically from that pursued before and after independence.[2]

The two critical changes that were initiated by the economic and cultural initiatives of the late 1950s and early 1960s were the opening up of the Irish economy to the outside world and the increasing self-confidence in Irish society.

A flavour of the full extent of the transformation in Irish society over the intervening sixty-five years can be seen in the following tables, which have been assembled from a wide range of sources including the Central Statistics Office (CSO), the Eurobarometer surveys carried out on a continuous basis in all EU countries, data obtained from leading Irish market research company Behaviour & Attitudes, and a London-based trend forecasting consultancy, Future-Foresight, who carry out regular, mainly consumer-based, surveys across Europe. They are divided into the following sections:

- Demographic
- Education
- Economic
- Inequality
- Ireland and Europe

2 Brian Nolan, Philip J. O'Connell and Christopher T. Whelan, eds, *Bust to Boom? The Irish Experience of Growth and Inequality* (Dublin: IPA Publications, 2000), 7.

- Religious observance and changing attitudes to moral issues
- National identity
- Well-being, happiness and quality of life

The statistical evidence will show a broadly positive position for Ireland in 2021. But the development strategy adopted in the late 1950s and its implementation during the succeeding decades has attracted continuous criticism from a range of economic, social and cultural commentators. These issues will be examined in Chapter 6. The initial criticisms were that Ireland had become increasingly unequal, materialistic and dependent on overseas investment, and as a consequence was in danger of losing a sense of identity and moral purpose. More recent critical comment concentrates on the unwise banking practices which only emerged in the final stages of the transformation. The regulatory framework surrounding the banking and wider financial services sector has now been addressed, but the recent scandal involving the largest stockbroker in the country shows that the financial sector still appears to be characterised by endemic malpractice. Underlying many of the criticisms was the issue of globalisation and its impact on the ability of small nations to conduct their own affairs and preserve a sense of national identity.

Statistical Overview of the Transformation of Irish Society from the late 1950s to the 2020s

1. Demographic

International comparative demographic statistics used to position Ireland in an unfavourable light at the undesirable end of whichever aspect of the population is under review: highest level of per capita emigration, high numbers of children per family, lowest marriage and mortality rates. But during the last fifty years, all of these positions have been reversed. The most dramatic reversal was in the size of the population itself, which showed an extraordinary 66 per cent increase between 1961 and 2021.

Table 1. Population (Millions) 1841–2021

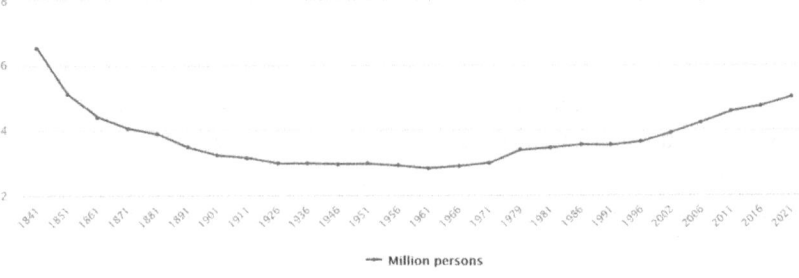

Source: CSO.

Since the mid-1990s there has been substantial net migration into Ireland, prompting the following comment from Paul Tansey: 'The reversal of the long-run population decline is perhaps the most important change engineered by the economic growth since the 60s.'[3]

Thus, the most heart-breaking feature of Irish life for well over two hundred years, involuntary emigration, had, by the twenty-first century, been eliminated or reduced to a trickle. As a result, it is difficult for today's generation of Irish citizens under sixty years of age to understand the misery and shame attached to the emigrant boat. There is still a trickle of people leaving the country, but in the main, it is far removed from the doleful experience of the mid-twentieth century. Most of today's leavers are well educated and have little difficulty in securing interesting and rewarding work wherever they go.

Table 2 shows changes in life expectancy in Ireland from the 1950s to 2017. The data show that Irish people are living longer: on average sixteen years longer than in 1950 and twelve years longer than in 1960.

---

3 Paul Tansey, *Ireland at Work* (Oxford: Oak Tree Press, 1998), 11.

Table 2. Life Expectancy at Birth 1950–2017

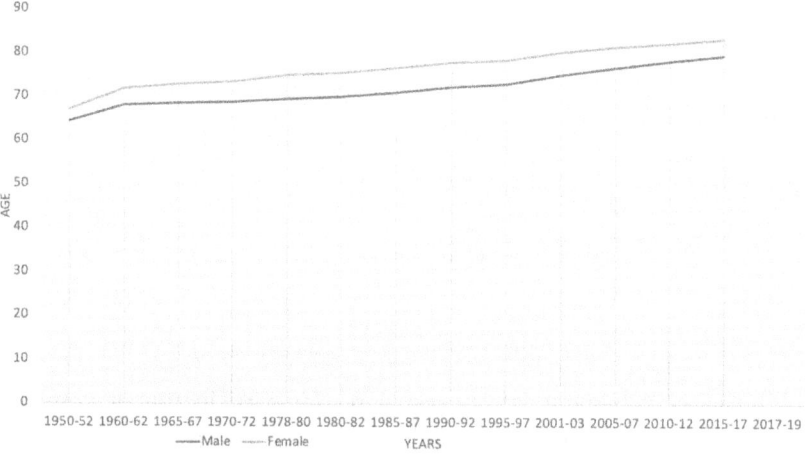

Source: CSO.

Women are not just living longer, they are living better. In the article by Whitaker quoted above he states that one of the most profound and welcome changes he has witnessed was the improvement in the status of women; 'it is difficult to believe that it is not all that long ago since women were degraded and disadvantaged in many ways, denied admission to universities and the professions, without voting rights, discriminated against in job access and pay treated in law as chattels'.[4] A vivid manifestation of this change is the rapid rise of women in the workforce.

---

4   Whitaker, 'We Have Come a Long Way', 10.

Table 3. Women in the Labour Force (21st century)

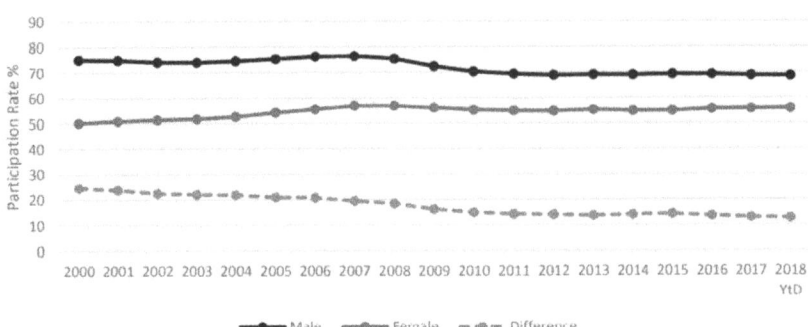

Source: CSO LFS *Quarterly figures annualised by average.

The rise in living standards and increasing participation of women in the workforce has been accompanied by a steep decline in the birth rate. Increasing levels of prosperity and openness to the rest of the world combined with the decline in authority of the Catholic Church has resulted in a rapid increase in the percentage of births now occurring outside marriage, which now account for approximately one in three of all births in Ireland.

Changing patterns of emigration and immigration are shown in Table 4. This table shows the very high levels of emigration in the 1950s tailing off in the 1960s and leading to net migration in the 1970s. Emigration returned in the 1980s but was replaced in the 1990s by very high levels of immigration.

Table 4. Net Migration 2009–2021

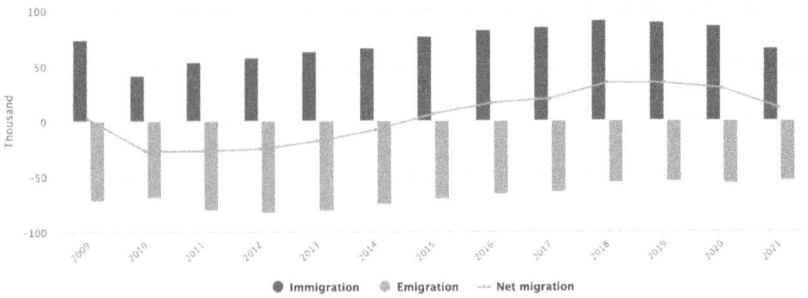

Source: CSO.

2. Education

A critical factor in the success of the economy, and in the enabling of women, has been the rapid expansion of second and third level education during the period under review. Table 5 shows the massive rise in the percentage of the population, with almost half the population having achieved a third level educational qualification. The gender breakdown shows men with slightly over 50 per cent and women at just over 45 per cent.

Table 5. Percentage of Adult Population Completing Third-Level Education 1960–2019

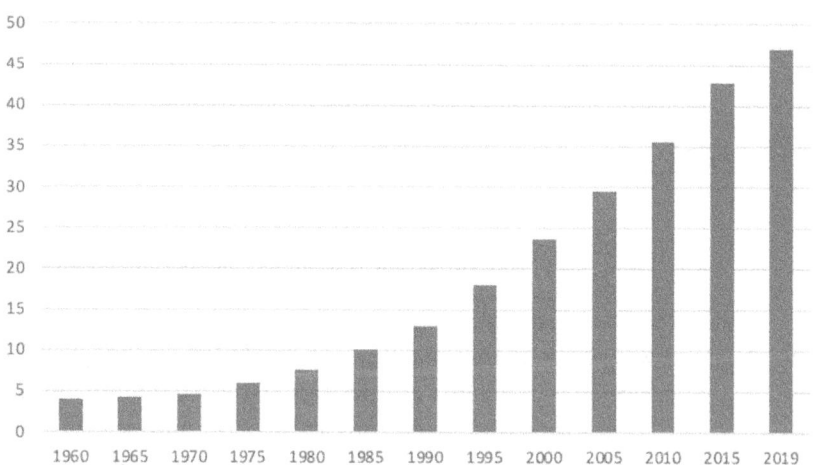

3. Economic

Two much quoted magazine cover stories sum up the Irish economic transformation between 1956 and 2006. The first from *Newsweek* in 2001 posed the question of what on earth Irish novelists would write about now that everyone had become so rich and happy: 'Prosperity has come to the land of Yeats and Joyce creating a land they could never have imagined; rich and happy.'⁵ The second from *The Economist* in 2004 made the point that

> surely no other country in the world has seen its image change so fast. Fifteen years ago Ireland was deemed an economic failure – Yet within a few years it had become the Celtic Tiger, a rare example of a developed country with a growth rate to match East Asia's as well as an enviably low unemployment and inflation, a low tax burden and a tiny public debt.⁶

Table 6. Constant GDP 1920–2020

Source: <https://www.rug.nl/ggdc/historicaldevelopment/maddison/releases/maddison-project-database-2020?lang=en>.

Table 6 shows strong rates of growth during the 1960s and 1970s, a significant slowing down in the 1980s and a huge take-off in the 1990s. The economic performance in the first two decades of the twenty-first century has been less spectacular, but is significantly ahead of the European average. Considerable controversy surrounds Ireland's economic performance, as our huge dependence on revenue from fixed direct investment, in the opinion of many economic commentators, distorts our true performance. Ever since the economic boom which began in the mid-1990s there have been regular outbreaks of celebratory cheers as the Irish economy reached new heights of growth and the whoops became louder as figures purporting to show that our economy had overtaken the UK's, making us wealthier than the 'old enemy'. More measured voices place us somewhere around

5   Cover story, *Newsweek* (20 April 2001).
6   Cover story, *The Economist* (14 October 2004).

half-way in the EU league, the most influential being Patrick Honohan, the former governor of the Central Bank. He has recently proposed an alternative measure, Active Individual Consumption (AIC), which tries to measure the goods and services that people actually consume, which puts us a little below the European average.[7] In a forthcoming paper by economic historians Ó Gráda and O'Rourke, reflecting on the performance of the Irish economy in the hundred years since partition, includes the following comments: 'In the late 1950s Ireland entered a period of economic growth which was to last for several years – Irish innovation showed clear signs of bullishness from the 1960s onwards – net emigration was lower between 1961–66 than in any inter-census period since independence.'[8]

4. Inequality

Inequality matters. Wilkinson & Pickett's definitive study of the subject around the world showed that there is a direct correlation between high levels of inequality and almost every social problem we face in the West; from obesity to crime, and from drug abuse to mental illness and from depression to stress.[9] But it is not the absolute levels of poverty and wealth that are the issue but the differentials in income levels from the highest to the lowest. More equal societies tend to be much less affected by these social maladies.

A second important aspect of inequality is that it is difficult to measure, partly because while it is relatively easy to describe in general terms, it is notoriously difficult to pin down. It is often measured in terms of the unequal distribution of economic resources such as income or wealth, but it can also be measured through other indicators of well-being, such as health, work satisfaction and even decision-making power. The most widely used

[7] Patrick Honohan, 'Is Ireland Really the Most Prosperous Country in Europe?' *Central Bank Economic Letter 1*, Central Bank of Ireland, 2021.
[8] Kevin O'Rourke and Cormac Ó Gráda, 'The Irish Economy during the Century after Partition', *Economic History Review*, forthcoming.
[9] Richard Wilkinson and Kate Pickett, *The Spirit Level: Why More Equal Societies Almost Always do Better* (London: Allen Lane, 2009).

method is probably the Gini Coefficient, which measures the level of inequality in a country on a scale from 0 (0%) to 1 (100%) by condensing the income distribution of a country to a single number between 0 and 1. The higher the number, the greater the level of inequality.

The independent Irish think tank for Action on Social Change, TASC, published a definitive guide to inequality in Ireland,[10] which presented a detailed run-through of the many different angles on the inequality debate, and concluded that Ireland occupies a mid-way position for income inequality among European countries. The report highlights the fact that workers in Ireland have relatively little bargaining power, trades unions are weak, employers have considerable flexibility, resulting in market incomes that are well below the European average, but that state transfers, family income, child support and jobseeker's allowance are generous by European standards, which has the effect of pulling Ireland up the rankings to occupy a mid-table positioning. The results of the TASC analysis shows that Ireland has the highest market income inequality after Greece, but the welfare state and a progressive tax system bring Ireland to be a little more unequal than most European countries, with a Gini coefficient of .3. An important point to note when considering inequality rankings is that the world, especially the Western world, has become more unequal since the libertarian political turn in the 1970s. Ireland followed this movement: we have a depressing tendency to follow the Anglo-American free market/minimum tax model as opposed to some of the more socially progressive continental European models.

Ireland has been a historically high inequality country. It has a set of institutions which predispose income to be more unequally distributed than in comparable countries. However, the TASC report goes on to say: 'Compared to the more equal countries in Europe it is not so much the poorest that fare badly, but Ireland is unusual in the low share of national income that goes to the working-to-lower-middle classes. The top decile does nicely, and the top one percent in particular.'[11]

---

10   TASC Report, *Inequality in Ireland Today* (Dublin: TASC Publications, 2018), 14.
11   TASC Report, *Inequality in Ireland Today* (Dublin: TASC Publications, 2018), 40.

More broadly based attempts to measure inequality across countries tend to show Ireland in a more progressive light. The Social Progress Index measures the extent to which countries provide for the social and environmental needs of their citizens. Based on the work of academics who have developed wider measures of well-being like Amartya Sen and Joseph Stiglitz, these studies cover three dimensions: basic human needs, foundations of human needs and degrees of opportunities. Once again, the Nordic countries fill the top slots, Norway, Denmark and Finland are the top three, but Ireland achieves a creditable twelfth position, again well ahead of the UK and US.

5. Ireland and Europe: From Calculation to Accommodation

Ireland officially joined the then European Economic Community on 1 January 1973, the country having passed a referendum to that effect in 1972 by an overwhelming majority – 83 per cent in favour, 17 per cent against, based on a turnout of 71 per cent. In seven subsequent European referendums, that turnout was never equalled, and in two - Nice 2001 and Lisbon 2008 - the proposals were defeated, necessitating follow-up referendums soon after which were successfully passed. The government of the day learned from the two defeats and campaigned more strategically and vigorously in the follow-up campaigns. Our initial reason to throw in our lot with Europe was almost exclusively functional and economic. The two main economic benefits were the Common Agricultural Policy, from which Irish farmers were a net beneficiary, and the membership of a large market which enhanced our appeal to mainly American fixed direct investment. In order to emphasise the initial functional nature of the relationship, on 1 January 1973, the government coordinated an extraordinary advertising campaign which involved a wide range of Irish state agencies and private businesses to produce over fifty different advertisements which were placed that day in the *New York Times*. Every single page of the edition contained one or more Irish advertisements. It was a clear signal to American businesses that Ireland was now a member of one of the biggest trading markets in the world, and our success in attracting

US investment over the last almost seventy years is testament to the success of that strategy.

The two referendum defeats in 2001 and 2008 were a reminder that our relationship with Europe couldn't be taken for granted, but the regular Eurobarometer surveys carried out for the EU showed consistently strong support for Europe among the Irish electorate until 2010 and 2011, when economic austerity measures were instigated as a result of the Troika oversight of the Irish economy following the collapse of the Irish banking system. The speed of Ireland's economic recovery from the recession has already been noted, and was accompanied by a recovery in our favourable attitude to the EU, which became even more marked in the aftermath of Brexit when Ireland's interests particularly in relation to the Good Friday Agreement required steadfast support from the European negotiators.

A Eurobarometer poll in 2019 showed that trust in the EU was higher than trust in national governments across Europe, but the difference was more pronounced than the average in Ireland. The same poll showed that 89 per cent of Irish people believed that the EU's voice in the world carried weight, and we were second only to Portugal, 94 per cent, on this issue. Irish respondents were also more optimistic than average at the time, with two-thirds believing that the economic situation was very good. The results from another Eurobarometer poll in 2021 were even more positive from a European perspective, and in relation to Ireland's increasingly favourable attitude to the EU. On average just under half, 49 per cent, of respondents across Europe expressed trust in the EU, but Ireland recorded a score of 74 per cent, second only to Portugal at 78 per cent and significantly ahead of Germany, 48 per cent and France, 39 per cent. In the same survey 91 per cent of Irish people were in favour of a European Monetary Union with the Euro as the single currency compared to an average score across Europe of 70 per cent. When asked about globalisation two-thirds, 66 per cent, of Irish respondents felt positive about it, the second most favourable response after Denmark, 78 per cent. The one area where Ireland is out of line with the top-performing European countries is climate change, with only 9 per cent of the population rating it a serious problem, well below the average.

These results suggest that Ireland is becoming a nation of 'good Europeans', more aware of the benefits above and beyond the purely economic.

Table 7. Perception of EU Responsiveness to Interests of Members

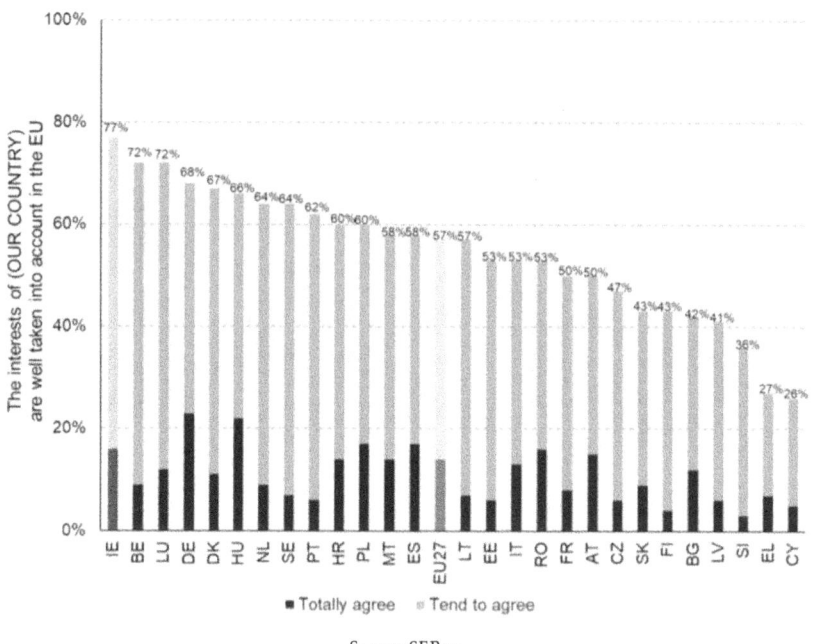

Source: SEB94.

Table 8. Trust in the EU by Member States

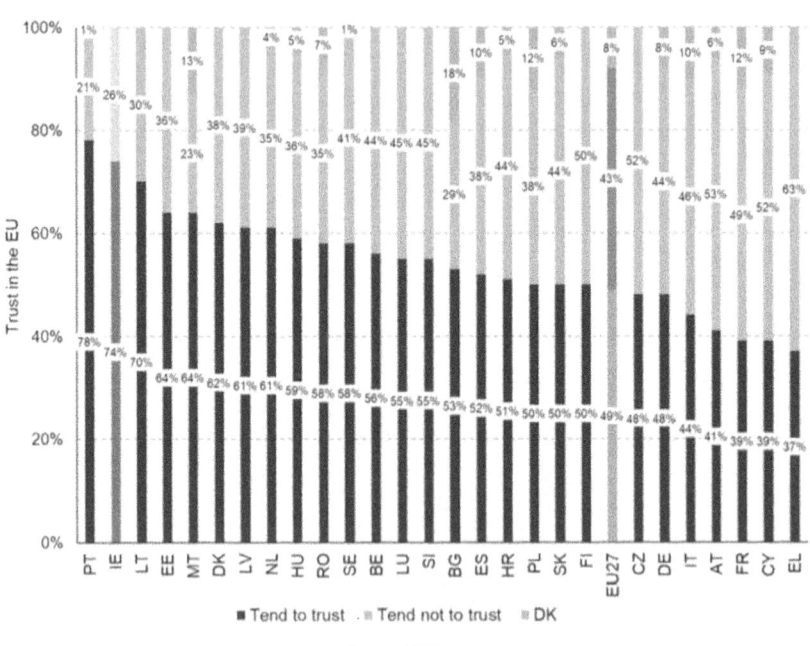

Source: SEB94.

6. Religious Observance and Moral Beliefs

Once an outlier famed for its high level of religious observance, Ireland has certainly become more European on all issues of faith and morals. The most dramatic manifestation of the change was the results of two landmark referendums: abortion in 2018 and divorce in 2019. Abortion, which had been a contentious and highly emotive issue in Ireland and around the world, passed off with remarkably little rancour, and was comfortably approved by a two-thirds majority. The divorce referendum, which had been the subject of a previously divisive election in the 1980s, passed in 2019 by an even more comfortable four-fifths majority. Ancient Ireland was truly dead and gone, with John Charles McQuaid in the grave.

These results were mirrored by successive surveys showing steep declines in weekly attendances at religious services. A detailed survey of Irish behaviour across a wide range of subjects in 1995 and repeated in 2015 by leading market research company Behaviour & Attitudes (B&A) showed that weekly attendance at church services/Mass had declined more than threefold from 73 per cent in 1995 to only 22 per cent in 2015. Analysis of the results by age in 2015 showed that the younger age groups were three times less likely to attend weekly services than the over 55s, which strongly suggests that the decline in weekly attendances is likely to increase in future.

Not surprisingly, the importance of religion/faith to an Irish sense of identity is also becoming closer to that of other European countries:

Table 9. Importance of Religion/Faith to Personal Identity

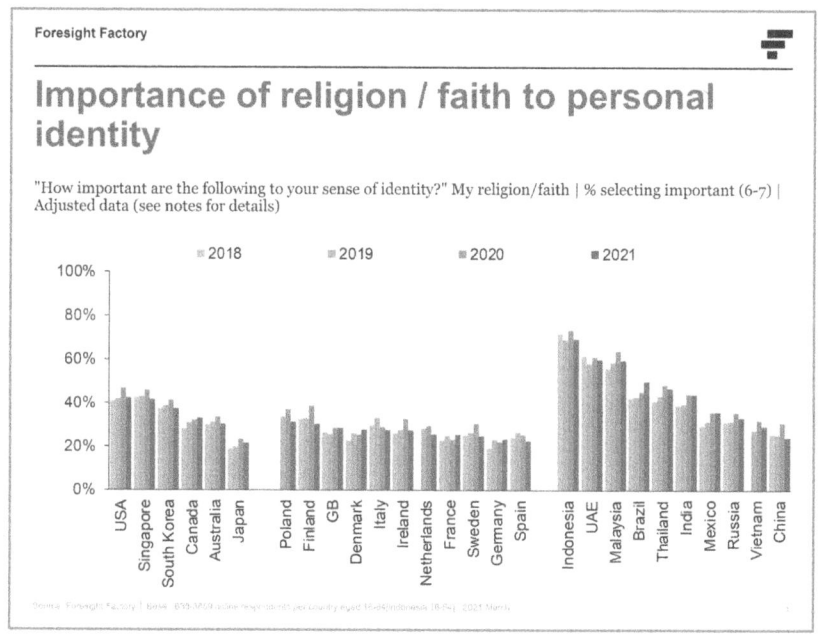

Source: Foresight Factory.

The B&A survey comparing attitudes in 1995 and 2015 also included a number of questions measuring changes in the Irish attitude towards moral issues. Once again, the results show the increasing liberalisation of the country in the twenty-year period.

Table 10. Changing Mores

	1995	2015
I believe couples should live together before they are married	42%	67%
I think sexual freedom of today is a good thing	46%	57%
Abortion is always wrong	53%	32%
Divorce is always wrong	28%	13%

Source: B&A Ireland 1995–2015 Survey.

Increasing levels of prosperity and openness to the rest of the world combined with the decline in authority of the Catholic Church resulted in a rapid rise in the number of births occurring outside marriage which now account for over a third of all births in Ireland.

Table 11. Births Outside Marriage

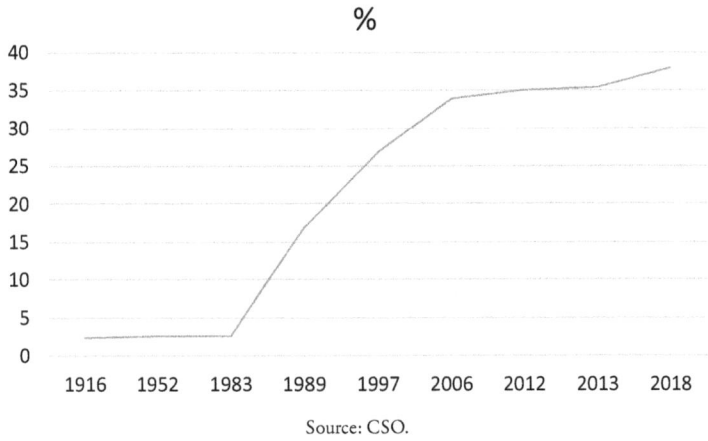

Source: CSO.

Statistical Analysis of the Transformation

7. Irish Pride

The Foresight Factory pan-European survey, carried out in 2019, included a series of questions designed to measure European citizens' assessment of the importance of nationality and sense of pride in their own country. In terms of the former, Ireland is close to the European average, with just under 60 per cent of respondents agreeing with the importance of nationality to their personal identity. In terms of being proud of their country, Ireland was above the European average, but below Finland, which recorded the highest score in Europe. A breakdown of the results by age shows that the older age cohorts are significantly more likely to feel proud of their country.

Table 12. Pride in Country

Source: Foresight Factory.

Two additional questions from the Foresight survey shed more light on Irish people's attitudes to their national identity. When asked 'what does the phrase "made in Ireland" mean to you', the four highest category responses were: makes me want to buy for the good of the country; makes me feel proud; makes me more likely to buy; and makes me feel proud. Just over half of all respondents also claimed that they intended to buy more locally produced food and drinks than in the past.

8. Quality of Life and Happiness Indices

The concept of the nation brand image has become more prominent in geo-political discourse especially since Joseph Nye coined the term 'soft power' in the 1980s – he elaborated on this concept in a 2004 publication.[12] His objective was to show that the more conventional forms of power, military and economic, were sometimes ineffectual compared to 'softer' forms of power, which are difficult to explain but often boil down to whether people like you or not. Not only is this hard to define, it is almost impossible to measure, but that hasn't stopped a wide range of international institutions and global marketing communications consultancies from commissioning annual surveys to measure the image of different countries and often branching out into alternative methods of measuring how well they are doing as opposed to the more standard measures of GNP, for example, the OECD's Better Life Index, the UN's World Happiness Index and *The Economist* magazine's Quality of Life Index. In spite of the widely different definitions and methodologies, Ireland's ranking is always remarkably consistent, coming in in most surveys around twentieth position out of on average 160 countries. Given our size and relative economic weight this is a very creditable performance.

One of the latest indices, the Portland Group's *Soft Power Index,* whose latest report features an introductory article on the increasing importance of soft power by Joseph Nye, has Ireland in nineteenth position, and includes the following comment: Both Ireland and New Zealand, as relatively

---

12 Joseph Nye, *Soft Power: The Means to Success in World Politics* (New York: Public Affairs US).

small countries, have put in relatively strong performances in the latest soft power rankings.

Another, similar survey, the Good Country Index, produced by Simon Anholt, who is one of the most prolific publishers on nation branding and soft power, shows Ireland featured prominently in recent years.

The latest Ipsos Global Trends survey reports on a wide range of political and cultural attitudes in twenty-five countries around the world and includes Ireland for the first time. The results were published in the *Irish Times*, with a comment on some of the main findings by Fintan O'Toole. He suggested that one of the most interesting results was that Ireland was the second lowest country, second only to China, for agreeing with the statement: 'I would like my country to be the way it used to be.' Our lack of nostalgia can be attributed to the fact that our immediate past was dominated by colonisation, famine, civil war, high levels of emigration and economic failure, but O'Toole suggests that it may account for the absence of any significant support for the far right in Ireland. He also comments on our comparatively open and welcoming attitude to immigration and globalisation and our above average pride in being Irish. His conclusion is revealing and supports the general thrust of other surveys quoted in this chapter:

> The broad feeling about Ireland from the study, then, is one of sober optimism. Irish people do not look back to a lost golden age or forward to an apocalyptic decline – they love their country enough to recognize its dark sides. They also love it enough to be happy to share it with those who hope it can give them a better life.[13]

Conclusions

The objective of this chapter is not to attempt a comprehensive statistical analysis of the demographic, sociological and cultural changes in Ireland

---

13 Fintan O'Toole, 'A Proud Nation that We are Happy to Share', *The Irish Times* (13 November 2021), 1–2.

between the late 1950s and the present day. It is designed to give some idea of the main changes that have taken place that support my conclusion that the second revival which began in the late 1950s succeeded in its main objective of stemming the tide of emigration, which at the time threatened the country's very future and succeeded in creating a society where all can thrive and flourish. Life expectancy has increased, with both men and women living over twelve years longer than they were sixty years ago. Educational opportunities have increased significantly, and almost half of the young adult population now have a third level qualification. Perhaps the most dramatic of all has been the change in the position of women in Irish society; almost all barriers to playing an equal role have been removed. Women now participate equally in all levels of education and in the workforce, and recent referendums have significantly increased their control of their reproductive rights.

Membership of the EU has brought huge economic and social benefits, and we are enthusiastic members. We are proud of our country and express a reasonable level of satisfaction with how the country is run and with its main institutions. Serious problems remain however, especially in the areas of healthcare and housing. Underpinning these problems is the cancer of inequality. In spite of efforts to alleviate the problem, through relatively progressive welfare payments, very little effort has been expended in tackling the root causes of inequality, with the result that too many people begin life in Ireland with a wooden spoon, while at the other end of the scale, the silver spoon cohort will thrive regardless of talent or effort. We are still not cherishing all the children equally.

Nevertheless, I believe that the evidence presented in this chapter shows that the seeds planted in the revival that took place from 1958 to 1966, in which the Mandarin, the Musician and the Mage played critical roles, has resulted in a society that is unrecognisable just over sixty years later. Within this period, as the demographic and economic data presented here shows, the population has almost doubled, emigration has been reduced to a mainly voluntary trickle and the economy is one of the better performing in Europe. But perhaps more importantly, Irish people were enjoying a high level of self-confidence, content with their membership of and active role in international institutions (especially the EU) and proud of their Irish identity. By 2019, Ireland was ranked second (to Norway) in the UN's Human Development Index.[14]

This transformation began in the late 1950s and 1960s. Eminent economic historians Kevin O'Rourke and Cormac Ó Gráda capture it well in their forthcoming history of the Irish economy quoted previously: 'in the late 1950s Ireland entered a period of economic growth which was to last for several years … Irish innovation showed clear signs of bullishness from the 1960s onwards'.[15] It is also significant that all this was achieved without resorting to the extremes of individualism experienced by other Western countries during the height of the neo-liberal era. In a recent opinion column, economist Dan O'Brien, writing about what he believed was an excessively cautious attitude to the COVID-19 pandemic by the Irish authorities, argued that it was due to 'the absence of a libertarian tradition here and the strength of collectivism – [Irish] society is cohesive and consensus orientated'.[16] I believe that the three men at the heart of the second revival would have applauded this conclusion.

---

14   Mark Henry, *In Fact: An Optimist's Guide to Ireland at 100* (Dublin: Gill Books, 2021), 367. (Henry does make the point that the UN Index is based on a nation's GDP, but even if adjusted to Patrick Honohan's proposed Gross National Income, GNI, index Ireland would still rank in eighth place.)
15   Ó Gráda and O'Rourke, 'The Irish Economy during the Century after Partition'.
16   Dan O'Brien, 'Covid-19 Has Brought out the Inner Catastrophist in Our National Psyche', *Sunday Business Post* (24 October 2021), 27.

PART III

The World in the 2020s and How Ireland Might Respond

CHAPTER 6

The Sceptics: Globalisation, Contents and Discontents

Irish society has been transformed since the publication of the *First Programme for Economic Expansion* over sixty years ago. From being one of the poorest performing economies in Europe at the time, Ireland's economic performance featured on the front cover of *The Economist* in 2007 under the heading 'Europe's Shining Light'. It is worth noting that that influential periodical has a history of taking a fairly baleful view of Ireland. The Great Recession of 2008 did more damage to the Irish economy than to most other countries, but it recovered strongly and is now, once again, one of the successful economies in Europe. But Ireland's opening out to the world, advocated by Whitaker in the late 1950s, had always attracted criticism from those who disagreed with the policy of attracting overseas fixed direct investment in the first place, to those who feared that although the economic consequences might be beneficial, the cultural effect on the character of the country and its people would be deleterious.

Early Sceptics

Two Trinity College economists, Raymond Crotty and Anthony Coughlan, were the most prominent early critics. Their arguments were mainly economic, believing that the Anglo-Irish Free Trade agreement and Ireland's accession to the then-EEC would merely perpetuate our long-standing economic dependency on more powerful economic forces. Crotty had little confidence that the multi-national businesses attracted by export tax concessions would contribute much to the Irish economy, dismissing them as 'enclave industries'.[1] In a wide-ranging history of the development of agriculture and capitalism from the earliest times to the present day, he argued that we were substituting subordination to the interests of the British market to a similar subservient role in servicing a European market:

> The ultimate consequence of the policy of reintegrating Ireland's former capitalist colonial economy with the economies of the metropolitan capitalist countries has been to intensify Irish economic dependence.[2]

The most persistent of the cultural critics was Desmond Fennell, who has been described as a 'writer who consistently challenges the orthodox views held in Ireland and the world generally'.[3] A fully fledged contrarian, he published a succession of books in the 1980s and 1990s which were bitterly critical of the side-effects of the modernisation of the economy and growth of fixed direct investment, which he argued had resulted in a deepening materialism and consumer ethos in Irish society. He believed in the essential rural characteristic of Irish life, 'a balanced material and spiritual existence – opposed to the contemporary dehumanising materialism',[4] which was responsible for increased levels of suicide, sexual license, violent crime and marriage breakdown. His second criticism was that these changes were accompanied by historical revisionism which was intent on betraying the ideals of the 1916 Rising. He was bitterly critical of the so-called 'Dublin 4 elite' and their cheerleaders, the *Irish Times* and RTÉ, and their crusade of de-nationalism of 'religion, the GAA, the Christian Brothers 1916 and the Gaelic Revival movement'.[5]

---

1 Raymond D. Crotty, *Ireland in Crisis: A Study in Capitalist Colonial Undevelopment* (Cork: Bandon Books, 1986), 90–92.
2 Ibid., 100.
3 Brian Arkins, 'Introduction', in Toner Quinn, ed., *Desmond Fennell: His Life and Work* (Dublin: Veritas Publications, 2001), 11.
4 Desmond Fennell, *The State of the Nation: Ireland Since the Sixties* (Dublin: Ward River Press, 1983), 74.
5 Desmond Fennell, *Heresy: The Battle for Ideas in Modern Ireland* (Newtownards: Blackstaff Press, 1993), 197.

Fennell's third criticism was that the new development strategy, by aligning Ireland more closely with the global economy, and in particular the US and UK, we were forfeiting the ability for independent thought. This is an important point mentioned by a number of commentators, and may still have some relevance. He quoted one critic who argued that in most public policy areas, from business to medicine, engineering to architecture, economic planning, to town planning, our thinking is derivative: 'One doubts if we have added anything of real importance to sociological, theological, philosophical or aesthetic thought.'[6] We have, in his colourful phrase, become 'mentally colonised'.

Unlike most of the critics, Fennell tried to follow his own beliefs, uprooting himself and his family to live in a remote part of Connemara, where he campaigned for more local democracy, greater use of local resources and a simpler lifestyle. Aware of his New Age movement choice, he recommended that Ireland should take a leadership role by using its spiritual resources: 'to turn our anachronisms into a virtue – paradoxically when the world is seeking for soul, for transcendence, for myth, we are being asked to seek a belated enlightenment.'[7] But in the face of the lure of the modern consumer world and the apathy of his Connemara community he acknowledged defeat: 'I feel I have laboured and wrote in vain and I grieve at being thrust by fate into such a malfunctioning, discouraging and sluggish intellectual environment.'[8] Fennell achieved none of his aims, but it was his misfortune to be writing at a time when Ireland was becoming more prosperous and in the grip of a dominant political and economic ideology completely at variance with his own views. Now that the neo-liberal ideology has been discredited and a new generation disillusioned by recession and austerity and more conscious of non-economic issues like climate change there could be a revival of interest in his formidable body of work.

6 Fennell, *The State of the Nation*, 63.
7 Fennell, *Heresy*, 55.
8 Ibid., 234.

Later Sceptics

Later sceptics had to cope with the reality of the so-called Celtic Tiger years from the mid-1990s to the Great Recession in 2008, so they concentrated their fire on what they regarded as the excessive consumerism and materialism that accompanied the economic boom. There were still some doubts being expressed about Ireland's dependence on a continuing flow of fixed direct investment, and Dennis O'Hearn, a Belfast-based economist, was to the fore in his view that the country's economic success was built on very flimsy foundations. Comparing the Irish model with the East Asian success stories like South Korea, Hong Kong, Singapore and Taiwan, he argued that indigenous businesses played a much stronger role in their success, making them less vulnerable to the inevitable swings and roundabouts of the world economic cycle. He argued that the shaky edifice that is the Irish economy was overly dependent on a handful of American corporations who could be here today and gone tomorrow in a world where low-cost tax havens are increasingly easy to access: 'It is barely an exaggeration to say that the Irish Tiger boils down to a few American corporations in computers and pharmaceuticals.'[9]

The perceived lack of indigenous business success stories was a recurring issue, and the subject of a series of high-profile government-commissioned reports designed to address the issue: Telesis (1982), Culliton (1994) and O'Driscoll (2005). Some of the proposals made in these reports were implemented, but in the meantime more and more successful indigenous Irish businesses were starting to make their presence felt across the globe. CRH, Ryanair, Kerry Group, Glanbia and many more made the Irish economy somewhat less dependent on overseas investment, and in turn made the sceptics' economic criticisms less relevant. The cultural sceptics, on the other hand, believed that economic success made their criticisms even more pertinent.

---

9   Denis O'Hearn, *Inside the Celtic Tiger: The Irish Economy and the Asian Model* (London: Pluto Press, 1998), 73.

Peadar Kirby, academic and former journalist, has written and co-authored a number of books on the subject of Irish transformation, and is mainly concerned by a belief that the economic boom had increased economic inequality, and that the rising tide wasn't lifting all boats. In support, he quoted from a Human Poverty Index compiled for eighteen developed countries, showing Ireland in second-last position, and an income inequality index ranking twenty-five OECD countries showing Ireland in eighteenth position. He is critical of the increasing encroachment of economic criteria and language in all aspects of life and the constant pressure to embrace the values of individualism, entrepreneurship and achievement-orientation which this entails. He concludes that the social costs of economic success are too great: 'The Celtic Tiger has prioritized the economy over society, the private over the public and the economic over the political'.[10]

Michael O'Connell is a social psychologist who published two books in the early twenty-first century which echoed some of Kirby's themes: 'Collective identity and a fear of God has given way to individualism and a fear of negative equity.'[11] He also argues that Ireland has become much more right-wing, exemplified by a visceral hatred of taxation and an increasingly hostile attitude towards immigrants. Like Kirby, he makes use of official statistics to make his point, claiming that Irish expenditure on Education and Health showed Ireland in the mid-1990s to be in the bottom end of European league tables. He paints a disconcerting portrait of twenty-first-century Irish society as materialist, individualist, smug and selfish, and worried that any sign of an economic downturn could exacerbate the situation: 'There are few more reactionary forces than a million pissed off yuppies who can't meet their mortgage repayments.'[12]

Joe Cleary, formerly of Maynooth University and currently attached to Yale, is also exercised by what he regards as the increasing marketisation of Irish society, but his particular concern is the almost complete lack of any alternative vision of a good society. Like the other sceptics, he opposes the

10 Peadar Kirby, *The Celtic Tiger in Distress: Growth with Inequality in Ireland* (London: Palgrave, 2002), 105.
11 Malcolm MacLachlan, 'Introduction', in Michael O'Connell, ed., *Right-wing Ireland?: The Rise of Populism in Ireland and Europe* (Dublin: Liffey Press, 2001), X.
12 Ibid., 8.

dominant neo-liberal agenda. He's particularly disappointed by what he claims is the absence of any attempt by the artistic and literary community to provide alternative visions for Irish society. He argues that 'the masses' have been bought off by rampant consumerism, which at best results in 'low-grade material benefits' and at worst end up in 'endemic frustration and dissatisfaction'.[13]

The Association of Irish Sociologists also entered the fray through their Irish Sociological Chronicles, seven editions of which were published between 1998 and 2010. Most of the contributions could be described as being fairly sceptical about the overall benefits to Irish society of the long-term economic boom. Echoing some of the previous critics, the main focus of the sociological contributions centre around consumerism and materialism and arguing that economic growth had been achieved at the expense of the wider interests of society: 'In both policy and popular discourse the country has become coterminous with the economy, pushing the concept of civil society to the sidelines.'[14] There are frequent allusions to Bauman's concept of the 'liquid society'[15] and Beck's notion of the increasing 'risk'[16] involved in everyday life, and they introduce their own metaphor, 'collision', claiming that the speed of the changes in Irish life has created its own problems: 'Collision is the central unifying metaphor which expresses the changes in Irish society today: collisions between the traditional and the modern, between the local and the global and between the values of the collectivist and individualist world views.'[17]

By 2006, just before the party ended, the tone of their anti-consumerist agenda was becoming more virulent: 'We find ourselves suspended in stasis betwixt and between political stability which is also corrupt and precarious; wealth that creates growing inequality; urban growth that is squalid and blighted; a liberal affluent culture that is shallow and vulgar – a

13   Cleary, *Outrageous Fortune*, 45.
14   Mary Corcoran and Perry Share, 'Introduction', in *Belongings: Shaping Identities in Modern Ireland, Irish Sociological Chronicles 6* (Dublin: IPA publications, 2008), 1.
15   Zygmunt Bauman, *Liquid Modernity* (Cambridge: Polity Press 2000).
16   Ulrich Beck, *The Risk Society* (New York: Sage Publications 1992).
17   Carmen Kuhling and Kieran Keohane, *Ireland Unbound: A Turn of the Century Chronicle: Irish Sociological Chronicles 5* (Dublin: IPA Publications, 2006), 105.

promiscuous and indiscriminate "openness" the new – a derision of past beliefs and ideals, softened by a note of nostalgia and willful romance for their passing and reassuring platitudes that the "spirit of community" is alive and well. Is this a description of true happiness, or is it the kind of feigned happiness that accompanies tragedy?'[18]

The relentless level of criticism eventually produced a response in the form of a comprehensive report comprising the work of twenty-one academics, mainly economists and most of them attached to the Economic and Social Research Institute. The report, significantly titled *The Best of Times?*, was published in 2007.[19] Given what was to happen a year later, it was wryly suggested that the inclusion of the question mark in the title was fortuitous. Nevertheless, the publication was a timely corrective to the sceptics and represented a more rounded perspective on the state of the nation exemplified by a much-quoted line from President Mary McAleese a few years earlier: 'If the men and women from Ireland's past could choose a time to live, there would be long queue for this one.'[20]

The publication coincided with a growing global debate on whether economic growth per se was a sufficient measure of overall happiness or a flourishing life. An influential book at the time by Richard Layard, *Happiness: Lessons for a New Science*, kick-started a new debate about the relevance of GNP or GDP which was referenced by some of the authors of the report, but concluded that while happiness may not always correlate with economic growth, it does tend to give us a 'generally optimistic and hopeful outlook – that preserves us from pessimism and narrowness and proneness to inter-group conflict and hatred when prosperity stalls'.[21] A chapter on the lives of residents in some of the new dormitory towns feeding into the Dublin employment market concluded that these new lives were

---

18 Mary Corcoran, *Uncertain Ireland: Irish Sociological Chronicles 5* (Dublin: IPA Publications, 2003/2004), 40.
19 Tony Fahey, 'How Do We Feel?: Economic Boom and Happiness', in Tony Fahey, Helen Russell and Christopher T. Whelan, eds, *The Best of Times?* (Dublin: IPA Publications, 2007), 11.
20 Ibid., 85.
21 Ibid., 25.

not dominated by 'anomie and alienation' but were characterised by supportive new ties and bonds.

The charge of increasing inequality is also met with the claim that Ireland had always been a more unequal society than the European average, and that the economic boom from the 1990s to the present hadn't changed the relative position of different segments of Irish society in any significant way, although there was some evidence that the higher income groups had extended their advantage somewhat, and the position of the very worse off had seen their position deteriorate further. They characterise traditional Irish policy on this issue as using taxation to provide funds to alleviate the problem rather than making any concerted effort to create greater equality, accepting that 'the occupational playing field remains substantially tilted in favour of children from more advantaged households'.[22]

The concluding chapter of *The Best of Times*, written by a Swedish Social Research Professor, pointed out that when societies experience a sudden increase in prosperity the results may not be to everyone's taste, but that on balance the results were positive, which led to the joint authors declaring: 'The evidence in this volume points to considerable improvements in the absolute welfare of most inhabitants in Ireland and that the Celtic Tiger, judged on the basis of its social as well as its economic impact certainly deserves at least two cheers and perhaps even three.'[23] Some of the earlier critics were not satisfied: Peadar Kirby, for example, argued that the facts presented in the report were not sufficiently grounded in sociological theory, and that the so-called 'facts' presented in the report were done so without a 'theory to guide classification and selection'.[24] Kieran Keohane made a similar point, arguing that the report's findings are disengaged from 'the main currents of sociological theory resulting in insularity and self-referential provincialism'.[25]

---

22 Ibid., 85.
23 Ibid., 10.
24 Peadar Kirby, 'The Best of Times or Besting the Critics? The ESRI on the Social Impact of the Celtic Tiger', *Administration* 55/3 (2008), 184.
25 Kieran Keohane, 'The Best of Times and Worst of Times', *The Irish Review* 38 (2008), 122.

The Sceptics: Globalisation, Contents and Discontents

Another assessment of the overall effects of the economic boom was published just before the crash: an IPA report of a meeting of over 200 senior administrators in workshops and roundtables in 2007. Writing in the introduction, Seán Dorgan observed: 'Writing in 2007 we can say that Ireland has experienced a period of exceptional economic growth, considerable social progress and profound transformation. The past two decades may be counted in many respects as the most successful in Irish history. Without entering into the complex question of how emigration, low standards of living and unemployment should be fully factored into an evaluation of what the quality of life truly was in an earlier Ireland the evidence is strong that Irish people are a notably content population by contemporary international standards.'[26]

On balance, I believe that those who argued in favour of the progress made during the economic boom have made a better case than the critics. It is true that the boom lifted some boats more than others and inequality remained at a high level in Ireland, but it could be argued that this had more to do with the neo-liberal ethos that characterised the Western world from the 1980s up to the Great Recession of 2008 than to any particular characteristic of the Irish economic boom. The critics also make great play with what they claim was the greater emphasis on consumerism in Irish life and resulting materialism of Irish culture. It is undoubtedly true that people had more money, and spent more money, and the craze of manic pre- Christmas shopping trips to New York would hardly make any sane nation proud, but too much of the sociologist's criticism was condescending and more than a little patronising. Roger Scruton has warned against the 'intellectual's natural revulsion at the getting and appending of others'.[27] The key word here is 'others': my purchases are considered necessary and tasteful; yours are thoughtless, wasteful and vulgar. In their 2005 book *Rebel Sell*, Canadian philosophers Joseph Heath and Andrew Potter comment: 'Whenever you look at the consumer goods that critics complain about, that people don't really need, they are invariably goods that

26   Seán Dorgan, 'Introduction to Public Service 2022', in Mark Callanan, ed., *Ireland 2022: Towards One Hundred Years of Self-Government* (Dublin: IPA Publications, 2007), 1.
27   Roger Scruton, *Modern Culture* (London: Continuum Books, 1998), 55.

middle-class, middle-aged intellectuals don't really need – consumerism always seems to be a critique of what other people buy – which makes it all too often thinly veiled snobbery or even worse, puritanism.'[28] The critics seem oblivious of the bourgeoning academic discipline of consumption studies which present a much more rounded view of consumption and in particular its role as an enabling mechanism in society. There is therefore a crucial distinction to be made between the increasing commoditisation of society as a result of the hegemony of neo-liberal policies which were powerful in the Western world from the 1980s to 2008 and the consumption of goods which is an inherent characteristic of all societies.

The transformation of Irish society did involve embracing the modern world, which inevitably leads to the age-old debate about whether the degree of modernisation and disruption involved in the attainment of economic growth is worth the price. This is a debate which has raged since the beginning of time in the classical mythological figures of Hermes and Hestia. The latter symbolises the circular hearth placed at the centre of the home, the closed sphere of the group drawn into itself, while Hermes is the god of the threshold and the door, but also the crossroads and town gates representing movement and relationships with others. In the last few decades, the concept of 'globalisation' has added a new dimension to the debate.

Ireland, Modernisation and Globalisation

In modern times, the most widely quoted representation of the debate between tradition and modernity is the nineteenth-century German sociologist Ferdinand Tönnies's distinction between *Gemeinschaft* and *Gesellschaft*, where the former represents the local community and the latter the outside world. Through his business trading activities he was acquainted with both worlds, and was conscious of the contradictions between the two:

---

28   Joseph Heath and Andrew Potter, *Rebel Sell: Why the Culture Can't be Jammed* (Oxford: Capstone, 2005), 138.

> In the Middle Ages there was unity, now there is atomisation, then the hierarchy of authority was solicitous paternalism, now it is compulsory exploitation, then there was sympathetic relationships among kinfolk and old acquaintances, now there are strangers and aliens everywhere, then society was made up of home and land-loving peasants, now the attitude of the businessman prevails, then man's simple needs were met by home production and barter, now we have world trade and capitalistic production, then there was permanency of abode, now there is great mobility, then there were folk art, music and handicrafts, now there is science – as in the case of the cool calculation of the businessman.[29]

Written almost two hundred years ago, these lines could also represent the cry of some twenty-first-century Irish communities who still regret the opening up of the world sixty-five years ago by Ken Whitaker and his colleagues. Marshall Berman's more recent study of this ancient conflict, *All that Is Solid Melts into Air*, also captures the dilemma raised by our Faustian act with modernity: 'The deepest horrors of Faustian development spring from its most honourable aims and its most authentic achievements. Faust sells his soul for knowledge and power and the catch is he can never trade them back. When freed from tradition we gain the ability to see good in it; integrity, stability, solidity, continuity, groundedness.'[30]

Whitaker, Ó Riada and Kinsella all managed to navigate the treacherous waters of modernity and progress while retaining their integrity, solidity, stability and groundedness, and although there have been lapses, notably from the mid-1990s to the Great Recession of 2008, Irish society as a whole has also managed this balance fairly well, in spite of having become one of the most globalised societies in the world. Some of the recent fallout from the Great Recession – rising disenchantment with democracy around the world, the rise of autocratic regimes and the Brexit and Trump explosions – have led some commentators to conclude that the phenomenon of globalisation is on the wane, but I believe that an examination of the origins and nature of the concept will suggest that this is not the case.

---

29 Ferdinand Tönnies, *Community and Association*, Trans. C. P. Loomis (London: Routledge & Keegan Paul, 1957), xi.
30 Marshall Berman, *All that is Solid Melts into Air: The Experience of Modernity* (London: Verso, 1983), 15.

Globalisation: Origins and Growth

What is globalisation? It is one of those portmanteau words into which all kinds of other words, quite often with different meanings, are deposited. A huge body of writing on the subject emerged in the last decades of the twentieth century, with many commentators describing the term itself as 'slippery': 'Globalisation is a hideous word of obscure meaning, coined in the 1960s, which came into its own in the 1990s and is extremely difficult to pin down.'[31] It was also pointed out that this difficulty means it can be used in too many different contexts, which in turn makes it even more difficult to define: 'A significant problem with discussions of globalization is that the term tends to expand infinitely its scope of reference; it is employed so loosely that almost anything can be used to illustrate its operation or be included in its embrace.'[32]

It has attracted widespread criticism on two main grounds: being a key driver of the political and economic ideology often referred to as neo-liberalism, and as a force that homogenises nation states. German sociologist Ulrich Beck summarises the first criticism: 'globalisation is the view that the world market eliminates or supplants political action; rule by world market, the ideological core of globalisation is that a basic difference of the first modernity, the distinction between politics and economics, is liquidated, the state is to be run as a company, an imperialism of economics'.[33] The second is summarised by Thomas Friedman, a *New York Times* op-ed writer who has written a number of best-selling books on the subject: 'Because globalization as a culturally homogenizing and environment-devouring force is coming on so fast, there is a real danger that in just a few decades it could wipe out the ecological and cultural diversity it took millions of years of human and biological evolution to produce.'[34] Before discussing

---

31 Martin Wolf, *Why Globalisation Works* (Yale: Nota Bene, 2005), 13.
32 Paul Hirst and Grahame Thompson, 'The Tyranny of Globalisation: Myth or Reality?', in Frans Buelens, ed., *Globalisation and the Nation State* (Cheltenham: Edward Elgar, 1999), 117.
33 Ulrich Beck, *What is Globalisation?* (Cambridge: Polity Press, 2000), 6.
34 Friedman, *The Lexus and the Olive Tree*, 221.

these criticisms in more detail, I want to briefly review some of the widely different views on the origins of globalisation.

When did globalisation begin? Responses to this question vary from ancient times to the 1980s via the Middle Ages. The Peace of Westphalia in 1648 is probably the most frequently mentioned starting point, but some argue that globalisation began almost 12,000 years ago, when small bands of hunters and gatherers reached South America; 'this event marked the end of a long process of settling all five continents'.[35] The most comprehensive classification of the different periods of globalisation is probably Steger's five-part plan,[36] beginning with a pre-historic phase from 10,000 BC, to 3,500 BC, during which small bands of hunters and gatherers reached the southern tip of South America, which meant that all continents were settled in a journey begun by our humanoid African ancestors more than one million years ago. The second stage, the pre-modern, lasted from 3,000 BC to 1,500 AD marked by two inventions critical to the progress of globalisation: the wheel and writing. The third 'early modern' stage, 1500–1750, included the Renaissance and the Enlightenment, and the next two centuries, 1750–1970, are referred to as the 'Modern' period, when world trade accelerated rapidly due to developments in transport: railways in the early nineteenth century and the steamship later.

It was in this period that the Industrial Revolution took place, starting in north-western Europe. Two British economists provided the intellectual impetus to the next stage of globalisation: Adam Smith and David Ricardo. Smith's *The Wealth of Nations*, one of the most influential works of political economy, proposed that in spite of the fact that free markets look chaotic in principle, they represent a more efficient method of creating the optimum supply of goods and services. Under the benevolent gaze of the 'invisible hand', the market would perform its magic, and any constraint on free market movement would result in inefficiencies, corruption and stagnation. John Kay has summed up the argument for contemporary audiences: 'Market economics did not succeed because business

---

35   Manfred B. Steger, *Globalisation: A Very Short Introduction* (Oxford: Oxford University Press, 2013), 20.
36   Ibid., 20–35.

people were cleverer than politicians, they succeeded because disciplined pluralism is more innovative and responsive of consumer needs than centralized decision-making.'[37]

Ricardo provided the second intellectual underpinning of the free market system: the theory of comparative advantage. This stipulates that if every nation or region specialised in the production of goods and services in which they had an in-built cost advantage, everyone would benefit. For the last three hundred years these theories have been applied successfully in the Western world. But they create two major problems which require correction on a regular basis: the tendency for markets to break down at regular intervals and to create rising levels of inequality. Both require government correction. Following the Great Depression and the Second World War, there was a concerted effort by the world's leading powers to create new global monitoring systems which would balance free trade with a more equitable distribution of wealth within societies and less risk of recurring crises. This resulted in the Bretton Woods agreement and the setting up of the IMF and the World Bank. A sustained period of growth followed until the so-called Arab Oil Crisis of the mid-1970s, which was partly responsible for the election of more ideological proponents of free market economics in the UK and US: Margaret Thatcher and Ronald Reagan.

This resulted in a more aggressive form of capitalism, variously described as 'neo-liberalism' or the 'Washington Consensus', which lasted until the Great Recession of 2008, which discredited the neo-liberal experiment. But globalisation continued to thrive and, if anything, intensify, encouraged by influential commentators. In *Globalisation Works*, the respected economics correspondent of the *Financial Times*, Martin Wolf, argued in favour of more, not less: 'The failure of our world is not that there is too much globalisation but that there is too little; the potential for greater economic integration is barely tapped, we need more global markets, not fewer, if we want to raise the living standards of the poor of the world.'[38] Thomas Friedman, the op-ed writer for the *New York Times*, was even more strident, coining two pithy aphorisms, 'the electronic herd' and

---

37   John Kay, *The Truth about Markets* (London: Penguin, 2004), 364.
38   Wolf, *Why Globalisation Works*, 4.

the 'golden straightjacket' to explain the new world order. The 'electronic herd' represents the increased financial flows that can now move around the world in an instant due to digitalisation, but, according to Friedman, if countries wish to attract this flow of investment, they must be prepared to don the 'golden straightjacket', a process he describes in some detail:

> A country must adopt or be seen to be moving towards the following golden rules: making the private sector the primary engine of its economic growth, maintaining a low rate of inflation and price stability, shrinking the size of its state bureaucracy, maintaining as close a balanced budget as possible, removing restrictions on foreign trade, privatizing state owned industries and utilities, deregulating capital markets, making its currency convertible, opening its industries, stock and bond markets to foreign ownership and investment, deregulating its economy to promote as much domestic competition as possible, opening its banking and telecommunications systems to private ownership and competition and allowing its citizens to choose from an array of competing pensions options and foreign run pension and mutual funds.[39]

During the end of this phase of globalisation, the arrogance of the neo-liberals knew no bounds, and while no country adopted the Friedman prescription in full, all faced pressure to move in this direction.

We have now reached the 'Contemporary' stage in the long evolution of globalisation, with information technology giving it another boost. Manuel Castells' monumental three-part work, *The Information Age: Economy, Society and Culture*, was the first comprehensive account of the nature and implications of the current age: 'We are living through one of those rare intervals in history – an interval characterized by the transformation of our material culture by the works of a new technological paradigm organised around information technology.'[40]

The Great Recession of 2008 prompted some comment that globalisation was in retreat and the growing populist movements around the world fuelled by austerity programmes introduced in the aftermath of the recession fuelled this speculation. The election of Donald Trump in the US and the Brexit referendum in the UK, combined with the electoral

---

39   Friedman, *The Lexus and the Olive Tree*, 87.
40   Manuel Castells, *The Rise of the Network Society* (Oxford: Blackwell, 1996), 28.

success of authoritarian 'strongmen' around the world, seemed to confirm this speculation. Stories about the retreat of democracy and the decline of the West multiplied, and there was ample evidence to prove both theses, but because the continuous increase in globalisation throughout the ages has been due mainly to advances in technology, it is difficult to see how the process can be stopped. As the Americans say: 'You can't put the toothpaste back in the tube.' The COVID-19 pandemic has demonstrated the extent of enhanced globalisation sustained through technological advances in digitalisation: offices, schools, courts and churches continued to function around the world in spite of lockdowns. Automation and the internet enabled businesses around the world to function more or less as normal.

Ireland and Globalisation

Ireland has been a huge beneficiary of the accelerated globalisation of the late twentieth century. Overseas businesses attracted to this country now account for approximately 80 per cent of total manufacturing, over 90 per cent of total exports and 50 per cent of employment in the manufacturing sector. Survey results from the Eurobarometer show that a majority of the population believe that globalisation has been very beneficial for Ireland. The Irish success has not gone unnoticed. Kenichi Ohmae, former head of McKinsey's, referred to Ireland as a 'harbinger of the coming shift in national economics,'[41] and Richard Florida, who has chronicled the rise of creative man in the twenty-first-century economy, sees Ireland as a much envied success story', having added a deliberate cultural dimension to its infrastructure, in order to attract the new creative industries: 'Traditional economic development efforts would not have worked if Ireland had not buttressed them with a major lifestyle effort.'[42] Even more favourable references have been made to Ireland's economic strategy by Robert Shapiro,

---

41 Kenichi Ohmae, *The Borderless World: Power and Strategy in the Interlinked Economy* (New York: Harper Business, 1999), 239.
42 Richard Florida, *The Rise of the Creative Class* (New York: Basic Books, 2012), 341.

a former member of the Clinton administration, whose book is littered with complimentary references to Ireland: 'The leading country for offshore outsourcing today as a share of its labour force is not India or China but Ireland – Ireland and Korea show that any country can create a place for itself in globalisation – strange as it may seem to traders in the Paris bourse or the Bank of China in Hong Kong, Ireland is a genuine hub in global capital markets.'[43]

Ireland's Long History of Globalisation

Ireland has had a long and intimate relationship with globalisation, having lived with it since the beginning of time. One of the most important works of Irish literature and history, which Kinsella makes extensive use of, is the *Lebor Gabála Érenn*, which literally translates as *The Book of the Taking of Ireland*, but is more commonly referred to as *The Book of Invasions*. It is a work comprising poetry, myths and stories about the successive waves of invasions of the island by different ethnic groups adding new chapters to the history of the country. But it hasn't all been one-way traffic: the Irish have an equally long history of 'invading' the rest of the world: 'Columbanus and Gallus to France, Switzerland and Italy in the 7th century, Marcellus, Scotus to the courts of Carolingian Europe in the 9th century', Catholic clergy and scholars to the Irish colleges in Salamanca, Paris, Prague and Rome in the 16th century, Toland, Berkeley, Burke, Cantilloon and Tyndal between 17th and 19th to Europe and America to Joyce, Beckett and Wilde to Europe in the 20th century. After all it was Joyce who wanted to Hibernicise Europe and Europeanise Ireland.'[44] Bradley and Kinnelly make a similar point: 'Globalisation was

---

43 Robert Shapiro, *Futurecast: 2020: A Global Vision of Tomorrow* (London: Profile Books, 2008), 101, 177, 200.
44 Richard Kearney, 'Where I Speak from: A Short Intellectual Autobiography', in Daniël P. Veldsman and Yolande Steenkamp, eds, *Debating Otherness with Richard Kearney: Perspectives from South Africa* (Cape Town: AOSIS, 2018), 39–42.

not unknown to the ancient Irish. During the Stone Age axes traveled long distances from the quarry sites in Rathlin Island off the Antrim coast while Bronze Age Ireland participated fully in the industrial revolution of the time traveling across Northern Europe and on to the Mediterranean.'[45] The most celebrated period of Ireland's influence on Europe occurred when the Continent was in a state of barbaric chaos after the Germanic tribes that had destroyed Roman rule in Northern Europe invaded Britain but stopped at the Irish sea: 'So Ireland was left unbarbarised – many of the literate and learned from Britain and the Continent fled there with the result that an amazing period occurred in Irish history – roughly the 6th, 7th and 8th centuries – when that island was an outpost of civilization in an otherwise uncivilized Europe.'[46] During this period knowledge of Latin and Greek survived in Ireland, and Irish scholars were involved in rescuing important literature which they later carried with them to Europe. The leading philosopher in Europe at the time was an Irishman, Eriugena, described by Bertrand Russell as 'the most astonishing person in the 9th century',[47] and his European intellectual exploits are featured in Kinsella's twelfth Peppercanister volume, *Out of Ireland* (1987).

Irish emigration on a much larger scale began later, following the Flight of the Earls in 1607. Miller has calculated that between 50,000 and 100,000 emigrated in the 1600s and a further 250,000 to 400,000 left for North America between 1700 and 1760.[48] The American Revolution interrupted the flow, but between 1783 and 1814 another 100,000 to 150,000 took flight to America. The pace quickened in the years before the Famine: between 800,000 to a million people left Ireland in the thirty years prior to 1845 and between 1851 and 1921 over 4.5 million Irish people emigrated, the vast majority to the United States. In addition to Irish people leaving to look for work for over one hundred and fifty years between 1850 until recently, Irish missionaries were dispatched by the Catholic Church, mainly

---

45 Finbarr Bradley and James J. Kennelly, *Capitalising on Culture, Competing on Difference* (Dublin: Blackhall, 2008), 15.
46 Bryan Magee, *The Story of Philosophy* (London: Dorling-Kindersley, 1998), 55–56.
47 Bertrand Russell, A *History of Western Philosophy* (Oxfordshire: Routledge Classics, 2004), 374.
48 Kerby A. Miller, *Emigrants and Exiles* (Oxford: Oxford University Press, 1985), 137.

to Africa and Latin America. More recently, the Irish pub phenomenon has been exported to every corner of the globe. The Centre for the Study of Diasporas at the Lowy Institute in Sydney estimates that the Irish diaspora is now over 70 million.

As a result of all this migration, Irish people have a dense network of contacts around the world, from friends and relations to churches and pubs. Much of that network was in place during the period from 1922 to the late 1950s and, as we have seen, the political and administrative establishment were not unduly disturbed by the continuing high levels of emigration that took place during this period. It was the reverse movement they worried about, particularly the movement and interaction of cultural, economic, scientific or political developments, ideas or philosophies which disturbed the pious certainties of Irish Catholicism. But there were always some dissenters. For example, in 1923, George Russell's *Irish Statesman* urged: 'We say we cannot merely out of Irish traditions to find solutions to all our modern problems. We shall find some inspiration and beauty in our own past, but we have to ransack world literature, world beauty, world science and study our national contemporaries and graft what we can learn into our national tradition, if we are not to fade out of the list of civilized nations.'[49] By the late 1950s a combination of the obvious failure of isolation, the growing impatience and frustration of a new generation and the onset of global media flows, primarily television, meant that Catholic Ireland could no longer be protected from the outside world. Whitaker, Ó Riada and Kinsella eagerly embraced that world, and its influence was to significantly shape their work and careers.

There seems little doubt that Ireland has benefitted economically from globalisation. Our geographic location was once seen as a serious impediment to economic success, but in a globalised, connected world that is no longer the case. The most successful phenomenon in the American alcoholic drinks market in the last three years is the hard seltzer category, dominated by the White Claw brand. The product development, marketing strategy, market research and marketing communications are all created in

---

49 Terence Brown, *Ireland: A Social and Cultural History* (New York: Harper Perennial, 2004), 121.

an office in Dublin 4. Digital has eliminated distance; with a computer and broadband access business can be carried out successfully from anywhere. But is there a downside? Thomas Friedman, who, as we've seen, has been one of the strongest advocates of globalisation, also warned that countries need to develop sufficiently strong cultural filters so that they can interact with the world without their culture being turned into a 'global mush'.[50] We also need to consider the larger question of whether the idea of the nation state itself is relevant in a global world.

Globalisation and the Nation State

When the term 'globalisation' became a major topic of debate in the 1990s, immediate fears were expressed about the future of the nation state, and some excitable voices, mainly from technological backgrounds, predicted that the end was nigh. Douglas wrote that, as a consequence of globalisation, 'State authority has leaked away, upwards, sideways and downwards, in some matters it seems to have gone nowhere, just evaporated'.[51] Nicholas Negroponte, a tech luminary at the turn of the millennium, put the case even more starkly: 'Like a mothball which goes from solid to gas directly I expect the state to evaporate – without question the role of the nation state will change dramatically and there will be as little room for nationalism as there is from smallpox.'[52]

Marxists, whose world view has always made them suspicious of nationalism, welcomes this development, as Hobsbawm demonstrates:

> After the excesses of the Second World War and the Cold War confrontation, the growth of vast globalising forces, transnational economic units, huge power blocs, international organisations, mass migrations and mass communications has

50   Friedman, *The Lexus and the Olive Tree*, 221.
51   Ian R. Douglas, 'Globalisation and the Retreat of the State', in B. K. Gills, ed., *Globalisation and the Politics of Resistance* (London: Palgrave Books, 2000), 111.
52   Nicholas Negroponte, cited in John Gray, *False Dawn: The Delusions of Global Capitalism* (London: Granta Books, 1999), 68.

undermined the efficiency of the nation state and rendered its boundaries obsolete, despite the temporary proliferation of divisive ethnic nationalisms.[53]

Ironically, the Marxists' most vocal bed-fellows are to be found in the business community, who welcome the demise of any borders which have the potential to interfere with the free flow of world markets:

> The emergence of the interlinked economy brings with it an erosion of national sovereignty as the power of information touches local communities, academic, professional and social institutions, corporations and individuals, it is this borderless world that will give participating economies the capacity for boundless prosperity.[54]

Hirst and Thompson echo these sentiments but express doubts about the conclusions:

> It has become fashionable to argue that the era of the nation state is over and that national level governance is ineffective in the face of globalised economic and social processes; that national politics and political choices have been side-lined by world market forces that are stronger than even the most powerful states.[55]

They go on to argue that nation states are still the key practitioners in the art of government as a means of legitimately distributing power. One of the most consistent advocates of the benefits of globalisation, Wolf, argues that the role of the state is just as important in a globalised world:

> Just as globalisation does not seem to make states impotent, it does not make them unnecessary either. On the contrary for people to be successful in exploiting the opportunities afforded by international integration, they need states at both ends of their transactions.[56]

---

53   Eric Hobsbawm, quoted in Anthony D. Smith, *Historiographical Debates about Ethnicity and Nationalism* (Cambridge: Polity Press, 2000), 2.
54   Ohmae, *The Borderless World*, 239.
55   Paul Hirst, Grahame Thompson and Simon Bromley, *Globalisation in Question: The International Economy and the Possibilities of Governance* (Cambridge: Polity Press, 1996), 176.
56   Wolf, *Why Globalization Works*, 227.

Smith provides the most persuasive argument in favour of the likely enduring power of the nation state. He points out that although the building blocks of most nations were constructed during the seventeenth and eighteenth centuries often through the creation of the 'story' of the nation determined by intellectuals at the time, they are usually bound together with a glue that stretches back into 'the mists of antiquity':

> The modern era resembles a palimpsest on which are recorded experiences and identities of different epochs and a variety of ethnic formations, the earlier influencing and being modified by the latter to produce the composite type of collective cultural unit which we call 'the nation'.[57]

He goes on to argue that some form of nationalism or ethnic community is the only realistic way to organise society:

> The myths, memories, symbols and ceremonies of nationalism provide the sole basis for social cohesion and political union in modern societies – by rehearsing the rites of fraternity in a political community in its homeland at periodic intervals the nation communes with itself and worships itself making the citizen feel the power and warmth of their collective identification ... a global culture seems unable to offer the qualities of collective faith, dignity and hope that only a 'religious surrogate' with its promise of territorial cultural community across the generations can provide.[58]

These arguments seem more convincing than the somewhat simplistic belief that nations are about to wither away, and the fact that membership of the United Nations has been steadily increasing over the last two decades during the intense period of globalisation would tend to support this case. But globalisation has undoubtedly increased pressure on nation states, and has subtly changed their role, from a preoccupation with the internal running of the country and allocation of resources among competing interest groups, to a more external function of maximising a country's appeal to outside businesses and investors. Thus, the real effect of globalisation on the nation state has been to turn them into 'competition states' and 'nation brands'. There is also increasing pressure

---

57   Anthony D. Smith, *Nations and Nationalism in a Global Era* (Cambridge: Polity Press, 1995), 59.
58   Ibid., 60.

on countries to adopt more of the policies on Friedman's list described earlier, although the pressure to deregulate financial markets has eased following the financial scandals at the heart of the 2008 recession.

Competition for transnational mobile investment has become so intense that countries must scramble to attract and retain the more rewarding high-tech businesses. Cerny, who coined the phrase 'competition state', has described the new demand on politicians:

> Politicians are now expected to act as institutional entrepreneurs in the modern world where international competitiveness is becoming the main criteria for policy success – there has been a shift away from the general maximisation of welfare to the promotion of enterprise, innovation and profitability in both public and private sectors.[59]

Ireland is a classic example of a 'competition state', and because we were one of the first to actively tailor an economic strategy to the attraction of overseas investment, we have become a role model for how to become a successful 'nation brand'. There are many domestic and international critics of these developments. They argue that the process has gone too far and that countries are too eager to put themselves at the mercy of powerful global businesses. However, the Nordic countries have shown how economic progress can be achieved in conjunction with equality and social harmony: 'All the Nordic countries share the following traits; strong extensive welfare states, social cohesion, their interconnectedness and collectivisation and economic equality.'[60] The phrase 'getting to Denmark' is now being used as a universally desirable aspiration; 'this phrase is now used as a metaphor for transforming a country into a prosperous, stable, well behaved, law abiding society.'[61] The authors of a recent study of the 'Nordic Model' concluded that the region provided no evidence that 'the forces of globalisation' had eroded the welfare state, and claimed that the

---

59 Philip Cerny, 'Reconstructing the Political in a Globalising World', in Frans Buelens, *Globalisation and the Nation State* (London: Edward Elgar, 1999), 130.
60 Michael Booth, *The Almost Nearly Perfect People: The Truth About the Nordic Miracle* (London: Jonathon Cape, 2014), 124.
61 Martin Wolf, 'Reviewing the The Narrow Corridor by Darren Acemogla and James A. Robinson', *Financial Times* (28 September 2019).

stability, transparency and efficiency of their political systems made them particularly attractive to global businesses.[62]

We must conclude therefore that globalisation will continue to put pressure on countries to maximise their attractiveness to overseas investment but that many of the worst fears of those who argue that the nation state has been diminished by the pressures exerted by the global business community have been exaggerated. The success and resilience of the 'Nordic Model' shows that not only is it a viable alternative to the 'Washington Consensus', it may turn out to be superior model as the current financial crises unfolds.

Before this crisis emerged, O'Sullivan was making the point that globalisation made the role of government more rather than less important; that more intervention would be required, not so much in a traditional left-wing sense of taking over sectors of the economy but in a strategic sense to maximise opportunities and minimise threats in a volatile global world:

> In Ireland's case the Global Question asks how a small open nation can manage the effects that globalisation has on its economy, society and public life balancing the impact of powerful external forces with independence of choice on the type of society, identity and public life they require – the challenges are similar to those posed by the National Question in earlier times.[63]

He is critical of what he regards as a tendency in recent years for Ireland to drift towards the 'Washington Consensus' neo-liberal camp through our cultural alignment with the two main countries in this category, Britain and the US, more by default than by any real analysis of alternative options. He defines the case for a more strategic role for the state in the following terms:

> What small countries need is: political entrepreneurship, imagination, patience here, impatience there and other varieties of virtu and fortuna.[64]

---

62 Carlos Buhigas Schubert and Hans Martens, *The Nordic Model: A Recipe for European Success? European Policy Centre Working Paper* 20, 2005, 42.
63 Michael O'Sullivan, *Ireland and the Global Question* (Cork: Cork University Press, 2006), 4.
64 Ibid., 12.

In other words, to survive in a global world, small countries need to become more Machiavellian, using all the strength, talent, ability and intelligence at their disposal to overcome the circumstances they can't control. For that, smaller countries need a strategy, one that matches the direction of the world with our own needs at any given time. Ireland's tendency to drift in the neo-liberal direction in recent years happened more by default than as part of any agreed strategy, but the present crossroads could present the ideal time for a more considered plan of action.

Globalisation and Culture

The influence of globalisation on culture, especially indigenous culture, is probably more familiar to more people than any other aspect of the subject, because so many have direct experience of two of the main drivers of the phenomenon, mass travel and mass media. Both lead to a vague feeling that everywhere and everything are becoming more alike; a feeling usually accompanied by a sense of disappointment. It is difficult to avoid an intuitive sense of unease about dilution or homogenisation, words that tend to be used in a pejorative context. Even advocates of the benefits of globalisation like Friedman accept this unease and argue that smaller countries need 'strong cultural and environmental filters' to withstand the pressure of the global tide.[65]

Much of this unease is due not only to a belief that globalisation can eliminate indigenous culture but that it invariably replaces it with some form of American cultural domination:

> The standardisation of world culture with local, popular and traditional forms driven out or dumbed down to make way for American television, American music, food, clothes and films has been seen by many as the very heart of globalisation.[66]

---

65 Friedman, *The Lexus and the Olive Tree*, 236.
66 Fredric Jameson, 'Globalisation and Strategy', *New Left Review* 4 (July/Aug 2000), 49–68.

> Authentic traditional and local culture in many parts of the world is being battered out of existence by the indiscriminate dumping of large quantities of slick commercial media products mainly from America.[67]

This book holds that this is an unduly pessimistic outlook that underestimates the strength and resilience of indigenous culture and the natural human reaction to resist imperialism of any kind. Increasing globalisation obviously puts local culture at risk, but the more uniform everything becomes, the more aggressively people will start defending the local. What we must also take into account is the human capacity for awkward stubbornness. Ignatieff has noted:

> The more evident our common needs become, the more brutal becomes the human insistence on difference – the centripetal forces of need, labour and science which are pulling us together as a species are counterbalanced by centrifugal forces; the claims of race, tribe, section, region and nation pulling us apart.[68]

The pessimists in this debate neglect the fact that, with the possible exception of some remote tribes in some as yet undiscovered part of the world, most cultures have at various stages of their existence been influenced by the outside world; as Kinsella puts it, we are all 'mongrel pure – what nation's not'.[69]

Two academics who have specialised in studying the effects of globalisation on culture are US Economics Professor Tyler Cowen and UK Sociology Professor John Tomlinson. Cowen argues that cultural globalisation is a positive development, and that most cultures are fundamentally hybrids to begin with:

---

67   Jeremy Tunstall, *Media are American* (Columbia: Columbia University Press, 1977), 57.
68   Michael Ignatieff, cited in Vince Cable, *The World's New Fissures* (London: Demos, 1994), 6.
69   Kinsella, *Collected Poems*, 137.

> Western cultures draw their philosophical heritage from the Greeks, their religions from the Middle East, their scientific base from the Chinese and Islamic worlds, and their core languages from Europe.[70]

One of his key conclusions is that, although globalisation will lead to more cultural diversity within societies, it will probably result in less diversity across societies. Globalisation allows more people to enjoy more diverse cultural experiences than ever before, through a combination of increased prosperity, low-budget travel and mass communication. The latter includes not just traditional media, print, radio, television and cinema but also the internet and mobile telephony, which have radically expanded the range of diverse cultural experiences now available to all but the very poorest societies. Cowen recognises that increasing globalisation will result in some 'clashing values': the paradox of diversity, the preference of many for particular markers of cultural identity and the common desire for cultural difference. Discussing the 'paradox of diversity', he makes the point that in 1450, to whatever extent the world was diverse, few people were able to enjoy that diversity:

> Modernity allows us to enjoy the diversity of the world to a very high degree, relative to previous ages even when it undercuts that diversity to some extent.[71]

He then points out that cultural markers and a desire for cultural difference are not incompatible with multiculturalism. He concludes by recommending a cautious embrace of a cosmopolitan multiculturalism as a guiding principle in the modern world.

Ultimately, homogenisation and heterogeneity are not mutually exclusive but are two sides of the same coin. Food provides interesting insights into the syncretic nature of all culture:

> All food is fusion cuisine and all dining is ethnic dining: Swiss chocolate is in reality Mexican in origin, where would German food be without the potato, Italian food

---

70 Tyler Cowen, *Creative Destruction: How Globalization is Changing the World's Cultures* (Princeton: Princeton University Press, 2002), 6.
71 Ibid., 147.

without the tomato or Thai food without the chillies, all originally products of the New World.⁷²

Tomlinson takes a different approach, arguing that the impact of globalisation on indigenous cultures tends to be overestimated. He considers the possible impact of mass-produced television programmes like *Dallas*, which was shown all over the world in the 1970s, becoming a byword for cultural imperialism. He makes the point that these programmes were made for profit not propaganda, and that repeated studies have shown that their portrayal of an American way of life was as likely to produce negative as positive responses. Market research studies of the effect of mass communications, especially advertising, repeatedly show that target audiences are far from being a *tabula rasa*; instead, they interact, disagree and distort, depending on their own cultural and personal dispositions, and critics who warn about their likely effect massively underrate the public's capacity to subvert their meaning. Culture does not transfer in this unilinear way; movement between cultural geographic areas always involves interpretation, translation, mutation, adaptation and 'indigenisation', as the receiving culture brings its own culture to bear in dialectical fashion upon cultural imports.⁷³

Ireland offers an interesting test case of how a 'receiving culture' reacts to the increasing pace of cultural imports that began in the 1960s. We have seen how the Whitaker-inspired opening up of the country to overseas investment in the late 1950s was quickly followed by the election of President Kennedy (1960), which resulted in a surge of pride and self-confidence, the launch of Teilifís Éireann (1961) opening a window to the rest of the world that could never be closed and the establishment of Vatican II (1962), which loosened the authoritarian grip of the Catholic Church. The result was full participation in the 'swinging sixties' and the global consumer society. Inglis surveys the impact of globalisation on Ireland and comes to the following conclusion:

---

72   Tyler Cowen, 'Modern Mix', *Forbes Global Magazine* (28 April 2003), 40.
73   John Tomlinson, *Globalisation and Culture* (Cambridge: Polity Press, 1999), 84.

> The main cultural transformation in Ireland over the last fifty years is that individuals have increasingly sought to create and establish difference through the consumption of globally produced goods and services – ironically it is this pursuit of difference through consumption that has made the Irish more like the rest of the world.[74]

But the fact that Ireland has become 'more like the rest of the world' by enthusiastically embracing the consumer society doesn't necessarily mean that it abandoned every aspect of cultural difference. Inglis concentrates on four quintessential aspects of Irish culture: religion, music, language and sport. In each of these areas the conflict between the homogenising tendencies of globalisation and the human tendency to insist on difference has been fought fiercely in Ireland over the last half century, often with surprising results. The statistical data examined earlier shows that there has been a significant weakening in religious affiliation, but Ireland had for a long time previously been a statistical outlier in terms of religion or, as O' Connell has somewhat indelicately observed, 'Ireland's love affair with Catholic institutions has been, frankly, totally OTT.'[75]

But in spite of moving closer to developed country norms, Inglis concludes that in Ireland: 'Although there has been a shift away from a Catholic to a consumer form of capitalism, Ireland is still a very Catholic country.'[76] Irish sport and the Irish language played a prominent part in the Revival at the end of the nineteenth century. Both the Gaelic League and the GAA played a prominent part in the struggle for independence, but they struggled themselves in the post-independence years, and by the 1950s they were becoming associated with the failure of Irish society generally. But the 1980s and 90s witnessed a revival of interest in both areas. It would be possible to plot a graph showing the rise in attendances at GAA matches, the rise in attendances at Gaelscoileanna and the rise in GDP with all three lines rising simultaneously. Thus, an increase in globalisation can often result in an increase in determination to preserve one's unique points of differences. Irish experience suggests that the process is helped rather than

---

74   Tom Inglis, *Global Ireland: Same Difference* (Oxfordshire: Routledge, 2008), 39.
75   Michael O'Connell, *Changed Utterly: Ireland and the New Irish Psyche* (Dublin: The Liffey Press, 2001), 59.
76   Inglis, *Global Ireland*, 251.

hindered by globally inspired economic growth; this is because economic self-confidence leads to cultural self-confidence:

> The propensity to cultural difference is a primordial attribute of the human species: human identities are plural and diverse by their very nature, as national languages are plural and diverse and they are always variations on particular forms of common life, never examples of universal humanity.[77]

Predictably, given its primacy in Irish culture, it is music that provides the most intriguing conflict between the local and global. We've seen in Part I that since Ó Riada's re-invention of tradition in the late 1950s music has been the international success story of Irish culture, and how one cultural commentator concluded that as a result the epicentre of Irish culture had crossed over the Liffey from the Abbey Theatre to Windmill Lane Recording Studios.

Not everyone is happy with the outcome of the conflict, which inevitably has changed the nature of the music as more global influences are brought into play:

> Irish traditional music is a victim of its own success – Irish music idiom is trendy 'Gucci Paddy' so to speak – central to the commercial invention known as the Irish pub – where it becomes largely aural wallpaper.[78]

But international acclaim will always bring protests from purists, and in the current literature on Irish music, the majority of practitioners and commentators argue that exposure to more global influences has been a positive experience:

> The 20th century influences of media and technology have set Irish music off in many directions, rock, country, electric rock, pop, blues and avant-garde – all of these Irish music forms are offsprings of the same traditional music parent.[79]

77 John Gray, *Enlightenment's Wake: Politics and Culture at the Close of the Modern Age* (Oxfordshire: Routledge Classics, 2007), 98.
78 Fintan Vallely, 'The Apollos of Shamrockery: Traditional Music in the Modern Age', in in Martin Stokes and Philip V. Bohlman, eds, *Celtic Music, Music at the Global Fringe* (Lanham, MD: Scarecrow Press, 2003), 205.
79 O'Connor, *Bringing It All Back Home*, 7.

The very fact that Irish music has become so popular around the world is proof that globalisation doesn't weaken local culture but can actually strengthen it.

Conclusions

The defining characteristic of the second revival was the opening up of the country to the rest of the world. Ken Whitaker, Seán Ó Riada and Thomas Kinsella were whole-hearted supporters of this initiative, confident that their embrace of the best of what the world had to offer would add to rather than subtract from their deep-rooted knowledge of and commitment to Ireland's literature and culture. I believe that their confidence was justified. By the end of the twentieth century, the population decline of the 1950s had been reversed, showing a more than 50 per cent increase compared to the 1961 census and from being one of the poorest countries in Europe we had become one of the richest.

We had even surpassed Britain in terms of per capita GNP, and although we had become a much more self-confident nation in the intervening period, the overtaking of our nearest neighbour was still a cause for quiet satisfaction. We had coped well with globalisation without surrendering too much of our national identity; we had managed to integrate significant numbers of 'new Irish' immigrants without major public outbreaks of racism; and we had enacted a body of new legislation which transformed our reputation from being one of the most socially conservative countries in Europe to one of the most progressive. In particular, we had removed most of the barriers to women's equality which had disfigured the country for so long. But the three men who are the subject of this book would not be complacent: the centenary of the 1916 Rising passed without the promise of the Proclamation being fulfilled. We had not guaranteed 'equal rights and equal opportunities to all citizens', nor could we claim to have 'cherished all the children of the nation equally'.

There are some signs that the left-wing 'turn' in the world created by the pandemic could redress the balance somewhat, but there is still a long way to go to fulfil the ideals of the 1916 Proclamation, let alone the enlightened Programme for the First Dáil. There have been calls from a number of quarters for a return to the example of the first revival to seek inspiration for some of the wider societal issues raised by the sceptics. For example, Mathews argues:

> At a time when the homogenizing pressures of globalization have registered as a major concern within cultural criticism, the achievements as well as the failures of the Irish revival may have much to teach us about the cultural dynamics of Ireland in the 21st century.[80]

More recently, Bradley & Kennelly make a similar point:

> Contemporary Ireland while awash with capability, confidence and resources, seems uninspired and faces significant social and environmental challenges. It appears badly in need of the driving vision that characterized the period some thirty years before the creation of Saorstát Éireann in 1922. Often described as the Irish Revival or the Irish renaissance it was an era of cultural cohesion, prodigious idealism, self-reliance, creativity and innovation.[81]

But perhaps the most consistent and persistent sceptic regarding Ireland's economic, political and cultural transformation was the Mage: Thomas Kinsella. Unlike the critics discussed in this section, Kinsella's critical perspective was different: more ethereal, less concerned with effecting immediate redress, more anxious to reintroduce the bardic role of the *file* in Irish life and society. As the most prolific modern translator of ancient Irish poetry, he was well qualified for this task. His first published work was a series of small Dolmen editions of Gaelic texts in the 1950s. His monumental translation of Ireland's great saga, *The Táin*, appeared in 1969, followed by translations of Irish poems from 1600 to 1900, *An Duanaire*, in 1981 and his *New Oxford Book of Irish Verse*, in which almost two-thirds of the content was pre-nineteenth-century work, appeared in 1986. This work gave him a thorough grounding in the position of the *file* in the Irish poetic tradition.

---

80   Mathews, *Revival*, 148.
81   Bradley and Kennelly, *Capitalising on Culture*, 2.

Declan Kiberd has suggested that he was, understandably, envious: 'Ó Rathaille's was the most striking voice to come to us from the eighteenth century, but there have been many more, so many as to provoke the envy of many writers of our own time, including the poet Thomas Kinsella.'[82] The reason for the envy was the high level of esteem and privileged position accorded to the *file:* 'A combination of a senator in the Roman Empire, a member of the Académie Française, a Minister of Culture and a member of the modern media, the poet is originally a seer who until the arrival of Christianity had been vested with pontifical powers.'[83] Fellow poet David Wheatly has also noted Kinsella's commitment to public engagement: 'The state of the nation has been a favourite Kinsella trope since well before Peppercanister days – like Ezra Pound there has always been something of the consigliere about Kinsella, keen to bend the ear of the nearest prince, or Irish government minister.'[84]

Kinsella's public interventions ranged from his bitter condemnation of the Widgery Tribunal's attempt to whitewash the killings of Bloody Sunday in Derry to his direct in involvement in the Wood Quay controversy, where, as a member of 'Friends of Medieval Dublin', he tried unsuccessfully to prevent the Corporation building on the ancient site. But although he decried his lack of success in direct intervention, he was conscious of the past power of the *file*. When asked in an interview whether the poet had a social function in current society, his reply was revealing; 'I believe not – as compared, for example, with the poet in Irish society in earlier times, when the bardic order fulfilled virtually an administrative function for the Irish aristocracy, helping to keep the ruler and the kingdom on a proper path and maintain a stable situation'.[85]

Apart from his public interventions, Kinsella was quietly but consistently critical of some of the consequences of Ireland's transformation. These could be grouped under three main headings. The first is historical provincialism: a lack of effort to understand our past, resulting in an inadequate

---

82   Declan Kiberd, *Irish Classics* (London: Granta Books, 2000), 54.
83   Leerssen, *Mere Irish or Fíor-Ghael*, 153.
84   David Wheatley, '"All is emptiness and I must spin": Thomas Kinsella and the Poetry of Romance and Decay', *Irish Studies Review* (August 2008), 329.
85   Michael Smith, 'Interview with Thomas Kinsella', *Poetry Ireland Review* 75.

ability to cope with the present. The second has now become a worldwide problem, a democratic deficit, that is, declining citizen participation in public affairs. The third issue is the more perennial concern of the artist: a critique of the philistine nature and conspicuous consumption of society in general. Kinsella's criticisms were often bitter and despairing; 'and it goes dark and we stumble / in gathering ignorance / in a land of loss / and unfulfillable desire'.[86] However, in his later twenty-first-century poems, his tone is more measured, urging his fellow citizens to 'a turning away / from regard beyond proper merit / or reward beyond real need / towards the essence and the source'.[87] I believe that Kinsella's concerns would also have been shared by the Mandarin and the Musician, and in the final chapter I will speculate on the type of measures all three men might have wished to consider if Ireland was to experience a new revival.

But any new revival will have to take account of the range of ominous issues that were gathering force at the dawn of the new millennium, making the consideration of a third revival even more urgent. It is to these issues I will turn next.

---

86   Kinsella, *Collected Poems*, 259.
87   Thomas Kinsella, *Late Poems* (Manchester: Carcanet, 2011), 62.

CHAPTER 7

The World from the Perspective of the 2020s

Virginia Woolf famously and precisely declared that the world changed at the beginning of the twentieth century: 'On or about December 1910 human character changed. I'm not saying that one went out, as one might in a garden and saw that a leaf had flowered or that a hen had laid an egg. The change was not sudden and definite like that but a change there was nevertheless.'[1] She was writing about the birth of modernism in art and writing. I believe that something of a similar nature happened at the end of the twentieth century; on or about December 1999, the world changed in ways that we still can't fully comprehend because the process hasn't concluded. However, the change is intimately linked to the information and digital revolution which was developing momentum at the turn of the century and was to change the world in ways with which we're still trying to grapple.

The change is also linked to the end of the neo-liberal era, which had been carefully planned at the Frederick van Hayek-inspired Mont Pelerin meeting in 1946. Attendees included Milton Friedman and Karl Popper. The fruits of this initiative were launched sporadically from universities and think tanks during the 1950s and 1960s but only came to fruition with the election of Ronald Reagan in the US and Margaret Thatcher in the UK in the late 1970s. From then on, it spread around the world, creating fortunes and havoc in equal measure until it crashed spectacularly in the Great Recession of 2008, a recession it was mainly responsible for causing in the first place.

Numerous attempts have been made to explain what happened 'on or about December 1999', but one of the most prescient was a commencement address given by an ex-Belgium Prime Minister, Mark Eyskens, in the same

---

1 Virginia Woolf, *Mr Bennett & Mrs Brown* (London: Hogarth Press, 1924), 3.

year. It began ominously: 'What we are witnessing, is nothing less than a fracture, a complete break from and with the past – the past provides no examples, the present offers no guarantees, the future generates no confidence.'[2] His main premise was that although the emerging information revolution would enhance the capabilities of the human mind including our creative capacity, the scale of the change would have unforeseen consequences. He predicted the rise of China and Asia in general at the expense of the Western world, and problems for democracy arising from demagoguery, corruption, inefficiency and the capriciousness of voter preferences. He worried that the neo-liberal revolution, set in train by van Hayek and his pals, had resulted in a belief that economic rationality now represented the entire aspiration of societal and human striving; 'profit and loss have become more important than good and evil. Friendship becomes a network of useful relationships. Beliefs are shaped by the job a person does. Ethics are a function of the situation in which a person finds themselves – the end always justifies the means. Young people brought up in this spirit will never see society as a community of people, but as a football field for their ambitions'.[3] Eyskens disagreed with the elevation of economic growth as the sole societal goal, pointing out that, although 'a social paradise cannot exist in an economic graveyard, neither can an economic orchard exist in a social desert'.[4] He was alert to the dangers of the financialisation of the economy and, as a result, society, but with his university audience in mind he was also conscious of the pressure in the new information society towards excessive specialisation, believing that the knowledge society 'also generates ignorance and incompetence', due to the law of diminishing relative knowledge: 'The average citizen understands an even smaller part of the reality around him and as a result acquires a distorted vision of that reality'.[5] His only proposed solution was that all students should be equipped with

2   Mark Eyskens, 'Idea for a University in the 21st Century', 1999, <http://www.eyskens.com/page103/page132/page134/page137/page137.html>, accessed 11 November 2021.
3   Ibid.
4   Ibid.
5   Ibid.

a knowledge of philosophy and the history of ideas, which would enable them to see how their specialist subjects fitted into a wider world.

As the twenty-first century progressed, Eyskens's pessimistic forecasts proved all too accurate, and after two decades, questions were being asked about the legitimacy of capitalism in the light of increasing inequality, and democracy itself was under scrutiny. Meanwhile, climate change and the future of our environment loomed larger in the public consciousness, as increasingly unpredictable weather patterns appeared. Then, in 2019, COVID-19 emerged from the environmental pressure cooker of South-East Asia.

Doubts about Democracy

The Great Recession of 2008 brought the neo-liberal experiment to an end, but brought austerity in its wake, thereby creating a sullen and sometimes angry mood among the population in many Western democracies and beyond. The concept of *ressentiment*, associated with Nietzsche and Kierkegaard, began to surface in opinion columns to explain the mood of envy, helplessness and powerlessness felt by many, as government austerity measures started to bite. But even when the Western economies began to recover, opinion polling results continued to register high levels of insecurity, pessimism and helplessness, with our idea of the future shifting from something we automatically associate with human progress to something we find threatening. It was regularly reported that today's younger generation was the first to expect that their future standard of living would not be as high as their parents.

These problems contributed to a declining faith in democracy, as what once seemed the inexorable march of an ideal was in retreat: twenty-five democracies failed since 2000. In a similar vein, Vladimir Putin boasted in an interview with the *Financial Times* in 2019 that 'The liberal idea has become obsolete. It has outlived its purpose.'[6] Since then he has further

---

6   Cover story, *Financial Times* (28 June 2019).

dismantled whatever vestiges of democracy remained in Russia. Books about the end/decline of democracy started to appear in rapid succession after the Brexit and Trump revolts of 2016. Anne Applebaum's *Twilight of Democracy*[7] chillingly reminded us that 'given the right conditions any society can turn against democracy. Indeed, if history is anything to go by, all our societies eventually will'. In *The Light that Failed*, Kraster and Holmes wrote that Western liberalism had become soaked in complacency and arrogance after the fall of communism in the late 1980s: 'Liberalism fell in love with itself and lost its way as East Europeans resented being told what to do.'[8] There is little doubt that the triumphalism that followed the 'fall of the wall' became irritating even to its own supporters, and following the 2008 recession, there was a sense of quiet satisfaction often accompanied by large dollops of schadenfreude among the increasing number of autocratic rulers who had chosen to eschew the democratic option. Public intellectuals in the West, especially in the US, rushed into print in an effort to explain what had gone wrong.

One of the most popular targets was the obsession with identity politics. The left in particular was accused of abandoning its traditional concern for the poor and underprivileged in favour of gender, race and sexual orientation issues. Mark Lilla's *The Once and Future Liberal* was particularly scathing about this trend, arguing that liberals had 'retreated into caves in what was once a great mountain; they have lost themselves in a thicket of identity politics'[9] which was in danger of damaging social cohesion. While lamenting the resulting absence of a broad political vision, he accepted that he admitted that identity politics often involved a preoccupation with the 'feeling self', which was itself a particularly American phenomenon.

A second target was the inherent fragility of democracy itself. Yascha Mounk pointed out in *The People Versus Democracy* that two components of democracy, individual rights and the popular will, have always been at

---

7   Anne Applebaum, *Twilight of Democracy* (London: Allen Lane, 2020), 14.
8   Ivan Kraster and Stephen Holmes, *The Light that Failed: A Reckoning* (London: Allen Lane, 2019), 3.
9   Mark Lilla, *The Once and Future Liberal: After Identity Politics* (New York: Harper Collins, 2017), 11.

war with one another.[10] This 'war' becomes more intense if one of the key underpinnings of democracy, continually rising living standards, starts to unravel, which it did after the 2008 recession. Mounk adds two additional factors to stagnating economies: fear of multi-ethnic identities and the rise of social media. The former is a consequence of globalisation, which as I pointed out earlier appears to be an inexorable process, but one that needs to be more carefully managed by political leaders. Above all, it needs to be consciously managed through active policies for integration. The social media issue involves the wider subject of the impact of digital platforms, which will be discussed later, but it has a malign influence on democracy because by its damaging effect on traditional media it has increased the level of extreme partisan polarisation in society.

There is general agreement that democracy cannot work without some level of toleration for political rivals, and that in the recent past there has been an increasing tendency to deny the legitimacy of people we disagree with. An interesting example of the degree of venom that has infected the political system in America is that, whereas in 1980 only 5 per cent of Republicans would have worried if their daughter married a Democrat, by 2018 that percentage had increased to 49 per cent. Another reason being advanced for the problems facing democracy is the way it is being manipulated by corporate interests and wealthy elites for their own purposes. In *Democracy for Sale*, Peter Geoghegan describes how the penetration of 'dark money' into democratic politics is distorting the process in favour of corporate lobbyists and wealthy individuals like the Koch brothers and Robert Mercer, who can by-pass the normal democratic process by planting ideas through well-funded think tanks and academic institutions.[11] He also details how unaccountable money can use the automated targeting advertising machines of social media to deliver precisely calibrated messages to voters. The Koch family are estimated to have spent over $1.5b on Republican causes up to 2019. Mercer is a reclusive right-wing libertarian

---

10 Yascha Mounk, *The People Versus Democracy* (Cambridge: Harvard University Press, 2017), 27.
11 Peter Geoghegan, *Democracy for Sale: Dark Money and Dirty Politics* (London: Head of Zeus, 2020), 4.

billionaire who was Trump's biggest donor and is trying to shape the world to his personal beliefs.

There is an encouraging level of convergence on how to begin addressing these problems among the wide range of commentators. A consistent theme is the need to re-educate people about the advantages and strengths of democracy. They express a feeling that when democracy was young, people were more enthusiastic about its possibilities and more vocal in its defence. Now it's being taken for granted and younger generations who have forgotten how difficult it was to achieve are either taking it for granted or are not especially concerned whether it's there or not, therefore we need a renewal of our democratic vows. Once we invested time and money into education for civic responsibility but that sense of mission seems to have passed. But we are also reminded of advice that goes back to Aristotle's time: it is very difficult for democracy to work in a society where there are large disparities of wealth.

Two of the most important contributions to the debate went back to first principles about the nature of liberal democracies in an attempt to tackle the root of the problem. In a long essay in *Prospect Magazine* Timothy Garton Ash began by reiterating the main principles of liberal democracy; free speech, free elections and an independent judiciary but argued that they were not currently equipped to address new problems of market fundamentalism, pandemics, climate change and the threat posed by China.[12] Digging deeper into the roots of liberalism, he defined it as a mix of values that were sometimes in conflict – universalism, individualism, egalitarianism and meliorism. In economic terms there is conflict between Keynesianism and Hayekian market philosophies, and there is a perennial conflict between equality and solidarity on the one hand and community and identity on the other. He argues that in the recent past liberals haven't been concentrating enough on keeping a balance between these, sometimes conflicting, values. For example, they have paid too much attention to the rest of the world and not enough attention to the rest of the country, yet in spite of that, they haven't managed to do very much

---

12   Timothy Garton Ash, 'The Future of Liberalism', *Prospect Magazine* (9 December 2020).

about climate change. He quotes a survey he carried out showing that 53 per cent of young Europeans felt that autocratic regimes were more capable of dealing with major problems. *The Economist* magazine went through a similar exercise agreeing with Ash's point that part of the liberal agenda should be to solve the inevitable conflicts that will occur between its constituent values thus providing the dynamism which is necessary if society is to progress. It concluded with a series of proposals designed to reduce concentrations of power, curb the role of lobbyists and the tech companies, introduce larger taxes on land and reduce property windfalls and eliminate anti-competitive practices.[13]

Doubts about Capitalism

One of the main reasons for the debate about the future of democracy is that its support is partly dependent on continually rising living standards and over the last two decades economic growth has been, especially in the major economies, patchy at best. Just as the problems with democracy have led to a flood of books analysing what went wrong, there have also been numerous attempts to account for capitalism's twenty-first-century crisis. 2019 was probably the year when capitalism was confronted with its biggest threat since the publication of *Das Kapital*.

In late 2018, Larry Fink, the CEO of Blackrock, an asset management company handling $1.7 trillion worth of funds startled the business world in a letter to shareholders: 'The time has come for a new model of shareholder engagement – companies must ask themselves what role do they play in the community, how are we managing our impact on the environment, are we working to create a diverse workforce, are we providing the re-training and opportunities that our employees and our business will need to adjust to an increasingly automated world.'[14] Then, in August 2019, the

---

13 'New Liberal Manifesto', *Economist* magazine (15 September 2018).
14 Alicia McElhaney, 'Larry Fink to CEOs: Contribute to Society or Lose BlackRock's Investment', *Institutional Investor*, 16 January 2018.

Business RoundTable – the most influential group of corporate leaders in the US – explicitly rejected the doctrine of maximising shareholder value and called for 'conscious capitalism', proposing that businesses needed to broaden their responsibilities to society and should consider the interests of their employees, customers communities as well as shareholders'.[15] In the same month, *The Economist* magazine ran a cover story, 'What are Companies For?' The four-page feature accepted that lower growth, inequality and environmental crisis were causing questions to be asked about the fundamental nature of capitalism. For *The Economist* to question the 'fundamental nature of capitalism' was the equivalent of the Pope querying his own infallibility.

On September 18, the *Financial Times* weighed in with an even more dramatic intervention. The front page consisted of one line: 'Capitalism: Time for a Reset.' The rest of a four-page wrap-around stated that, although businesses must be profitable, they should also serve a wider purpose, and that the paper intended to start a debate on the nature and implications of that purpose, under the general heading, 'The New Agenda'. Inside the paper the chief economics editor, Martin Wolf, summed up the problems facing capitalism as slowing growth and soaring inequality caused by a small elite being able to extract disproportionate wealth from everyone else, concluding that 'something has gone very wrong'.[16]

Two books published in 2018, one American and one British, came to very similar conclusions about the mounting problems of capitalism. Joseph Stiglitz's *People, Power and Profit: Progressive Capitalism for an Age of Discontent* makes it clear that widening inequality in the US is evolving into an economy of 'the 1%, for the 1% by the 1%', and arguing that the neo-liberal experiment involving tax cuts, deregulation and minimum state intervention had failed.[17] At the heart of his analysis is an intriguing paradox: free markets cannot operate without government guidance, and

---

15   Rebecca Henderson, *Re-imagining Capitalism in a World on Fire* (New York: Public Affairs, 2020), 10.
16   Martin Wolf, 'Re-think the Purpose of Capitalism', *Financial Times* (12 December 2018).
17   Joseph Stiglitz, *Power, People and Profit: Progressive Capitalism for an Age of Discontent* (London: Penguin, 2019), 1–2.

at times direct intervention to ensure competition is working efficiently and fairly, but ardent free marketers don't believe in government and try to limit and hamper it at every turn, ergo capitalism is in crisis. The roots of the problem are clearly visible in the most successful capitalist enclave in the US: Silicon Valley. The tech giants make it their business to hobble the capitalist system through predatory pricing and pre-emptive mergers. A good example was Facebook's purchase of a potential challenger, Instagram, for $1 billion when it had only thirteen employees, and a few years later paying an astonishing $19 billion for the fledgling WhatsApp. As Peter Theil, one of the high priests of the Valley has often stated, competition is for losers. It is also worth noting that he has also argued that 'freedom and democracy are probably incompatible'.[18]

Written from a UK perspective, Paul Collier's *The Future of Capitalism* is more blunt in summing up of the problem: 'Modern capitalism has the potential to lift us all to unprecedented prosperity but is morally bankrupt and on track for tragedy.' [19] He wants to restore a greater sense of morality in all areas of society – state, family, business and the world at large. He believes there has been a decline in mutual reciprocity and a sense of shared identity across society, which has in turn weakened the obligation felt by the fortunate for the less fortunate. Like Stiglitz, he favours more stringent regulations on business, but he doesn't hold out much hope for their adoption, noting that: 'Every regulation can be subverted by clever box-ticking and every tax can be reduced by clever accounting.'[20]

In 2019, another UK professor from the Oxford Business School, Colin Mayer, while again accepting the potential contribution business can make to society, 'the main creator of our wealth, employment and new technologies',[21] echoed Collier, adding that business was the main source of 'inequality, deprivation and environmental degradation and the problems are getting worse'. Mayer is in no doubt who's to blame: Milton Friedman

---

18 Peter Theil, Article in *The Economist* (4 June 2016).
19 Paul Collier, *The Future of Capitalism: Facing the New Anxieties* (London: Allen Lane, 2018), 25.
20 Ibid., 99.
21 Colin Mayer, *Prosperity: Better Business Makes the Greater Good* (Oxford: Oxford University Press, 2018), 76.

and his insistence that maximising shareholder value is the sole objective of a business enterprise. Mayer points out that, in the long centuries-old history of business enterprises, the obsession with shareholder value is a relatively new phenomenon which coincided with the financialisation of the economy in the last quarter of the twentieth century. He traces the long history of corporations which were originally created to undertake voyages of discovery around the world.

In the UK the great Quaker enterprises of the late nineteenth century, Cadburys, Rowntree, Barclays and Clarks, not only made a range of consumer products and provided employment, but also built housing and other social amenities for thousands of workers in England. According to Mayer, the primacy of shareholder value destroyed many of these enterprises; 'the corporation is inhumane, because we have taken humans and humanity out of them and replaced them with anonymous markets and shareholders over which we have no control'.[22] In his book he presents an ambitious plan for revitalising capitalism. Pointing out that most businesses comprise different kinds of capital – human, natural, social, intellectual and financial – and typically only the latter is measured on a continuous basis. He proposes that all types of capital should be audited, which would force businesses to pay more attention to the workforce and the environment. He also advises that all businesses should articulate their purposes in their articles of association and demonstrate how their corporate structures and conduct promote their purpose.

A year later, in 2020, Harvard Professor of Management Rebecca Henderson's *Reimagining Capitalism for a World on Fire* went even further, with a more comprehensive programme designed to transform capitalism. Like the previous authors, she opens with a statement of the benefits and weaknesses of capitalism: 'One of humanity's greatest inventions and the greatest source of prosperity the world has ever seen – and – a menace on the verge of destroying the planet and destabilising society.'[23] Her comprehensive proposals for change involve a five-part plan which would re-engineer the corporation, paying more attention to social and

---

22 Ibid., 23.
23 Henderson, *Re-Imagining Capitalism*, 7.

environmental externalities, re-wiring finance to facilitate this, building co-operation between different businesses in the same sector to ensure all are playing by the same rules and closer partnering with government to ensure that all of society is represented in a new deal.

Doubts about Societal Future

It's not just democracy and capitalism that need a re-boot, but there is evidence from consumer surveys in Western countries that doubts about democracy and capitalism are compounded by a general feeling of helplessness about the pace of globalisation and digitisation, for instance: 'I don't recognise my own country anymore', 'I don't understand what's going on and I feel I'm under surveillance', and the looming threat of environmental collapse, 'why are there more extreme weather conditions?' The COVID-19 pandemic is the most serious manifestation of these trends. Reflecting the general despair, leading novelists have turned to dystopian subjects as science fiction became fact.

We've already seen that, in spite of a new breed of autocratic rulers determined to preserve the ethnic 'purity' of their countries, globalisation is likely to be an inexorable force that most societies will have to come to terms with one way or another. Fears that climate change could make large parts of the earth uninhabitable, leading to mass migration which overwhelms borders, are common. Apocalyptic novels like Michel Houellebecq's *Submission*, in which a Muslim political leader sweeps to power in France, bringing Islamic law to the country, add to the general unease that the times are out of joint. The onward march of digitalisation leaves many older people confused as they struggle to keep pace with the constant 'updates'. A growing realisation of being under surveillance by digital platforms creates further pressure. Shoshana Zuboff's *The Age of Surveillance Capitalism* argues that if the first phase of the digital revolution involved tracking our every move with the objective of enabling advertisers to send messages to the right person, in the right place at the right time, they are now using advanced analytic capacity to modify our behaviour to suit the demands of business: 'If the industrial revolution flourished at the expense of nature and now threatens to cost us the earth an information civilisation shaped by surveillance capitalism will change at the expense of human nature and cost us our humanity.' [24] Yuval Noah Harari echoes a similar theme when he argues that our choices are no longer our own: 'their range is being determined by enhanced algorithms as the surveillance capitalism practiced by Google, Amazon and Facebook become even more contagious'.[25]

But the threat to our societal future that has captured the most attention is the threat to our environment from climate change. We have now reached the Anthropocene age, a new epoch in geological time in which human activity is considered such a powerful influence on the environment, climate and ecology of the planet, that it will leave a long-term mark. It has been argued that the collective activity of humanity is now 'sapping the ecological basis of civilisation – and no collective agency capable of reckoning with this fact can yet be discerned'.[26] The scale of the problem became apparent in the 1990s, when the 'Hockey stick diagram' made its appearance, showing that records of mean temperatures from the year 500 to 2000 showed a long-term cooling trend changing to a rapid rise in temperature in the recent past; that the 1990s were the hottest decade ever; and that 1998 was the warmest year in the last thousand. In a review of Roberto Calasso's *The Unnameable Present*, the novelist John Banville wrote: 'For those of us living at this moment, the most exact and acute sensation is one of not knowing where we are treading from day to day – we are living in an unnameable present, one of growing incidence of political and social bizarrerie to the next.'[27]

One of the most ambitious attempts to understand these 'bizarreries' was Ross Douthat's *The Decadent Society*. He's been a lead columnist at the *New York Times* for the last six years and was the youngest ever to be

24 Shoshana Zuboff, *The Age of Surveillance Capitalism: The Fight for a Human Future at the New Frontier of Power* (New York: Profile Books, 2019), 470.
25 Yuval Noah Harari, 'The World after Coronavirus', *Financial Times* (20 March 2020).
26 Ibid.
27 John Banville, 'Review of Roberto Calasso's the Unnameable Present', *Financial Times* (28 September 2019).

appointed to one of the most prestigious journalistic posts in the world. Most writing on our current discontent tend to start somewhere around the early 1990s, when the liberal moment was at its height. Douthat begins in 1969, the year of the moon landing, and argues that since then our ambition has stalled: 'For the first time since 1482, we have found the distances too vast and the technology too limiting to take us somewhere undiscovered.' [28] He believes that loss of optimism and faith in institutions has been responsible for the drift and resignation which has characterised the world for the last sixty years, and as a result we have entered into a state of decadence. He discusses different forms of decadence, but believes our variety is made up of a combination of economic stagnation, institutional decay and cultural and intellectual exhaustion, and that while the speed with which we experience events may have quickened, the actual change has not. He discusses the four horsemen of decadence: stagnation, sclerosis, sterility and repetition. Stagnation and sclerosis have been dealt with earlier. He believes that declining fertility is due to our current exhaustion and lethargy, and references Sally Rooney as an example of younger people having difficulties in committing themselves to settled relationships. In the chapter on repetition, he notes the decline in originality in films, pop music and novels, which increasingly rely on a succession of repeats while the 1960 rockers who are still alive are still filling more concert seats than their successors.

Douthat doesn't think we're coping all that well with these difficulties. We're moving indoors with electronic and virtual entertainment, using porn and video games as a substitute for the real thing, and relying on a range of pharmaceuticals to keep us tranquilised in the manner of Huxley's Soma. The result: 'People growing old unhappily together in the glowing light of tiny screens'.[29] He seems fixated by Auden's reflection on the fall of the Roman Empire, which lasted for another four centuries but without 'creativity warmth or hope'. The remainder of the book speculates on possible scenarios that might unfold for us.

28   Ross Douthat, *The Decadent Society: How We Became the Victims of Our Own Success* (New York: Avid Reader Press, 2020), 13.
29   Ibid., 13.

Things get a little confusing here, as the different scenarios are not spelt out in any clear sequence, but the world the author refers to is the Western world. In trying to unravel the last third of the book I can detect three possible directions that the world might choose or be forced to take: Stasis, Apocalypse or Renaissance. Stasis is the most obvious option, because it requires no immediate action: we just muddle through as before, enjoying a life of quiet stagnation on the lines of the Roman Empire, relaxed on a diet of gentle drugs and a variety of electronic diversions, fondly remembering past glories but starved of any ambition to emulate them or revolutionise the world. He accepts that this form of decadence doesn't necessarily lead to irrelevance; human beings can live vigorously amid a general stagnation, be fruitful amid sterility, be creative amid repetition, and build good and fully human lives that offer a challenge to decadence. The main task would be to limit expectations and live within self-imposed means. It is not always made clear that this benign option is available only to the West, but he goes on to argue that stagnation is an illusion in today's volatile world, and that there are too many threats from the rest of the world, not to mention an impending environmental catastrophe, for it to be realistic.

This is where the apocalyptic option comes in. This results in a more ominous discussion of what might happen when the inevitable competition between the West and the rest boils over. A number of unexpected catastrophes are discussed, such as an incidence of technology-terrorism that goes wrong, artificial intelligence technology that over-reaches itself, a Y2K-type meltdown, more pandemics or economic crisis caused by the unsustainability of the world's debt-financed policies. Some of these possibilities could interact: a Chinese slow-down leading to financial problems for over-leveraged tech companies in Silicon Valley, which in turn leads to economic meltdown in Europe, leading to more authoritarian leaders in Europe. Meanwhile, unprecedented droughts followed by floods make large parts of the southern hemisphere uninhabitable, leading to unprecedented migration, which becomes politically untenable.

The Renaissance option would mean adopting technological solutions to all our problems, allowing us to live a life of cultivated leisure as envisaged for his grandchildren almost one hundred years ago by Keynes. If we could lift ourselves from our current stasis we could and we already have the means: an energy revolution that radically cheapens transportation and energy production, a robotics revolution that reduces the need for human labour, a medical and biotechnology revolution that extends lifespans and a revolution in space flight that enables us to live on Mars. If there is a level of agreement on the possibility of fulfilling Keynes's vision, why hasn't it happened? Douthat suggests an intriguing reason: the decline of religious idealism, believing that our liberal ideas don't do enough to satisfy the human heart, resulting in an exhausted sense of stasis and stagnation. No civilisation, he argues, has thrived without a belief that there was more to the human story than just the material world as we understand it, and therefore a renaissance would be more likely if there was a revival of the religious tradition that Christianity once displaced. He detects signs of such a revival which could be described as neo-paganism, involving a general belief in an immanent divine possibly, deriving from the ancient tradition of intellectual and aesthetic pantheism.

Douthat's conclusions may raise eyebrows in our liberated post-religious Western world, but a revival of some form of pantheism might lead us into a more caring attitude to our only planet, and the overall sweep of his analysis deepens our understanding of our strange times. It is also worth noting that the British philosopher, John Gray, has recently come to a similar conclusion: 'The most necessary task at the present time is to accept the irreducible reality of religion – the need for religion is generically human – human beings will not cease to be religious any more than they will stop being sexual, playful or violent.'[30]

One final book on the subject worth considering is Toby Ord's aptly titled *The Precipice*, which reviews a range of existential threats and comes to the conclusion that if in the twentieth century there was a one in a hundred chance that that we faced extinction, the odds have now reduced to one in six.[31] He describes the main threats as: nuclear war, climate change, other environmental dangers, engineered pandemics and unaligned artificial intelligence. Ord believes that the slow slide to an AI-controlled future is

30 John Gray, *Black Mass: Apocalyptic Religion and the Death of Utopia* (London: Penguin, 2007), 293–294.
31 Toby Ord, *The Precipice: Existential Risk and the Future of Humanity* (London: Bloomsbury, 2020), 58.

probably the most serious of all the threats. He argues that we are 'precariously close to self-destruction', and that safeguarding humanity's future is the defining challenge of our time, but that we are not taking these threats seriously enough: 'We can say with confidence that humanity spends more on ice cream every year than on ensuring that the technologies we develop do not destroy us.'[32] His main recommendation to avoid falling off the precipice is to strengthen our international institutions or face the greatest ever tragedy of the commons. Although recent events don't augur well for a new Bretton Woods agreement, the one thing all these writers are agreed on is that none of the existential risks that we are exposed to are going to respect national borders.

Conclusions

The prevailing tone of the post-Great Recession commentary has been pessimistic, bordering on apocalyptic. In one of his last poems, Derek Mahon characterised our time as 'an age of unbeauty, rage and fear'.[33] The 'end of the world is nigh' is regularly forecast, as the main pillars of the Western world, democracy, capitalism and the general liberal values of a free press, an independent judiciary and individual human rights come under attack from opponents as wide-ranging as autocratic opportunist politicians, to the surveillance activities of the new data-enriched tech businesses.

Proposals to prevent the further erosion of the Western liberal values seem to lack conviction, but as the twenty-first century comes of age in 2021, some green shoots of optimism are beginning to make an appearance. The election of the fundamentally decent Joe Biden as President of what is still the most powerful economic and military power in the world, by a majority that turned out to be substantially greater than looked likely on election night, is a clear signal that democracy is still in good working

32 Ibid., 58.
33 Derek Mahon, *Against the Clock* (Oldcastle: Gallery Press, 2018), 38.

order. There are signs that the advance of the so-called alt-right in Europe has been halted, and the return to power of the ultra-centrist Mark Rutte in Holland, where a strongly pro-EU party attracted a surprising level of support, suggested that the mood of *ressentiment* may be on the wane.

There are grounds for even more optimism in the world of business, where there is almost complete agreement that the neo-liberal experiment conceived almost seventy-five years ago in Mont Pelerin is, for the foreseeable future at least, well and truly buried. Reviewing a new book by Mark Carney,[34] ex-Governor of the Bank of England, Will Hutton wrote:

> If 25 years ago someone had suggested that one of the world's most prominent ex-Central Bankers would launch an intellectual broadside at free market fundamentalism, for shredding the values on which good societies and functioning markets are based I would have been amazed. If, in addition, he would go on to argue that shareholder capitalism, socially motivated investing, and business putting purpose before profit were the best ways to put matters right I would have considered it a fairy tale.[35]

There are also indications that leading businessmen are taking heed of Louis Brandeis's warning from the early twentieth century: 'We must make a choice – we may have democracy or we may have wealth concentrated in a few hands, but we can't have both.'[36] It is no coincidence that Brandeis was the lawyer used by President Woodrow Wilson (and later President Roosevelt) to break up the powerful rail and banking monopolies in the US. History may be beginning to repeat itself, because now governments are at last beginning to move against the increasingly monopolist power of the tech titans. In the US politicians of the left and right, in a rare instance of alignment, are calling them to account, threatening them with some diminution of their powers of surveillance. In July of 2020, the heads of Google, Amazon, Facebook and Apple stood in front of Congress for a hearing on antitrust, monopoly and political bias, among other things.

---

34 Mark Carney, *Value(s)* (Glasgow: William Collins, 2021).
35 Will Hutton, 'Value(s) by Mark Carney Review – Call for a New Kind of Economics', *The Observer* (21 March 2021).
36 Louis Brandeis, quoted in Irving Dilliard, ed., *Mr. Justice Brandeis, Great American: Press Opinion and Public Approval* (Saint Louis: Modern View Press, 1941), 42.

In Australia, the government have forced a reluctant Facebook to hand over revenue derived from the tech giant's casual appropriation of content from traditional media back to those media outlets. Early in 2021, Uber workers in the UK won a landmark case in the Supreme Court affirming their right to be treated as employees, with all the legal protection that implied under UK law, rather than as independent contractors, which had let the company off the hook of responsibility for any civilised employment standards.

There are also more encouraging signs in relation to climate change, but this time the pressure is coming from the public, especially younger people, who are increasingly bringing businesses to account in relation to their commitment to sustainability and the future protection of the planet. An international study by Unilever showed that a third of consumers prefer sustainable brands based on perception of good social and environmental behaviour. Unilever then mapped these claims against actual purchases. The results showed a lower degree of 'sustainable brand' purchases than claimed, but it was still as high as 30 per cent.[37] Against these encouraging signs, however, seemingly intractable problems for younger generations around the world, arising from the 2008 recession, remain. A recent survey carried out by the *Financial Times* concluded: 'A sense of insecurity is changing the way younger generations see the world – housing and education are more expensive, jobs feel more competitive and insecure, pensions less adequate and the environment imperilled – a feeling that their parents' wealth is becoming a more important determinant of their prospects than their own efforts. Job insecurity is a common theme especially those on temporary, fixed-term agency or zero-hour contracts.'[38] These are the challenges facing political leaders today.

---

37 'Sustainability 2030', *Copenhagen Institute for Future Studies* (CIFS), 2021, 8.
38 Sarah O'Connor, '"We are Drowning in Insecurity": Young People and Life After the Pandemic', *Financial Times*, 25 April 2021.

Ireland in the Twenty-First Century

The twenty-first century has seen dramatic changes in Ireland's fortunes, but if Napper Tandy was to emerge from his Castlebellingham final resting place and repeat his famous question: 'How's poor old Ireland and how does she stand?', he would probably be surprised by how favourable the answer is: 'Not too bad Napper, all things considered'. At the turn of the new millennium, we were brimming with a historically high level of self-confidence and wealth in relation to other European nations. The first seven years of the new century were probably the most economically successful in the country's history. The Celtic Tiger became a global phenomenon, resulting in admiration tinged with envy in the world's press: 'Over the past decade in particular Ireland's Celtic Tiger has featured so prominently in the French press that it risks joining in the compendium of Irish cliches along with bad weather, red hair and pints of Guinness.'[39]

However, the Great Recession in 2008 was a severe setback, partly because of the severity of the economic downturn, but more importantly because a combination of administrative incompetence and personal greed lay at the heart of the crisis. Ó Riain[40] argues that three features of contemporary capitalism, financialisation, globalisation and neo-liberalism, combined to make Ireland's crisis particularly dramatic. We engaged in an orgy of financial property speculation during the boom, we had for some time been the 'most globalised country in the world' and we have, more by default than conscious decisions, tended to adopt the US/UK capitalist model rather than the more social or even Christian democratic economic models favoured in continental Europe. He points out that Ireland shared the main characteristics of the neo-liberal economies: 'Centralised

---

39 Grace Neville, 'In at the Death: The French Press and the Celtic Tiger', in Eamon Maher, ed., *Cultural Perspectives on Globalisation and Ireland* (Bern: Peter Lang, 2009), 8.
40 Seán Ó Riain, 'The Road to Austerity', in William K. Roche, Philip J. O' Connell and Andrea Prothero, *Austerity and Recovery in Ireland: Europe's Poster Child and the Great Recession* (Oxford: Oxford University Press, 2017), 36.

government power and weak civic institutions, welfare states based on transfers rather than services, structural budget deficits and a macroeconomic strategy based on domestic consumption rather than export production'.[41]

In the end, Ireland had to be bailed out by the European Central Bank, which resulted in an embarrassing loss of sovereignty for two years with effective control of the economy being transferred to a Troika of the ECB, the IMF and the EU. The price to be paid was a stringent austerity programme resulting in deprivation rates across all households in the population soaring from 13.7 per cent in 2008 to 30 per cent in 2013. Even more humiliating was the fact that the programme came with a world of continuous and surveillance involving precise targets and benchmarks.

Three interesting conclusions emerge from the debacle. First, in spite of the Troika attracting a large share of opprobrium, a number of commentators have stressed that Ireland's austerity programme was very much driven by the Irish authorities themselves: 'To a greater extent than is commonly acknowledged Ireland's austerity was auto-austerity'.[42]

The second conclusion is that Ireland made a surprisingly rapid recovery from recession, leading to its designation as a 'poster child' of austerity. Stephen Kinsella, a Senior Lecturer in Economics in Limerick University, has tempered this appellation slightly by arguing that Ireland was in reality more of a 'beautiful freak': 'a case marked by highly unusual and historically specific features and influences that acted in concert and shaped a pathway to recovery unlikely to have been or to become available to other countries affected by economic calamity'.[43] Kinsella goes on to argue that the unique openness of the Irish economy was a critical factor in the recovery. The sum of exports and imports as a proportion of GDP was higher in Ireland than in the other bailout countries, as was the impact of foreign direct investment. As a result, he concludes that 'Ireland was able to absorb the impacts of austerity in ways that Greece, Portugal and Spain could not'.

41 Ibid., 38.
42 William K. Roche, Philip J. O'Connell and Andrea Prothero, 'Introduction: "Poster Child" or 'Beautiful Freak?' in *Austerity and Recovery in Ireland*, 2.
43 Stephen Kinsella, 'Economic and Fiscal Policy', in *Austerity and Recovery in Ireland*, 58.

Honohan, in his analysis of the period from his prospective as Governor of the Central Bank, comes to a very similar conclusion: 'As one of the most globalised economies on the planet, the way Ireland has dealt with its international economic relations has been crucial – Ireland experienced a somewhat faster macroeconomic recovery from the crisis than the other most stressed Euro area countries. This can be attributed to a degree of underlying dynamism in the economy, to the persistence of government pursuing credible adjustment policies.'[44]

Two other features of Ireland's austerity and recovery are worth noting: the relative fairness in the way that austerity medicine was shared out among the population, and the relative lack of protest and social unrest that ensued. Kinsella suggests that one of the reasons why Ireland was a 'beautiful freak' was the relatively high levels of expenditure on social programmes which served to cushion the impact of austerity. Specialists in inequality studies are more critical, but believe that inequality has been a feature of Irish society since the foundation of the state – 'Ireland is one of the most class-divided, unequal countries in Europe'[45] – but their analysis of changes in income by social class decile in the five years after the crash show very little movement across social classes. Honohan backs up this argument: 'Fiscal policy could have been more progressive – but it did limit the worsening of aggregate disposable income inequality as conventionally measured.'[46]

However, he too notes that inequality in the distribution of net wealth was higher than that of other EU countries. He concludes his analysis of this turbulent period with a characteristically balanced summary: 'On the whole Ireland has prospered in an era of globalisation. Benefits have accrued to most sections of society. But, although public policy has helped contain the rise in income inequality to a greater extent in Ireland than elsewhere, the resources of the nation have not been deployed as effectively as they might to spread the fruits of national prosperity more widely.'[47]

---

44   Patrick Honohan, *Currency, Credit and Crisis: Central Banking in Ireland and Europe* (Cambridge: Cambridge University Press, 2019), 343.
45   Kathleen Lynch, Sara Cantillon and Margaret Crean, 'Inequality', in *Austerity and Recovery in Ireland*, 254.
46   Honohan, *Currency, Credit and Crisis*, 337.
47   Ibid., 252.

The above analysis partly explains why the years of austerity were not marked by more social unrest, but most commentators agree that there were also deeper sociological factors at work. Some refer to the fundamentally conservative nature of Irish society. It was no accident that the founders of the Irish state over one hundred years ago were referred to as 'the most conservative revolutionaries who ever lived'. The poet Michael O'Loughlin, who had lived for many years in Amsterdam, recently bemoaned the fact that, apart from the water charges demonstrations, there was a relative lack of civic unrest during the worst years of austerity. The only conclusion that emerged from this debate was that, as a very small interconnected country with easily accessible politicians, we could make our grievances known very quickly to the relevant parties. Brigid Laffan suggests a more likely explanation: 'A deeply rooted political and administrative culture of pragmatism'.[48] Honohan has also made the same point in relation to the aftermath of the 2008 recession, referring to 'the pragmatic response of the general public who though very angry with the damage that the elites had done were well informed and realistic about what the best solutions for the country could be'.[49]

Two extraordinary manifestations of this pragmatism were on display in the last decade. The first was the celebration of the centenary of the 1916 Rising. Given the still febrile situation in Northern Ireland, this event had the potential to inflame passions and re-open barely recovering wounds. Instead, a confident Irish body politic handled the situation with calmly assured dignity by subtly making it a cultural rather than a political commemoration. Even more impressive was the way the country dealt with the potentially even more divisive issues of abortion and same-sex marriage by the imaginative use of Citizens' Assemblies. As cracks appeared in democracy around the world, the idea of examining other forms of democracy to augment parliamentary elections was beginning to appear. President Macron's series of town hall meetings across France in an attempt to halt the 'gilets jaunes' protests were a good example. The political website Politico

---

48   Brigid Laffan, 'International Actors and Agencies', in *Austerity and Recovery in Ireland*, 186.
49   Honohan, *Currency, Credit and Crisis*, 343.

reported on similar experiments from Sydney to Gdansk, and concluded that 'The Irish experiment has been hailed as the most widely publicised success.'[50]

The idea is based on the premise that a small but representative group of citizens, randomly selected to reflect the age, education level, gender and wealth, can represent the population as a whole. Exactly the same model is used all over the world on a continuous basis by market research companies carrying out surveys for their clients. The first experiment in Ireland was in 2012, when a Consolidated Convention comprising thirty-three politicians and sixty-six citizens were charged with recommending how to overhaul the constitution. They recommended legalising gay marriage, which was passed overwhelmingly in a referendum in 2015, the first such case in the world. Then in 2017, a Citizens' Assembly consisting of ninety-nine randomly chosen citizens recommended ending the constitutional ban on abortion, and this too is now law. The most remarkable aspect of these events was that they were accomplished with a minimum of rancour, and indeed with relieved and joyful celebration.

As Ireland emerges from successive pandemic lockdowns into an uncertain economic future, the Mandarin, the Musician and the Mage are no longer with us. As we have seen, the Musician suffered a tragically early death, the Mandarin lived long enough to reach his 100th birthday in 2017 and the Mage died in 2021 at the age of ninety-three. They would undoubtedly be amazed by their country's progress since the dark days of the late 1950s, but being the type of men they were, they would also be only too willing to offer advice about how to proceed from here. In the next chapter I will speculate on what form this advice might have taken.

---

50   Naomi O'Leary, 'The Myth of the Citizens' Assembly', *Politico*, 2019 <https://www.politico.eu/article/the-myth-of-the-citizens-assembly-democracy/> accessed 23 October 2021.

CHAPTER 8

Possible Lessons from the Mandarin, the Musician and the Mage for a New Revival

Introduction

In both of the earlier revivals, debate was not confined to cultural and social issues, but was also concerned with politics and economics. The first revival encompassed a range of innovative initiatives in commerce, agriculture, natural sciences and sport, as well as in theatre, literature, art and language. The second revival was initially focused on the economy, given the dismal prospects at the time, but it was also a time of cultural and artistic awakening and renewal. During both periods many of the leading participants were curious about developments in the outside world and how they might be relevant to Ireland, and whose lessons might be applied in Ireland. But in spite of these periods of intense debate on choices facing the country, Ireland's reluctance to engage in sustained intellectual debate on alternative strategic options has been widely noted.

The celebrated 'Perspectives' section in Joe Lee's history of the twentieth century is littered with laments for a lack of strategic thinking about the future direction of Irish society, as he asks, 'Why was the market for ideas in independent Ireland so small?' and he concluded, 'the incapacity of the Irish mind to think through the implications of independence for national development derived largely from and was itself a symbol of the dependency syndrome that had wormed its way into the Irish psyche during the long centuries of foreign dominance'.[1] Tom Garvin came to a similar conclusion: 'There was a clear anti-modernist streak in Irish official and clerical thinking generating a reluctance to engage seriously with the modern world – more importantly the notion of a static unchanging order was regarded as the ideal.'[2]

This conclusion wasn't just noted by academics. Former Taoiseach Garret FitzGerald also expressed his despair at the reluctance to engage in ideas: 'As a people we are I think resistant to, indeed somewhat afraid of, ideas. Certainly, it has been my experience over many years that attempts either in lectures or articles to put forward ideas evoke remarkably little response. There is a strong Irish preference for the concrete over the conceptual.'[3] This issue hasn't been resolved, and it played a significant role in the loss of control over our own economy following the 2008 recession. London-based financial commentator on Irish affairs, Michael O'Sullivan, again reiterated this weakness: 'The credit crisis has highlighted the lack of serious strategic thinking on the part of the political and policy-making classes, not just in the past six months but in a habitual way. By and large the skills and incentives of our political class draw them towards small local issues and leave them unprepared for the "bigger picture" ones.'[4] One can only conclude that we are much better at fighting our way out of a problem than at anticipating the problem in advance.

The two earlier revivals had three elements in common: intense intellectual curiosity, a deep sense of community spirit and a wide-ranging knowledge of and attachment to Irish cultural traditions and heritage. In considering how these elements might be applied to a new revival, using the careers and achievements of Whitaker, Ó Riada and Kinsella as a catalyst, I will refer to them by their Gaelic names: *fiosracht*, representing intellectual curiosity, *meitheal*, representing community spirit and active citizenship and *dinnseanchas*, representing knowledge of local history and traditions.

---

1 Lee, *Ireland 1912–1985*, 627, 631.
2 Garvin, *Preventing the Future*, 10.
3 Garrett FitzGerald, quoted in Fennell, *Heresy*, 250.
4 Michael O'Sullivan, 'We Need a Political System that Encourages Strategic Thinking', *The Irish Times* (14 April 2009), 10.

Fiosracht

The lack of intellectual curiosity in Irish life which has intrigued so many commentators is most in evidence at General Election time. In the recent past, elections have been exclusively consumed by which party were most likely to increase the gross national product while promising the most generous welfare payments and the most enticing tax concessions. No competing visions were offered as to how Irish society might evolve, or what type of society we wanted to develop, or what Ireland should stand for in the world. The most recent attempt to define a vision was that deathless phrase repeated ad nauseam by the then-Taoiseach Enda Kenny: 'the best little country to do business in'. Yeats's invocation of the 'greasy till' couldn't have been more apt to describe this hideously pathetic goal. The only consolation is that we didn't succumb to the temptation that befell so many countries who looked to a dangerously idealised past and strived to 'make their country great again'.

There was little danger we would fall into that trap. When we look at our past we see a long history of failure, civil war, famine, emigration, seven hundred years of colonial rule, successive failed revolts and the catastrophic psychological effect of the loss of language. But in considering what lessons we could learn from the three men who contributed so much to the second revival and think of what ideas they might inspire for a new revival, we might start with a variation of Thomas Kinsella's 'and I always remembered who and what I was' by considering 'who and what we want to be'.

The previous chapter summarised the extremely febrile state of the world in an age of anger and the need for great clarity of purpose for small countries who have no option but to engage in this world. Small countries have even more need to engage in the wider world than large ones; Maalouf sums up the rules of engagement: 'globalization is not the tool of some "new order" that "some people" are trying to impose on the world. It is more like a huge arena, open on all sides, in which a thousand jousts and combats are taking place all at the same time, making an indescribable and shattering din, an amphitheatre in which anyone is free to enter with his own motto or theme tune and whatever banner or other paraphernalia he chooses'.[5] We need to have the confidence that our banners, mottos and tunes will thrive in this amphitheatre. Our record is good; we have seen earlier how we have embraced the European Community project, and detailed statistical evidence has been presented which shows that we are one of the most enthusiastic participants in the EU. We have also been active participants in the United Nations, and before that the League of Nations, from the foundation of the state. Since 1958, not a single month has passed without Irish involvement in UN peacekeeping operations, and in 2021 Ireland was elected to the UN Security Council for a two-year period. This was the fourth time Ireland has held a seat on this important body, which has prompted *The Economist* magazine to note: 'In proportion to its size Ireland could now claim to be the world's most diplomatically powerful country.'[6]

We also start with a huge reservoir of goodwill; we're better known than most countries of our size, and we're well liked. It is often commented that Ireland's gross national likeability is significantly higher than its gross national product, and UK cultural critic Terry Eagleton has commented wryly that 'the Irish were put on earth for other people to feel romantic about'.[7] But this romantic notion of Ireland didn't just happen by accident; it was a deliberate construct formed by many of the writers and artists during the first revival in the late nineteenth and early twentieth centuries. They created an attractive and coherent image or reputation for Ireland based on an artistic and creative society with a heightened consciousness of the real meaning of life and a reduced emphasis on the material world. W. B. Yeats, the most prominent literary figure of the first revival, was always conscious of the fact that he was creating a reputation, or what we would now refer to as a 'brand image', for Ireland. Foster makes it clear how deliberate the construction of this image was, referring to Yeats as 'concentrating on hard-headed marketing', and arguing that 'inventing tradition came easily

---

5   Amin Maalouf, *On Identity* (London: Harvill Panther, 2000), 114.
6   'How Ireland Get Its Way: An Unlikely Diplomatic Superpower', *The Economist* (18 July 2020).
7   Terry Eagleton, 'A Row of Shaws', *London Review of Books* (21 June 2018).

to WBY'.⁸ A century later, Kiberd was able to confirm the success of Yeats's 'marketing' initiative:

> That enterprise achieved nothing less than a renovation of Irish consciousness and a new understanding of politics, sport, language, philosophy and culture in its widest sense. It was the grand destiny of Yeats' generation to make Ireland once again interesting to the Irish, after centuries of enforced provincialism following the collapse of the Gaelic order in 1601. No generation before or since lived with such conscious national intensity or left such an important legacy.⁹

Two aspects of this reputation were to prove important in the second half of the twentieth century: it was very distinctive, enabling Ireland to stand out from other, often much bigger, countries in the market for overseas investment and tourism, and it was attractive, providing an antidote to the type of contemporary Western concerns of anxiety, alienation and anomie chronicled by Bauman (2003–2006) in his analysis of the 'liquid' nature of modern society.¹⁰ The staying power of the Irish image has meant that it managed to survive in spite of the changes wrought by the economic transformation of the country since the 1960s. Thomas Friedman, the *New York Times* columnist whose best-selling books on globalisation we have already noted, commented in one of his columns:

> People all over the world are looking to Ireland for its reservoir of spirituality hoping to siphon off what they can feed to their souls which have become hungry for something other than consumerism and computers.¹¹

North American humanities professor Michael Mays, who does notice the changes that have taken place, is still able to detect elements of Yeats's more romantic, less materialist vision. Here he alludes to the travel writer Pete McCarthy:

---

8   R. F. Foster, *The Apprentice Mage, 1865–1914: W. B. Yeats: A Life, Vol. 1* (Oxford: Oxford University Press, 1997), 69.
9   Kiberd, *Inventing Ireland*, 3.
10 Bauman, *Liquid Modernity*.
11 Thomas L. Friedman, 'Op-Ed Article', *New York Times* (3 August 2001).

McCarthy discovers in his travels, and is drawn to, a set of qualities – a combination of hospitality and sociability, of laissez faire acceptance and relaxed good-naturedness – an Irishness that is genuine, palpable and real, an Irishness genuinely suffused with warmth and conviviality, a commodity that has proved itself time and time again and long before the concept of globalisation was ever dreamt of to be remarkably portable, far and away Ireland's most valuable marketing export.[12]

In the aftermath of the Great Recession, overseas commentators were still in thrall to the image established over one hundred years ago: 'in the eyes of post-modern gurus Ireland still corresponds to the image conveyed by the late 19th century and early 20th century nationalists – spirituality has become along with cream liqueur and traditional music one of Ireland's signature exports'.[13] Comments like Friedman's and Mays's quoted above are often linked with the notion that Ireland's distinctive cultural and political background could be used to set an example to the world in the aftermath of the Great Recession. Simon Anholt, an expert in nation branding, suggested that Ireland could 'position' itself as the society and economy at the end of the neo-liberal era to 'pilot and promote a new form of capitalism; more moral, more fair, more balanced, more human'.[14]

Unfortunately, not everyone took such a benign view. The economic boom from the mid-1990s to the 2008 recession saw the emergence of a new dimension to the Irish nation brand image: the cute hoor. In Jungian terms this 'dark shadow' of our personality was always there; we managed to ignore it, but as the economic boom developed our neighbours were quick to notice: 'a country that had lovingly portrayed itself as uniquely oppressed is rich – an average of 7 per cent growth for the last decade – the result – ugly bungalows, seedy businessman, American investors, flexible politicians, low corporate tax – a wholly centralised government with wholly un-ideological politics, skilfully marketing its business-friendliness which was facilitated by cash in brown envelops handed over with a nod and

12   Michael Mays, 'Irish Identity in an Age of Globalisation', *Irish Studies Review* 13/1 (2005), 9.
13   Catherine Maignant, 'The Global Irish Spirit', in Eamon Maher, ed., *Cultural Perspectives on Globalisation and Ireland* (Bern: Peter Lang, 2009), 34–35.
14   Simon Anholt, quoted in John Fanning, 'Brand Ireland should be Rethought and Replaced', *The Irish Times* (27 February 2012).

a wink'.[15] Michael O'Sullivan, the London-based financial commentator, was less sarcastic but came to a not dissimilar conclusion, describing the new Irish business class as 'fast aggressive and shiny, not unlike the newly monied classes of other emerging economies'.[16]

This is a far cry from the vision of the spiritually minded, non-materialistic people developed by Yeats and eagerly appropriated by politicians in the newly independent state. Inevitably, these tendencies in Irish society were gleefully picked up by European commentators when the full extent of the Irish economic collapse became apparent in the early months of 2009. A leading French geo-political commentator writing in the *Financial Times* made a similar point: 'The gold medal for selfishness may once more be given to the Irish, who have followed their ingratitude of their "No" vote on the Lisbon Treaty with absolute contempt towards the search for a collective solution to the financial crisis.'[17] The Irish government decision at the height of the crisis to underwrite the entire deposits of the six main banks operating in Ireland also raised more than a few eyebrows. The French reaction was typical: 'Centuries of consistently benign French commentaries on Ireland came shuddering to an abrupt halt ... Ireland can no longer bask in the warm glow of admiration ... it is possible that the old France-Ireland alliance may never be the same again.'[18]

The more recent controversy over the US's proposal to increase corporation tax on business and the EU's attempt to have a uniform corporate tax rate has once again plunged Ireland in difficulties, as these proposals represent a direct threat to the country's totemic 12.5 per cent corporate tax rate. The Irish government is fighting a massive rearguard action, defending the right of small countries to use corporate tax as a competitive weapon. But however valid this argument might have been when we were a poor country, now that we are relatively rich it seems like a very negative strategy

---

15 'Top of the Morning: Review of *Luck and the Irish* by R. F. Foster', *Economist* magazine (18 October 2007).
16 O'Sullivan, *Ireland and the Global Question*, 83.
17 Dominique Moïsi, 'A Global Downturn in the Power of the West', *Financial Times* (5 October 2008).
18 Grace Neville, 'In at the Death', 65.

to adopt, and one that is completely at odds with the positive aspects of our worldwide reputation.

Given the importance of protecting the positive aspects of this reputation in a competitive global world, I am suggesting that the Mandarin, the Musician and the Mage would advise adopting a more conciliatory attitude to higher and uniform corporate tax rates, and would accept that using corporate tax as a competitive weapon merely serves to encourage a race to the bottom which will have the inevitable effect of reducing the amount governments across Europe will have at their disposal for schools, hospitals, roads and social welfare. In order to recover the damage caused to our reputation by our dog-in-the-manger attitude to the dreaded 12.5 per cent tax rate, we might also consider new initiatives that would position us in a more favourable light.

In the previous chapter I tried to summarise the febrile state of the world today and the particular challenges faced by small open economies like Ireland. A consistent theme, inspired by Thomas Kinsella, has been that we always need to maintain an acute understanding of 'who and what we are' if we are not to become unstuck in a global world. But maybe it is now time to pay more attention to 'who and what we want to be'. I've made the point that our past provides no inspiration, even if we define that past in hundreds of years. But we could look beyond all that for inspiration as Whitaker, Ó Riada and Kinsella did on a regular basis. This would however bring us back to the 'island of saints and scholars', a phrase guaranteed to produce either acute embarrassment or stifled guffaws. But it does represent a real truth about our history. In Bertrand Russell's monumental *History of Western Philosophy* there is a full chapter on Ireland in the fifth, sixth and seventh centuries written in straightforward and non-condescending language, making the point that we did indeed help to 'save civilisation'.[19] With that in mind I suggest that we might consider a new initiative of setting an 'Education Corps' along the lines of President Kennedy's Peace Corps initiative in the 1960s. Young Irish graduates and people in their 50s and 60s who would welcome a career change would sign up to teach in less developed countries for a two-year period. There

---

19   Russell, *A History of Western Philosophy*, 374–379.

are obvious precedents; Irish missionaries fulfilled this role for much of the twentieth century, and Irish businesses operating in less developed markets have often enjoyed the benefits of the goodwill built up over the years from grateful citizens of these countries, who prospered as a result of their education in Irish-run schools.

Meitheal

Meitheal can be defined as joint purposeful communal activity or the spirit of the community. The term comes from the traditional rural custom of a group of neighbours coming together to help each other with tasks such as saving the hay or gathering the harvest. Each family would help their neighbours, who in turn would reciprocate. The first revival was characterised by a wide range of voluntary organisations established to galvanise the energy and talent of a people lacking self-confidence and self-esteem. At the heart of the first revival were two self-help organisations, one business and one social, which were to have a lasting and hugely beneficial impact on the country.

Horace Plunkett's agricultural co-operative movement survives today in its modern metamorphosis in the two giant food-based businesses, Kerry Group and Glanbia, and in the one Irish food brand to have succeeded internationally, Kerrygold. Nine years before Plunkett founded the Irish Agricultural Co-operative Agency Society, Michael Cusack and a small group of men met in Miss Hayes' Commercial Hotel in Thurles to establish the grandly named Gaelic Athletic Association for the Preservation and Cultivation of National Pastimes, an association that achieved instant success and which continues to gain in strength 125 years later.

The self-help organisations of the second revival were the semi-state bodies which, as we have seen, played a significant role in that revival, and some of them, such as the IDA, CTT (now Enterprise Ireland and Bord Bia), BIM, Bord na Móna and Bord Fáilte (now Tourism Ireland), are still central to Irish economic and social life.

The neo-liberal era, which lasted from the 1970s to the 2008 recession, and emphasised individualism, competition and market values in all areas of life, was by definition inimical to co-operation and communal values. The tide has now turned, and the 2019 pandemic has demonstrated just how interdependent the world is. The excesses of neo-liberalism have resulted in a revival of interest in the philosophy of civic republicanism, which could be regarded as providing an intellectual underpinning of the Irish concept of *Meitheal*.

In the course of a wide-ranging article in the *Irish Times* in December 2001 to coincide with his eighty-fifth birthday, Ken Whitaker commented on the many improvements that had transformed the country since the dark period of the 1950s. He also commented on some of the unfortunate side-effects of our new prosperity, and in particular on what he felt was a decline of standards in public life:

> As one who had taken for granted the selfless dedication to duty of those prominent in public life, I was shocked by the recent revelations of corruption, of the sacrifice of integrity to greed, in a number of cases.[20]

When interviewed by the present author, he was asked to elaborate, and although a discreet mandarin veil descended over the subject, he did venture the following tale from the 1940s:

> I was working late with a superior when he excused himself to make a call from the phone on his desk. He proceeded to explain to his wife that he would be home a little late, replaced the phone on the hook, rummaged in his pockets for some coppers and placed them in a small box beside the phone. He must have noticed my look of curiosity and explained that as it had been a personal call he felt the money should be returned to the state.[21]

He made no further comment, but it was obvious that he believed that this little anecdote would be almost incomprehensible to the current generation of civil servants. To some extent this is only to be expected: increased prosperity, greater exposure to global trends and the new

---

20   Whitaker, 'We Have Come a Long Way', 10.
21   Thomas Kenneth Whitaker, Interview with author, 22 February 2007.

individualism have created a very different ethos in Irish society compared to that of the late 1950s. One of the main 'sceptics' earlier treated, O'Connell, has pinpointed individualism as a problem:

> There is a spectre haunting Ireland ... the spectre of individualism ... we have escaped the choking grasp of the Church but in doing so we have also abandoned the positive pro-social element of this message ... this is the negative element of freedom ... voracious individualism that pushes all else to one side.[22]

There is always a danger that this line of thought is merely an expression of nostalgia for a past which is basically unrecoverable. Although few who remember the despair and desolation of the 1940s or 1950s would wish to re-visit those days, we may have thrown out some good attributes with the 'unrecoverable' bathwater. Detailed interviews with some of the leading participants of the second revival of the late 1950s and early 1960s suggest two distinct characteristics that set apart that earlier era from our own:

1. greater involvement among administrative and business leaders in extra-curricular economic, business and cultural organisations.
2. greater awareness of a sense of 'nation-building' compared to what would now be referred to as 'networking' in these organisations.

We have seen in the second revival how formal institutions like the IMI and informal groupings like Tuairim and 'The Murphies' acted as catalysts in this process, and how the three men featured in this analysis were actively involved in 'nation building'. The three men at the centre of this book were highly successful in their chosen careers, but they were all involved in the civic arena in a way that transcended those careers, and in all three cases their extra-curricular roles stemmed from a deep knowledge of and love of Irish history, literature, language and culture. Ken Whitaker's love of the language came from his native Irish-speaking mother, an inspirational teacher in the Christian Brothers in Drogheda and regular holidays in the Donegal Gaeltacht:

---

22   O'Connell, *Changed Utterly*, 181.

> This opened up a new world of interest strengthening my commitment to the Irish language. I have been enriched by a knowledge of its poetry and folklore. I have written elsewhere of my part in the evolution of official policy in relation to the language. One initiative, which gave me great satisfaction, was persuading two poet friends – Seán Ó Tuama and Thomas Kinsella – to collaborate in preparing *An Duainaire*, an anthology of poems in Irish by the 'dispossessed', the leaderless Irish speakers after the years after Kinsale (1601). My purpose was to bring knowledge and appreciation of this great heritage to a wider circle.[23]

This kind of direct intervention in the cultural life of the country was also practised by Ó Riada and Kinsella. Both were equally determined to 'bring knowledge and appreciation of this great heritage to a wider circle'. After retirement from the Department of Finance in 1969 Ken Whitaker became Governor of the Central Bank, retiring from that position in 1976 only to take on the Chancellorship of the National University of Ireland. He was the Taoiseach's nominee in the Senate from 1977 to 1982, and during the 1980s and 1990s he continued to 'give the state some service' by chairing a succession of government commissions. This level of official civic service could hardly have been matched by Sean Ó Riada and Thomas Kinsella, but they, in their own different ways, were equally committed to making a contribution to the society in which they lived which was beyond the confines of their chosen careers.

Ó Riada's working life was spent almost exclusively in the public sector – RTÉ, the Abbey Theatre and UCC – but this was probably due mainly to the lack of alternative employment opportunities for musicians at the time. Like the other two men, Ó Riada was imbued with the sense of being an interdependent member of a community which involved wider responsibilities than merely obeying the laws of the land and paying taxes. He wanted to contribute to the betterment of the society in which he was a citizen, and he approached this objective in much the same way as his friend Thomas Kinsella: the restoration of an old indigenous tradition in the hope that contemporary society would develop a renewed interest and feel a renewed sense of pride. He was also conscious that he lived in a society which had not only turned its back on its own culture and traditions,

---

23 Whitaker, *Retrospect 2006–1916*, 8.

either through ignorance or lack of confidence, but which had become isolated from the main European classical music tradition. Marcus defines his ambition in the following way:

> Ó Riada was born in a country that had missed two centuries of European musical development ... Ireland had long been isolated by geography, history and an element of choice from the upheavals of Western culture ... Ó Riada was well versed in the mind of Europe ... his compositions were littered with elements of ancient Greece, the Renaissance and German poetry.[24]

Marcus goes on to compare Ó Riada's objective to Joyce's; both had to create a new language in which to express their ambitions: 'They both struggled with the problems of the Irish artist who aspires to see the universe in the lineaments of his own land.' As we have seen, Ó Riada achieved his objective, transforming Irish people's attitude to traditional music and helping to create a sense of pride in their culture. In 1963 he moved himself and his family to the West Cork Gaeltacht, where he maintained his active civic involvement, making films and writing music, involving himself in the life of the community, where he formed a choir and wrote a special Mass for them.

Kinsella's ambition on behalf of the community was similar to Ó Riada's: the restoration of the Gaelic literary tradition and its presentation in a form that would be more appreciated by modern audiences. This project occupied him from the early 1950s to the publication of the *New Oxford Book of Irish Verse* in 1986. We have also seen his adoption of the role of the conscience of the people and his frequent poetic interventions in contemporary affairs right up to the end of his life. He intervened directly in the Wood Quay controversy in the 1970s and in local protests near his home in Dublin 2 around the same time.

All three men therefore played an active civic role throughout their lives, and this may have been due to the spirit of the times, in particular the formative period of their careers in the mid-to-late 1950s. The results

---

24   Louis Marcus, 'Seán Ó Riada and the Ireland of the Sixties', in Bernard Harris and Grattan Freyer, eds, *The Achievement of Sean Ó Riada* (Ballina: The Irish Humanities Centre and Keohanes Ltd Ballina, 1981) 15.

of interviews with leading businessmen also confirm that in the immediate aftermath of the crises of the public finances in 1956 there was a much greater awareness of the need for concerted effort if the state was to survive. Whitaker has recalled being simultaneously frightened and inspired by a cartoon in a popular satirical magazine in 1957:

> I was spurred on by a cartoon in *Dublin Opinion* showing Ireland as a still beautiful but somewhat bedraggled old lady asking a fortune-teller: 'Have I a future?'[25]

When the very survival of the state was being questioned, as was the case in the mid-1950s, people were faced with a stark choice: emigrate or work together to solve the problem. Many took the first option, but many more opted to remain and build a new society. Although those who remained may not have been conscious of the philosophy of civic republicanism, they were all in their own way adopting some of its core precepts. Since that time Irish society has become much less receptive to these ideas, but it is a premise of this book that civic republicanism should not be confined to times of crisis. A brief outline of the history and ideas of this philosophy will attempt to explain why.

Civic republicanism is a philosophical concept that dates back to the ancient Greeks, who placed public participation and civic pride at the heart of the body politic, and who took a dim view of anyone who was not an active citizen or who had no time for public affairs. A belief in civic republicanism would involve a commitment to active citizenship, a belief that there needs to be a significant body of citizens who are prepared to continually take into account the interdependence of citizens in any society:

> A satisfactory society cannot be realised on the basis of an exact and narrow adherence to the law – there needs to be a significant body of citizens who are prepared to take into account in their actions the common good or wider interests e.g. culture or the environment they share with others.[26]

Advocates of civic republicanism also argue that its necessity is not just a case of recognising society's interdependent nature, but that it is also

---

25   Whitaker, *Retrospect 2006–1916*, 14.
26   Iseult Honohan, *Civic Republicanism* (Oxfordshire: Routledge, 2002), 19.

beneficial to our own nature: that for an individual to flourish, to experience the Aristotelian ideal of *eudaemonia*, they must realise their potential in society, which can only be achieved by active participation.

Civic republicanism went into decline during the Dark Ages, and only re-emerged in Renaissance Italy, where the rise of the city state made it relevant once again with Machiavelli, and later in seventeenth-century Britain with Harrington, in France with Rousseau's 'social contract' and in the fledgling United States with some of the Federalist Papers. Civic republican ideals remained dormant for most of the nineteenth and twentieth centuries as the battle between free market capitalism and communism and socialism took centre stage, but they started to re-emerge in the post-Second World War period in the writings of Hannah Arendt and Charles Taylor. Arendt in particular re-emphasised Aristotle's belief that free political activity and civic engagement represented 'the fullest realisation of human nature because it provides recognition of individual identity'. She wanted to restore the public space and decried the devaluation of politics to 'national housekeeping'.[27]

Honohan has acknowledged that, in spite of the efforts of Arendt and Taylor, the late twentieth century was not particularly conducive to the ideas and ideals of civic republicanism:

> In modern commercial society there is a real threat that people will become indifferent to politics. Social life will become characterised by the sort of civic privatism de Tocqueville called 'individualism' – having created a small self-contained society for his own use he willingly abandons the larger society to itself ... the idea of an extensive responsibility to the larger political community does not chime easily with contemporary ways of thinking.[28]

Dunne also argued that 'the current reduction of civic virtue to competence as a lobbyist is damaging to the quality of democracy'.[29]

---

27 Ibid., 127.
28 Ibid., 114–115.
29 Joseph Dunne, 'Citizenship and Education: A Crisis in the Republic', in Peadar Kirby, Luke Gibbons and Michael Cronin, eds, *Reinventing Ireland: Culture, Society, and the Global Economy* (London: Pluto Press, 2002), 81.

Renewing Our Civic Republican Vows

Contemporary advocates of civic republicanism are always conscious of not wanting to appear too authoritarian in their efforts to achieve greater participation in civic life. Writers on the subject often quote Oscar Wilde's wry put-down of socialism, 'it requires too many evenings', and they are often painfully aware of the possible sacrifices they may be demanding:

> Any commitment to civic virtue and the common good may be seen as subordinating the individual to society, or private life to public life in a way that is incompatible with modern concerns for individual fulfilment. The requirement of civic virtue may be seen as anachronistic, oppressive, moralistic or unrealistic.[30]

Nevertheless, the arguments in favour of encouraging today's citizens to follow the example of Whitaker, Ó Riada and Kinsella are compelling, and the need for more civic republicanism has to some extent been officially recognised with the setting up of a Taskforce on Active Citizenship in 2006 by the then-Taoiseach Bertie Ahern. The taskforce produced a comprehensive report in 2007 which began by acknowledging the problems that existed in Irish society, in spite of the economic transformation of the country:

> Many of the social, economic and cultural changes are welcome. Some changes are less welcome, especially those that may have eroded aspects of community spirit and human well-being. For example, concerns exist about the level of inequality in Irish society, and its impact on solidarity between individuals and communities. It is not obvious that we are today more caring, engaged, friendly, relaxed and happier than we were in the recent past.[31]

These are interesting admissions in an official government report, and the taskforce recommended a wide-ranging set of proposals to remedy

---

30 Honohan, *Civic Republicanism*, 148.
31 'Report of the Taskforce on Active Citizenship', *The Wheel: Building Stronger Communities* (2007), <https://www.wheel.ie/sites/default/files/media/file-uploads/2018-08/Report%20of%20the%20Taskforce%20on%20Active%20Citizenship.pdf> accessed 10 November 2021.

Lessons from the Mandarin, the Musician and the Mage 223

the situation and the setting of targets to be achieved in the immediate future:

> An increase in the pool of active people in the community by 60,000 each year for the next three years ... to increase the number of adults involved in at least one 'civic activity' by 60,000 each year for the next three years ... to improve voter turnout among 18–24 years and overall voter turnout to over 80% at general elections.[32]

These are ambitious targets, but the economic crisis that engulfed the country as the report was in preparation appears to have weakened official resolve, and to date the recommendations have not been implemented. This should be remedied as soon as possible. A greater commitment to civic republicanism can only improve the prospects of success for whatever measures are taken to solve Ireland's economic problems.

The examples of Whitaker, Ó Riada and Kinsella are very relevant to this debate. They all lived exemplary civic republican lives. They have been honoured by their peers, their achievements have been recognised by their fellow citizens and their lives have been accomplished and fulfilled as a result. They have heeded Kinsella's warning:

> In a disordered and misguided community
> it is the accomplished and the more fulfilled
> who are to be found to one side
> unwilling to take part.[33]

The Taskforce on Active Citizenship introduction quoted above alludes to Kinsella's point: the danger that the people who benefitted most from the economic transformation become 'unwilling to take part' and can afford to sit on the sidelines, thus weakening the quality of civic life. That accusation could not be applied to the three men at the core of this book. They all 'took part'.

The ease with which democracy can come under threat was mentioned in the previous chapter, and has an obvious relevance to the debate

---

32 Ibid.
33 Thomas Kinsella, *Belief and Unbelief: Peppercanister 27* (Dublin: Dedalus Press, 2007), 22.

on active citizenship. Applebaum[34] reminds us of two critical dangers to modern democracies, the presence of what she calls 'restorative nostalgias': mythmakers who want the past back and the damage to the political system from the increasingly cantankerous, continuous nature of modern discourse facilitated by digital platforms. We have been mercifully free of the former, there is no political support for 'making Ireland great again', but the coarsening effect of social media has made its presence felt here, leading some, mainly female, politicians to consider whether active political engagement is worth the hurt caused by these unregulated platforms. Applebaum warns that history is circular and human nature is flawed, so we must always be on our guard to prevent a slide back towards tyranny. Encouragement of active citizenship and the spirit of *Meitheal* would be a positive step in that direction.

Dinnseanchas

> Our imaginations are inhabited by ghosts, the past haunts us, but to change our lives for the better we need to understand that fact better. The mind is a refuge for ideas dating from many different centuries, just as the cells of the body are of different ages.[35]

The Gaelic word *dinnseanchas* represents the lure and lore of the local, the intense attachment people feel towards the immediate townland or neighbourhood in which they grew up. But it can also embody the emotional, social and cultural ties that bind people to that place. Nuala Ní Dhomhnaill describes *dinnseanchas* in the following terms:

> *Dinnseanchas* has long been one of the great branches of knowledge of the Gaelic world. For countless millennia in the oral tradition and for the fifteen hundred years of the written Irish-language tradition, it has been central to the culture.[36]

---

34 Applebaum, *Twilight of Democracy*, 74.
35 Theodore Zeldin, *An Intimate History of Humanity* (New York: Vintage, 1998), vii.
36 Oona Frawley, ed., *Nuala Ní Dhomhnaill: Selected Essays* (Dublin: New Ireland, 2005), 26.

Access to this 'great branch of knowledge' is not possible without a detailed commitment to the language, culture and history of that world. Many of the leading figures of the first revival were ardent Irish language enthusiasts, and were well versed in Irish history and culture. The same was true of the three men featured here as exemplifying the second revival. Kinsella in particular, because of his extensive translations of Gaelic poetry, welcomed the re-discovery of his poetic forbearers: 'It's a commitment to tradition, an understanding of them as part of our past, it is an understanding of our totality.'[37]

A core element of the first revival was the re-discovery of the Irish cultural tradition. The results of this 'recovery' were still in evidence up to the 1950s, transmitted by enthusiastic proselytisers in the education system, where the spirit of the struggle for national identity and independence was still very much alive. It would be difficult for today's cosmopolitan student generation to imagine the patriotic pride and fervour of a Christian Brothers education in Ireland during the 1930s, 1940s and 1950s, where the words of 'Faith of our Fathers' and 'A Nation Once Again' were drilled into every schoolboy and sung with gusto on a regular basis in the classroom. Few pupils left in any doubt about 'who and what [they were]'. Today a more calculated ethos prevails in an education system dominated by 'points' and an 'audit culture'.

Bradley & Kennelly (2008) contrast the Irish education system in this respect compared to Finland:

> It is instructive to compare the role in education of the national epic of Finland the *Kalevala*, with Ireland's closest equivalent, the *Táin Bó Cuailnge*. The *Táin* … is virtually ignored in education [in Ireland], contrast this with Finland where the *Kalevala* is studied extensively in schools at all levels serving as an ethnic memory for the Finns and providing a coherent national identity. By presenting a compelling view of the Finnish past it has provided a guide to the modern development of Finnish culture. It is at the root of Finnish consciousness, shaping the language, inspiring independence and serving as a source of the flowering of Finnish art and literature.[38]

---

37 Haffenden, 'Interview with Thomas Kinsella', *Viewpoint*, 112.
38 Bradley and Kennelly, *Capitalising on Culture*, 226–7.

Thomas Friedman, the US political commentator and arch proponent of globalisation, has warned against the danger of ignoring heritage and roots: 'Without a sense of home and belonging life becomes barren and rootless, and life as a tumbleweed is no life at all.'[39] The implication of Friedman's quote is that it is easier to operate in a global world if you have a self-confident sense of your own identity. There was no question of Whitaker, Ó Riada or Kinsella lacking a secure sense of identity or living 'life as a tumbleweed', and it may be that the greatest impetus to another revival would be a much greater awareness among the wider population of our cultural history and heritage. Mathews has noted the connection between cultural and economic rejuvenation in the first revival:

> the Gaelic League actively concerned itself with the material problems of the Irish nation and recognised a link between the language revival and the regeneration of the Irish economy ... the pages of *An Claidheamh Soluis* were frequently used to drum up support for 'native manufacturers' and to advance the argument that there was a link between the decline of the language and the loss of industry in rural Ireland.[40]

There are a number of reasons why a greater awareness of our cultural heritage, represented by the concept of *dinnseanchas*, should be considered a vital component of a new revival. It would provide a much-needed impetus to indigenous businesses, firstly by reminding us of our rich heritage, culture and native resources; it also would encourage domestic businesses to innovate and encourage domestic consumers to buy Irish goods. Secondly, it could encourage us to adopt more sustainable economic and consumption practices by bringing us closer to what we need to protect. Thirdly, it would remind us that increasing inequality is not compatible with continuing support for democracy, and finally, it could make us question whether economic growth is the only realistic societal goal.

---

39 Friedman, *The Lexus and the Olive Tree*, 27.
40 Mathews, *Revival*, 28.

Creating a More Vibrant Indigenous Business Sector

The importance of creating an indigenous entrepreneurial culture was highlighted over thirty years ago in an influential study by Birch (1987), which came to the, at the time, surprising conclusion that over 80 per cent of all new jobs in the US were created by small rather than large businesses.[41] From then onwards most developed countries, including Ireland, put more official emphasis on encouraging an entrepreneurial culture. It has often been assumed that for historical and deep-rooted cultural reasons Ireland lacks an entrepreneurial culture. Michael Casey, former assistant director general of the Central Bank, has argued that 'risk aversion is hard-wired into us'.[42] Lee comes to a very similar conclusion when he makes the point that the insecurity of nineteenth-century Ireland resulted in a 'possession mentality which stifled a performance ethos'. He then makes an even more damning judgement:

> A variety of factors have contributed to the poor performance of native Irish businesses, but the sheer intellectual inadequacy counts among the basic weaknesses. A first-class business mind would be a joy to behold. There were too few of them in Ireland.[43]

There is now new evidence to suggest that the last three decades have seen the emergence of a strong entrepreneurial culture, particularly among younger people. The Global Enterprise Monitor, an annual survey of entrepreneurial activity in OECD countries, while acknowledging a weak Irish entrepreneurial culture in the past – in particular a failure to look beyond the home market and an unwillingness to develop business beyond the point where a comfortable living can be made – now reports

41 David Birch, *The Job Generation Process* (1979). University of Illinois at Urbana-Champaign's Academy for Entrepreneurial Leadership Historical Research Reference in Entrepreneurship, Available at: <https://ssrn.com/abstract=1510007> (accessed 11 November 2021).
42 Michael Casey, 'Fear and Cultural Quirks to Blame for Ireland's Lack of Enterprise', *The Irish Times* (23 May 2006).
43 Lee, *Ireland 1912–1985*, 577.

that Ireland ranks within the top five countries in Europe in terms of early stage entrepreneurial activity.

The main change that has occurred over the last few decades is a significant increase in self-confidence, which is most clearly evidenced by the number of entrepreneurs who think globally from the beginning. The astonishing success of the Collison brothers in having their tech company Stripe valued at $90 billion in Silicon Valley is the most spectacular example of Irish entrepreneurial ambition and achievement, and the fact that they were born and educated in a small rural village in Tipperary has been widely noted in the huge media coverage that has accompanied their success. Less spectacular, but equally significant, is the success of Gunpowder Gin from a new Irish distillery based in the picturesque village of Drumshanbo in Co. Leitrim. Founded in 2015, it was designed for a global market from day one, but its marketing communications are steeped in local lore from the rich heritage of the surrounding countryside. Michael Porter, the Harvard Professor whose *Competitive Advantage of Nations* is a key text on this subject, argues that successful clusters of businesses in most countries are often based on cultural factors within these countries.[44]

Daniel Pink, an American political and business commentator, has provided an interesting schema of how the dominant paradigms in the global economy have changed over the centuries: from an agricultural age in the eighteenth century, to an industrial age in the nineteenth century, to an information age in the twentieth century, to a conceptual age in the twenty-first century. This means we are now in the process of moving from:

> An economy and a society built on the logical linear computer-like capabilities of the information age to a society built on the inventive, empathic, big-picture capabilities of what's rising in its place; the conceptual age.[45]

He goes on to quote another business commentator, Harman, who argues that the businesses of the conceptual age will require the ability to detect

---

44   Porter, *The Competitive Advantage*.
45   Daniel Pink, *A Whole New Mind: Why Right-Brainers will Rule the Future* (New York: Riverhead Books, 2006), 2.

broad patterns, to create artistic and emotional beauty and be able to craft stories:

> Poets are our original systems thinkers. They contemplate the world in which we live and feel obliged to interpret and give expression to it in a way that makes the reader understand how the world turns. Poets, these unheralded systems thinkers are our true digital thinkers. It is from their midst that I believe we will draw tomorrow's business leaders.[46]

Bradley and Kennelly argue that the core of their *Capitalising on Culture, Competing on Difference* thesis is that:

> Culture, tradition and identity are powerful resources that lead to innovation, creativity entrepreneurship and global advantage. Such qualities, founded on meaning, rooted in place and catalysed by forward-thinking public policy, can create conditions necessary for the creation of the vaunted knowledge or learning society.[47]

Facing up to Environmental Catastrophe

The full extent of the environmental catastrophe that lies in wait for everyone has now been laid bare by the recent publication of the Intergovernmental Panel on Climate Change. Quoting directly from the report, the *Guardian* ran a banner headline, 'Global Climate Crisis: Inevitable, Unprecedented and Irreversible'. The Chief Scientist from Greenpeace in the UK issued a stark warning: 'this is not the first generation of world leaders to be warned by scientists about the gravity of the climate but they are the last that can afford to ignore them.'[48] Pictures of melting polar ice caps and the virtual disappearance of some popular species of fish have convinced all but the most recalcitrant that we can no longer assume that nature is there to be 'defeated' and that natural

---

46   Sidney Harman, *Mind Your Own Business: A Maverick's Guide to Business, Leadership and Life* (New York: Crown Business/Currancy Doubleday, 2003), 10.
47   Bradley and Kennelly, *Capitalising on Culture*, 2.
48   Front cover, *The Guardian* (9 August 2021).

resources are inexhaustible. James Lovelock's concept of Gaia, of the world as a self-sustaining whole, is now becoming widely accepted.[49]

Philosopher Mary Midgley, a fierce critic of the atomistic reductionism which was at the heart of the enlightenment, has become a champion of the concept of Gaia, of the world as a self-maintaining whole:

> For three centuries we had been encouraged to consider the earth simply as an inert and bottomless larder stocked for our needs. To be forced to suspect now that it is instead a living system, a system on whose continued activity we are dependent, a system which is vulnerable and capable of failing, is extremely unnerving.[50]

The environment is now at the forefront of the political agenda in most of the developed countries, and would appear to have developed enough momentum to stay there. Although difficult to verify, it seems reasonable to assume that a greater understanding of the 'lure and lore of the local' would lead to greater concern for the environment, because it would make people more aware of the natural history and landscape of the country.

Concerns about Inequality

A commitment to *dinnseanchas* would not sit easily with a high level of inequality in our society. During the decades of the neo-liberal era, inequality seemed to expand in line with the economy as the rich became progressively richer while the rest of the population struggled to keep pace. Measuring degrees of inequality is always a contested area, but there is general agreement that Ireland's rate of inequality is somewhat above the European average and, more importantly, as in most other European countries the gap in wealth between the top 10 per cent of society and the rest has been steadily growing.

---

49   James Lovelock, *The Ages of Gaia* (Oxford: Oxford University Press).
50   David Midgley, ed., *The Essential Mary Midgley* (Oxfordshire: Routledge, 2005), 350.

We've already seen how Wilkinson & Pickett's *The Spirit Level* demonstrated that inequality is not only unfair, it's unhealthy. Having collected comparable data from a range of countries for the following social problems, level of trust, mental illness, life expectancy, obesity, children's educational performance, teenage births, homicides, imprisonment rates, and social mobility, they conclude that 'there is a very strong tendency for ill-health and social problems to occur less frequently in the more equal countries'.[51] They argue that the greater the level of inequality in any one country, the greater the pressure to keep up appearances by consuming more. Also, greater inequality leads to higher levels of status anxiety:

> Average income levels don't matter, spending on high-tech health care doesn't matter ... income inequality does ... what matters in determining mortality and health in a society is less the overall wealth of that society and more how evenly wealth is distributed ... the more evenly wealth is distributed the better the health of that society.[52]

Dinnseanchas per se is not necessarily a levelling agent, but in its absence, when the 'shared understandings, myths, rituals and narratives' of a society are weakened, the barriers against the natural tendency for the rich to become richer and the poor poorer are also weakened. By strengthening the bonds of community and of knowledge of locality, a greater spirit of *dinnseanchas* would reduce a society's tolerance of inequality. Ní Dhomhnaill makes the following case: '*Dinnseanchas* ... can also become a way of uniting factions, of breaking barriers – the stories, the *dinnseanchas* were a material held in common, and were the cement that kept the community together and distinct.'[53]

---

51   Wilkinson and Pickett, *The Spirit Level*, 267.
52   Ibid., 81.
53   Frawley, *Nuala Ní Dhomhnaill: Selected Essays*, 40–42.

More Balanced Approach to GDP and Economic Growth

The Great Recession of 2008 and the resulting years of austerity soon followed by the COVID pandemic has meant that politicians of all parties are desperately searching for a way back to 'normal' economic growth. But long before the recession there was a growing chorus of dissent about the wisdom of the single-minded pursuit of economic growth. If the main ideological battles of the twentieth century were between competing theories of how to maximise growth, it looks like the main ideological battles of the twenty-first century will be between those who want a quick return to economic growth and those who question the wisdom and practicality of such growth.

There has been a renewed focus of attention on limiting economic growth since concerns about the environment began to surface leading to speculation that humans can flourish and at the same time consume less. A 'nascent disaffection with consumerism' has been noted, leading some commentators to speculate that we may be at the beginning of a new creative age. Leadbeter (2009) has analysed how the internet could change society by unleashing a wave of creative potential; by expanding the possibility for intellectual discovery, personal growth and making a contribution that is valued by others, the new technology could reduce the importance currently attached to consumption: 'In the 20th century almost everyone in the industrialized world was a worker and a consumer in the mass production economy: a worker by day for a wage, a consumer at night and at the weekends. By the end of the 21st century our grandchildren are more likely to see themselves as participants, contributors and innovators.'[54]

This could be accelerated by the realisation that more people in society will be faced with the prospect of a hundred-year life, and that one of the most important roles for government in the future will be to provide continuous education for a population who will be engaging in multiple careers rather than providing for continuous increases in gross national product.

---

54   Charlie Leadbeater, *We-Think: Mass Innovation, not Mass Production* (London: Profile Books, 2009), 231.

It could be argued that we have seen all this before. The great Victorian critics like John Ruskin and J. S. Mill were making very similar points in the nineteenth century. In his *Principles of Political Economy* (1848), Mill was even advocating a 'stationary state', one without economic growth. However, the notion of 'de-growth', although being widely discussed at the moment, is likely to be practically and certainly politically impossible in the immediate future. Mill's 'stationary state' never materialised, but doubts about our obsession with economic growth are gathering pace. However, recent questioning of what exactly we are measuring when referring to growth is likely to become more urgent.

Richard Easterlin's 1974 paper *Does Economic Growth Improve the Human Lot?* advanced the view that, having attained a certain level of income, people don't feel any better or happier.[55] Critics were quick to point out that it's not the absolute level of income or wealth people obsess about, it's their level compared to other people's, especially their close relatives and friends. However, the paper spurred a number of attempts to come up with more realistic measures of human progress, and a variety of new indices have been proposed in the last twenty-five years, ranging from the Human Development Index with input from Nobel Prize-winning expert Amartya Sen to the OECD's Better Life Index.

One of the most provocative discussions of this subject was David Pilling's *The Growth Delusion*,[56] in which the award-winning journalist began by saying that after twenty-five years of reporting for the *Financial Times* from five continents he had reached the conclusion that 'seeing everything through the prism of economic growth was distorting our view of what is important'. He makes a compelling case that GDP was never an objective measure of economic reality in any country, and that it presents an even more distorted view in a digital age as we progress from 'an economy based on manufacturing to services to an ethereal and unaccountable present'.[57] He reviews attempts at developing more accurate indices, finding

---

55 Richard Easterlin, 'Does Economic Growth Improve the Human Lot?' in Paul A. David and Melvin W. Reder, eds, *Nations and Households in Economic Growth* (Salt Lake City: Academic Press US, 1974), 89–125.
56 David Pilling, *The Growth Delusion* (London: Bloomsbury, 2018), 14.
57 Ibid., 92.

none of them entirely satisfactory, and concludes that we need to be very sceptical about what GDP is capable of measuring today, and therefore broaden the conversation to encompass a much wider range of measures which would provide some indication of a country's progress. This might result in placing less emphasis on the limited and crude type of growth we are currently pursuing.

Ireland's Investment in Dinnseanachas

It has now been argued that a reduction in our continuing dependence on overseas investment for business development and a reduction in our dependence on economic growth per se would be facilitated by a greater understanding of our history, heritage and culture. There is some evidence to suggest that this understanding has been weakened since the second revival, as market forces penetrated more deeply into every area of our lives. The heightened consciousness of history, heritage and culture that are required to protect communities from the exigencies of everyday life and which characterised the first and second revivals are far less prevalent today. Gray has warned of the way a single-minded pursuit of economic growth threatens our shared understanding of the past:

> By imposing on people a regime of incessant change and permanent revolution, unencumbered market institutions deplete the stock of historical memory ... which disrupts, or empties of the significance the narratives in terms of which people make sense of their lives.[58]

Eyskens has made an impressive analysis of the problems facing the educational system in an era of information overload, arguing that the average citizen now understands an ever-smaller part of the reality that surrounds them, resulting in a distorted view of that reality. His solution is to equip

---

58   John Gray, *Enlightenment's Wake*, 160.

everyone with a basic grounding in history and philosophy in order to cultivate a spirit of synthesis:

> Our education system in the past has planted too many exclamation marks and too few question marks ... the truth emerges from questioning and enquiry ... ideally, we need to study the philosophy of civilizations or cultural philosophy ... in which the history of the great civilizations would be used for discussing the great existential questions of mankind.[59]

It is therefore encouraging to note recently circulated proposals from the National Council for Curriculum Development for the addition of a Politics and Society Syllabus, designed to promote social cohesion (and help in the growth of civic republicanism) by studying a wide range of philosophical ideas from the ancient Greeks to the present day. This seems to be very close to what Eyskens was proposing, but it would be strengthened by a parallel module on Irish Studies designed to correct some of the deficiencies identified above by Kinsella and by Bradley and Kennelly.

Some form of renewal will be required to re-connect people with their history, heritage and culture. Gray argues that societies which will thrive in the future will be those who succeed in combining liberal traditions with a common national culture, and who come to terms with the danger of what he refers to as 'the incessant change demanded and promoted by market forces' which 'nullifies the significance of precedent and destroys the authority of the past'.[60] The most obvious way to re-establish the authority of the past would be the inclusion of an obligatory Irish Studies module in the education curriculum. Combined with the Politics and Society Syllabus already under consideration, it would equip the next generation with a greater sense of continuity with the past, which in turn would equip us better to cope with the future:

---

59   Mark Eyskens, 'Idea for a University in the 21st Century', 1999, <http://www.eyskens.com/page103/page132/page134/page137/page137.html>, accessed 11 November 2021.

60   Gray, *Enlightenment's Wake*, 160.

> A fundamental principle of sustainability is that no part of the system exists independently of any other part. Cultural capital therefore makes a contribution similar to that of natural capital. Just as neglect, overuse, disregard or under-investment of natural capital can lead to an ecosystem breakdown, so too with cultural capital. A failure to sustain the cultural values that provide individuals with a sense of identity and meaning in their lives can lead to loss of well-being and economic output. The heart of an innovative culture is really a frame of mind or way of thinking rather than the discovery of new knowledge.[61]

As we approach the end of the first quarter of the twenty-first century, Ireland, in common with other smaller European countries, faces a number of strategic options. The first is the degree to which the single-minded pursuit of economic growth should be the sole determinant of the nation's performance, partly in view of environmental and sustainability concerns, but also because of increasing concerns about the ability of material prosperity on its own to ensure the well-being of a nation's citizens and their capacity to flourish.

The second strategic issue concerns Ireland's level of engagement with the rest of the world. Here this book argues for an enhanced curiosity and learning from what the best of the world has to offer, combined with increasing emphasis on Ireland's own economic resources based on a renewed engagement with the country's history, heritage and culture. Martin McLoone, discussing identity and media in Ireland, summarised this latter point in the following terms:

> The challenge, then, is quite clear. It is not to surrender abjectly to the universal culture driven by market forces, nor to pursue a national essence through narrow and restrictive policy, but to seek out a third way, contingent upon releasing the submerged experiences of diverse social communities.[62]

---

61 Finbarr Bradley, 'Defining Education in the Engaged University', in Lorraine McIlrath, Alison Farrell, Jean Hughes, Seamus Lillis and Ann Lyons, *Mapping Civic Education with Higher Education in Ireland* (Dublin: All Ireland Society for Higher Education and Campus Engage, 2009), 53.

62 Martin McLoone, ed., *Culture, Identity and Broadcasting in Ireland: Local Issues, Global Perspectives* (Belfast: Queen's University of Belfast, 1991), 25.

Bibliography

Acton, Charles, 'Obituary for Seán Ó Riada', in Bernard Harris and Grattan Freyer, eds, *The Achievement of Seán Ó Riada* (Ballina: The Irish Humanities Centre and Keohanes Ltd Ballina, 1981), pp. 161–164.
Andrews, Elmer, ed., *Contemporary Irish Poetry: A Collection of Critical Essays* (New York: Macmillan, 1992).
Applebaum, Anne, *The Twilight of Democracy* (London: Allen Lane, 2020).
Arkins, Brian, 'Introduction', in Toner Quinn, ed., *Desmond Fennell: His Life and Work* (Dublin: Veritas Publications, 2001), pp. 11–19.
Ash, Timothy Garton, 'The Future of Liberalism', *Prospect Magazine* (9 December 2020).
Banville, John, 'The Island of de Valera and O'Faolain', *The Irish Review* 17/18 Winter (1995), pp. 142–152
_____, 'Review of Roberto Calasso's The Unnameable Present', *Financial Times* (28 September 2019).
Barrington, Donal, Interview with author, 9 April 2009.
Barry, Frank, *The Celtic Tiger: Delayed Convergence or Regional Boom. ESRI Quarterly Commentary* (Summer 2002).
Bauman, Zygmunt, *Liquid Modernity* (Cambridge: Polity Press, 2000).
Beck, Ulrich, *The Risk Society* (New York: Sage Publications, 1992).
_____, *What is Globalisation?* (Cambridge: Polity Press, 2000).
Berman, Marshall, *All that is Solid Melts into Air: The Experience of Modernity* (London: Verso, 1983).
Bhreathnach-Lynch, Síghle, *Ireland's Art, Ireland's History: Representing History 1845 to Present* (Omaha: Creighton University Press, 2007).
Birch, David, *The Job Generation Process* (1979). University of Illinois at Urbana-Champaign's Academy for Entrepreneurial Leadership Historical Research Reference in Entrepreneurship, Available at: <https://ssrn.com/abstract=1510007>, accessed 11 November 2021.
Black, Cathal, *Korea* (Dublin: Cathal Black Films Ltd, 1995).
Bodley, Seoirse, 'The original Compositions: An Assessment', in Bernard Harris and Grattan Freyer, eds, *The Achievement of Seán Ó Riada* (Ballina: The Irish Humanities Centre and Keohanes Ltd Ballina, 1981), pp. 30–40.
Booth, Michael, *The Almost Nearly Perfect People: The Truth About the Nordic Miracle* (London: Jonathan Cape, 2014).

Bradley, Finbarr, Interview with author, 28 January 2009.

———, and Kennelly, James J., *Capitalising on Culture, Competing on Difference* (Dublin: Blackhall, 2008).

———, 'Defining Education in the Engaged University', in Lorraine McIlrath, Alison Farrell, Jean Hughes, Seamus Lillis and Ann Lyons, *Mapping Civic Education with Higher Education in Ireland* (Dublin: All Ireland Society for Higher Education and Campus Engage, 2009).

Brown, Terence, *Ireland: A Social and Cultural History 1922–2002* (New York: Harper Perennial, revised edition, 2004).

Cable, Vince, *The World's New Fissures* (London: Demos, 1994).

Carney, Mark, *Value(s)* (Glasgow: William Collins, 2021).

Casey, Michael, 'Fear and Cultural Quirks to Blame for Ireland's Lack of Enterprise', *The Irish Times* (23 May 2006).

Castells, Manuel, *The Rise of the Network Society* (Oxford: Blackwell, 1996).

Cerny, Philip, 'Reconstructing the Political in a Globalising World', in Buelens, Frans, ed., *Globalisation and the Nation State* (London: Edward Elgar, 1999), pp. 89–138.

Cleary, J. 2007. *Outrageous Fortune: Capital and Culture in Modern Ireland* (Dublin: Field Day Publications, 2007).

———, and Connolly, Claire, eds, *The Cambridge Companion to Modern Irish Culture* (Cambridge: Cambridge University Press, 2005).

Collier, Paul, *The Future of Capitalism: Facing the New Anxieties* (London: Allen Lane, 2018).

Cooney, John, *John Charles McQuaid: Ruler of Catholic Ireland* (Dublin: O'Brien Press, 1999).

Corcoran, Mary, *Uncertain Ireland: Irish Sociological Chronicles 5* (Dublin: IPA Publications, 2004).

———, and Share, Perry, 'Introduction', *Belongings: Shaping Identities in Modern Ireland, Irish Sociological Chronicles 6* (Dublin: IPA publications, 2008), pp. 1–16.

Corkery, Daniel, *Synge and the Anglo-Irish Literature* (Cork: Cork University Press, 1947).

Crossan, Seán, 'The Given Note: Traditional Music, Crisis and the Poetry of Seamus Heaney', in Anne Karhio, Seán Crossan and Charles I. Armstrong, eds, *Crisis and Contemporary Poetry* (London: Palgrave Macmillan, 2008).

Crotty, Raymond D., *Ireland in Crisis: A Study in Capitalist Colonial Undevelopment* (Cork: Bandon Books, 1986).

Cowen, Tyler, *Creative Destruction: How Globalization is Changing the World's Cultures* (Princeton: Princeton University Press, 2002).

———, 'Modern Mix', *Forbes Global Magazine* (28 April 2003).

Cox, Tom, *The Making of Managers: A History of the IMI 1952–2002* (Oxford: Oak Tree Press, 2002).
Cromien, Seán, *History of the Murphies.* Unpublished correspondence (2005).
Crowley, Ethel, 'Finding Myself at the Cultural Crossroads: An Interview with Mícheál Ó Súilleabháin', in Ethel Crowley and Jim MacLoughlin, eds, *Under the Belly of the Tiger: Class, Race, Identity, and Culture in the Global Ireland* (Dublin: Irish Reporter Publications, 1997), pp. 125–138.
Cunningham, Tony, Interview with author, 10 February 2009.
Dawe, Gerald, *Against Piety: Essays in Irish Poetry* (Derry: Lagan Press, 1995).
De Fréine, Seán, *The Great Silence* (Cork: Mercier Press, 1965).
Denman, Peter 'Significant Element: Songs of the Psyche and Her Vertical Smile', *Irish University Review* 31/1 (Spring / Summer 2001), pp. 95–109.
De Paor, Liam, 'Ireland's Identities', *The Crane Bag* 3/1 (The Question of Tradition: 1979), pp. 22–29.
Dilliard, Irving, ed., *Mr. Justice Brandeis, Great American: Press Opinion and Public Approval* (Saint Louis: Modern View Press, 1941).
Dorgan, Seán, 'Introduction to Public Service 2022', in Mark Callanan, ed., *Ireland 2022: Towards One Hundred Years of Self-Government* (Dublin: IPA Publications, 2007), pp. 1–5.
Douglas, Ian R., 'Globalisation and the Retreat of the State', in B. K. Gills, ed., *Globalisation and the Politics of Resistance* (London: Palgrave Books, 2000), pp. 110–132.
Douthat, Ross, *The Decadent Society: How We Became the Victims of Our Own Success* (New York: Avid Reader Press, 2020).
Dowling, Michele, 'The Ireland that I Would Have: De Valera and the Creation of an Irish National Image', *History Ireland* 2/5 (Summer 1997), pp. 37–41.
Dunne, J. 'Citizenship and Education: A Crisis in the Republic', in Peadar Kirby, Luke Gibbons, and Michael Cronin, eds, *Reinventing Ireland: Culture, Society, and the Global Economy* (London: Pluto Press, 2002), pp. 69–88.
Easterlin, Richard, 'Does Economic Growth Improve the Human Lot?' in Paul A. David and Melvin W. Reder, eds, *Nations and Households in Economic Growth* (Salt Lake City: Academic Press US, 1974), pp. 89–125.
Eyskens, Mark, 'Idea for a University in the 21st Century' (1999) <http://www.eyskens.com/page103/page132/page134/page137/page137.html>, accessed 11 November 2021.
Fahey, Tony, 'How Do We Feel?: Economic Boom and Happiness', in Tony Fahey, Helen Russell, Christopher T. Whelan, eds, *The Best of Times?* (Dublin: IPA Publications, 2007), pp. 11–26.
Fallon, Brian, *An Age of Innocence: Irish Culture, 1930–1960* (Dublin: Gill & Macmillan, 1998).

Fanning, Bryan, *The Quest for Modern Ireland: The Battle for Ideas 1912–1986* (Newbridge: Irish Academic Press, 2008).
Fanning, John, 'Brand Ireland should be Rethought and Replaced', *The Irish Times* (27 February 2012).
Fanning, Ronan, 'The Genesis of Economic Development', in J. C. B. Mc Carthy, ed., *Planning Ireland's Future: The Legacy of T. K. Whitaker* (Dublin: Glendale Press, 1990), pp. 74–111.
_____, Article in *The University Observer* (8 February 2005), 3.
Fennell, Desmond, *The State of the Nation: Ireland Since the Sixties* (Dublin: Ward River Press, 1983).
_____, *Heresy: The Battle for Ideas in Modern Ireland* (Newtownards: Blackstaff Press, 1993).
Ferriter, Diarmaid, *The Transformation of Ireland 1900–2000* (London: Profile Books, 2004).
Finn, Tomás, *The Influence of Tuairim on Intellectual Debate and Policy Formation in Ireland 1954–1975*, PhD dissertation: NUI Galway, December 2008.
FitzGerald, Garret, *State-Sponsored Bodies* (Dublin: IPA Publications, 1961).
_____, *Planning in Ireland* (Dublin: IPA Publications, 1968).
_____, 'Grey, White and Blue: A Review of Three Recent Economic Publications', in Basil Chubb and Patrick Lynch, eds, *Economic Development and Planning* (Dublin: IPA Publications, 1969), pp. 118–271.
_____, Interview with author, 9 September 2009.
Fitzsimons, Andrew, 'Interview with Thomas Kinsella', *Journal of Irish Studies* 19 (2004), pp. 71–82.
_____, 'The Sea of Disappointment: Thomas Kinsella's "Nightwalker" and the New Ireland', *Irish University Review* 36/2 (Autumn/Winter 2006), pp. 335–352.
_____, *The Sea of Disappointment* (Dublin: University College Dublin Press, 2008).
Flanagan, Ian, Interview with Thomas Kinsella, *Metre* 2 (Spring 1997), pp. 108–115.
Florida, Richard, *The Rise of the Creative Class* (New York: Basic Books, 2012).
Foster, R., *The Apprentice Mage, 1865–1914: W. B. Yeats: A Life, Vol. 1* (Oxford: Oxford University Press, 1997).
Frawley, Oona, ed., *Nuala Ní Dhomhnaill: Selected Essays* (Dublin: New Ireland, 2005).
Friedman, Thomas L., *The Lexus and the Olive Tree* (London: Harper Collins, 1999).
_____, 'Op-Ed article', *New York Times* (3 August 2001).
Garvin, Tom, *Preventing the Future: Why Ireland was Poor for so Long* (Dublin: Gill & Macmillan, 2004).
Geertz, Clifford, *The Interpretation of Culture* (London: Fontana Press, 1993).
Geoghegan, Peter, *Democracy for Sale: Dark Money and Dirty Politics* (London: Head of Zeus, 2020).

Goodby, John, *Irish Poetry Since 1950* (Manchester: Manchester University Press, 2000).
Gray, John, *False Dawn: The Delusions of Global Capitalism* (London: Granta Books, 1999).
_____, *Black Mass: Apocalyptic Religion and the Death of Utopia* (London: Penguin, 2007a).
_____, *Enlightenment's Wake: Politics and Culture at the Close of the Modern Age* (Oxfordshire: Routledge Classics, 2007b).
Grene, Nicholas, *The Politics of Irish Drama* (Cambridge: Cambridge University Press, 1999).
Haffenden, John, *Viewpoint: Poets in Conversation with John Haffenden* (London: Faber & Faber, 1981).
Harari, Yuval Noah, 'The World after Coronavirus', *Financial Times* (20 March 2020).
Harman, Sidney, *Mind Your Own Business: A Maverick's Guide to Business, Leadership and Life* (New York: Crown Business/Currancy Doubleday, 2003).
Heaney, Seamus, *Opened Ground: Poems 1966–1996* (London: Faber & Faber, 1998).
Heath, Joseph, and Potter, Andrew, *Rebel Sell: Why the Culture Can't be Jammed* (Oxford: Capstone, 2005).
Henderson, Rebecca, *Re-imagining Capitalism in a World on Fire* (New York: Public Affairs, 2020).
Henry, Mark, *In Fact: An Optimist's Guide to Ireland at 100* (Dublin: Gill Books, 2021).
Hirst, Paul, and Thompson, Grahame, 'The Tyranny of Globalisation: Myth or Reality?', in Frans Buelens, ed., *Globalisation and the Nation State* (Cheltenham: Edward Elgar, 1999), pp. 139–178.
Honohan, Iseult, *Civic Republicanism* (Oxfordshire: Routledge, 2002).
Honohan, Patrick, *Currency, Credit and Crisis: Central Banking in Ireland and Europe* (Cambridge: Cambridge University Press, 2019).
Hutton, Will, 'Value(s) by Mark Carney review – call for a new kind of economics', *The Observer* (21 March 2021).
Inglis, Tom, *Global Ireland: Same Difference* (Oxfordshire: Routledge, 2008).
Jackson, Thomas, *The Whole Matter* (Dublin: Lilliput Press, 1995).
Jacobi, Jolande, *The Psychology of C. J. Jung* (New Haven: Yale University Press, 1973).
Jameson, Frederic, 'Globalisation and Strategy', *New Left Review* 4 (July/August 2000), pp. 49–68.
John, Brian, 'Imaginative Bedrock: Kinsella's One and the Lebor Gabála Érenn', *Éire-Ireland* 20 (Spring 1985), pp. 109–132.
Johnson, Dillon, *Irish Poetry after Joyce* (Notre Dame: University of Notre Dame Press, 1985).

Jones, E. L., 'The Revival of Cultural Explanation in Economics,' *Economic Affairs* 23/4 (2003), pp. 7–13.
Jung, Carl, *Modern Man in Search of a Soul* (London: Routledge Classics, 2001).
Kay, John, *How Markets Work* (London: Penguin Books, 2003).
_____, *The Truth about Markets* (London: Penguin, 2004).
Kavanagh, Patrick, *Collected Poetry* (London: Allen Lane, 2004).
Kenny, Ivor, *In Good Company: Conversations with Irish Leaders* (Dublin: Gill & Macmillan, 1987).
Kearney, Richard, 'Myth and Modernity in Irish Poetry', in Elmer Andrews, ed., *Contemporary Irish Poetry* (London: Macmillan, 1992), pp. 41–62.
_____, *The Irish Mind* (Dublin: Wolfhound Press, 1985).
_____, 'Where I Speak from: A Short Intellectual Autobiography', in Daniël P. Veldsman and Yolande Steenkamp, eds, *Debating Otherness with Richard Kearney: Perspectives from South Africa* (Cape Town: AOSIS, 2018), pp. 39–42.
Kelly, Ronan, *Bard of Erin: The Life of Thomas Moore* (Dublin: Penguin Ireland, 2008).
Keohane, Kieran, 'The Best of Times and Worst of Times', *The Irish Review* 38 (2008), pp. 118–132.
Kiberd, Declan, *Inventing Ireland* (London: Jonathan Cape, 1995).
_____, *Irish Classics* (London: Granta Books, 2000).
King, Philip, Interview with the author, 1 April 2007.
Kinsella, Stephen, 'Economic and Fiscal Policy', in William K. Roche, Philip J. O'Connell, and Andrea Prothero, eds, *Austerity & Recovery in Ireland: Europe's Poster Child and the Great Recession* (Oxford: Oxford University Press, 2017), pp. 40–61.
Kinsella, Thomas, 'The Irish Writer', *Éire-Ireland* (Summer 1967), pp. 8–15.
_____, 'The Divided Mind', in Seán Lucy, ed., *Irish Poets in English* (Cork: Mercier Press, 1973), pp. 208–218.
_____, *Fifteen Dead* (Dublin: Dolmen Press/Oxford University Press, 1979).
_____, 'Introduction', in Thomas Kinsella and Tomás Ó Canainn, eds, *Our Musical Heritage* (Dublin: Dolmen Press, 1982), pp. 9–12.
_____, ed., *The New Oxford Book of Irish Verse* (Oxford: Oxford University Press, 1986).
_____, *The Dual Tradition: An Essay on Poetry and Politics in Ireland* (Manchester: Carcanet, 1995).
_____, *Collected Poems 1956–2001* (Manchester: Carcanet Press, 2001).
_____, *Collected Poems* (Winston-Salem: Wake Forest University Press, 2006a).
_____, *A Dublin Documentary* (Dublin: O'Brien Press, 2006b).
_____, *Belief and Unbelief: Peppercanister 27* (Dublin: Dedalus Press, 2007).
_____, *Prose Occasions 1951–2006* (Manchester: Carcanet, 2009).

_____, *Late Poems* (Manchester: Carcanet, 2011), 62.
Kirby, Peadar, *The Celtic Tiger in Distress: Growth with Inequality in Ireland* (London: Palgrave, 2002).
_____, 'The Best of Times or Besting the Critics? The ESRI on the Social Impact of the Celtic Tiger', *Administration* 55/3 (2008), pp. 171–190.
Krastev, Ivan, and Holmes, Stephen, *The Light that Failed: A Reckoning* (London: Allen Lane, 2019).
Kuhling, Carmen and Keohane, Kieran, *Ireland Unbound: A Turn of the Century Chronicle: Irish Sociological Chronicles 5* (Dublin: IPA Publications, 2006).
Laffan, Brigid, 'International Actors and Agencies', in William K. Roche, Philip J. O' Connell, and Andrea Prothero, eds, *Austerity & Recovery in Ireland: Europe's Poster Child and the Great Recession* (Oxford: Oxford University Press, 2017), pp. 177–193.
Leadbeater, Charlie, *We-Think: Mass Innovation, not Mass Production* (London: Profile Books, 2009).
Lee, Joseph J., 'Society and Culture', in Frank Litton, ed., *Unequal Achievement: The Irish Experience 1957–1982* (Dublin: IPA Publications, 1982), pp. 201–218.
_____, *Ireland 1912–1985*: Politics and Society (Cambridge: Cambridge University Press, 1989).
Leerssen, Joep, *Mere Irish and Fíor-Ghael: Studies in the Idea of Irish Nationality, Its Development and Literary Expression prior to the Nineteenth Century* (Cork: Cork University Press, 1996).
Lilla, Mark, *The Once and Future Liberal: After Identity Politics* (New York: Harper Collins, 2017).
Liston, Jerry, Interview with the author, 11 February 2007.
Lockhart, Jim, Interview with the author, 8 November 2007.
Lynch, Kathleen, Cantillon, Sara, and Crean, Margaret, 'Inequality', in William K. Roche, Philip J. O' Connell, and Andrea Prothero, eds, *Austerity & Recovery in Ireland: Europe's Poster Child and the Great Recession* (Oxford: Oxford University Press, 2017), pp. 252–271.
Lynch, Patrick, 'The Economist and Public Policy', *Studies: An Irish Quarterly Review* 42/167 (Autumn 1953), pp. 241–274.
Lyons, F. S. L., *Ireland Since the Famine* (London: Fontana Press, 1973).
Maalouf, Amin, *On Identity* (London: Harvill Panther, 2000).
MacSharry, Ray, and White, Patrick, *The Making of the Celtic Tiger: The Inside Story of Ireland's Boom Economy* (Cork: Mercier Press, 2000).
Magee, Bryan, *The Story of Philosophy* (London: Dorling-Kindersley, 1998).
Mahon, Derek, *Against the Clock* (Oldcastle: Gallery Press, 2018).
Maignant, Catherine, 'The Global Irish Spirit', in Eamon Maher, ed., *Cultural Perspectives on Globalisation and Ireland* (Bern: Peter Lang, 2009), pp. 31–51.

Marcus, Louis, 'Seán Ó Riada and the Ireland of the Sixties', in Bernard Harris and Grattan Freyer, eds, *The Achievement of Seán Ó Riada* (Ballina: The Irish Humanities Centre and Keohanes Ltd Ballina, 1981), pp. 64–71.

Mathews, P. J., *Revival: The Abbey Theatre, Sinn Féin, the Gaelic League and the Co-Operative Movement* (Cork: Cork University Press/Field Day Publications, 2003).

Mayer, Colin, *Prosperity: Better Business Makes the Greater Good* (Oxford: Oxford University Press, 2018).

Mays, Michael, 'Irish Identity in an Age of Globalisation', *Irish Studies Review* 13/1 (2005), pp. 3–12.

Mazarr, Michael J., *Global Trends 2005: An Owner's Manual for the Next Decade* (London: Macmillan, 1999).

McCarthy, Marie Frances, *Passing it On: Music and Irish Culture* (Cork: Cork University Press, 1999).

McElhaney, Alicia 'Larry Fink to CEOs: Contribute to Society or Lose BlackRock's Investment', *Institutional Investor* (16 January 2018).

McGowan, Kieran, Interview with author, 9 September 2009.

McLoone, Martin, ed., *Culture, Identity and Broadcasting in Ireland: Local Issues, Global Perspectives* (Belfast: Queen's University of Belfast, 1991).

Midgley, David, ed., *The Essential Mary Midgley* (Oxfordshire: Routledge, 2005).

Miller, Kerby A., *Emigrants and Exiles: Ireland and the Irish Exodus to North America* (Oxford: Oxford University Press, 1985).

_____, 'Emigration, Capitalism and Ideology in Post-Famine Ireland', in Richard Kearney, ed., *Migrations: The Irish at Home and Abroad* (Dublin: Wolfhound Press, 1990), pp. 91–108.

Moïsi, Dominique, 'A Global Downturn in the Power of the West', *Financial Times* (5 October 2008).

Montague, John, *The Rough Field* (Dublin: Claddagh Records, 2003).

_____, *The Pear is Ripe: A Memoir* (Dublin: Liberties Press, 2007).

_____, *New Collected Poems* (Loughcrew: Gallery Press, 2012).

Morrison, George, 'Film Making', in Bernard Harris and Grattan Freyer, eds, *The Achievement of Seán Ó Riada* (Ballina: The Irish Humanities Centre and Keohanes Ltd Ballina, 1981), pp. 64–71.

Mounk, Yascha, *The People Versus Democracy* (Cambridge: Harvard University Press, 2017).

Moynihan, Maurice, *Éamon De Valera: Speeches and Statements, 1917–1973* (Dublin: Gill & Macmillan, 1980).

Murphy, John A., *Ireland in the Twentieth Century* (Dublin: Gill & Macmillan, 1975).

Mjøset, Lars, *The Irish Economy in a Contemporary Institutional Perspective* (Dublin: NESC Report, 1992).

Neville, Grace, 'In at the Death: The French Press and the Celtic Tiger', in Eamon Maher, ed., *Cultural Perspectives on Globalisation and Ireland* (Bern: Peter Lang, 2009), pp. 53–66.

Nolan, Brian, O'Connell, Philip J., and Whelan, Christopher T., eds, *Bust to Boom? The Irish Experience of Growth and Inequality* (Dublin: IPA Publications, 2000).

Nye, Joseph, *Soft Power: The Means to Success in World Politics* (New York: Public Affairs US).

O'Brien, Dan, 'Covid-19 Has Brought Out the Inner Catastrophist in Our National Psyche', *Sunday Business Post* (24 October 2021), p. 27.

O'Brien, John A., *The Vanishing Irish: The Enigma of the Modern World* (London: W. H. Allen, 1954).

O'Callaghan, Margaret, 'Language, Nationality and Cultural Identity in the Irish Free State: 1922–1927', *Irish Historical Studies* 24/94 (November 1984), pp. 226–245.

O'Connell, Micheal, *Changed Utterly: Ireland and the New Irish Psyche* (Dublin: The Liffey Press, 2001a).

———, *Right-Wing Ireland?: The Rise of Populism in Ireland and Europe* (Dublin: Liffey Press, 2001b),

O'Connor, Nuala, *Bringing it All Back Home: The Influence of Irish Music* (London: BBC Books, 1991).

O'Connor, Sarah, '"We are drowning in insecurity": Young People and Life after the Pandemic', *Financial Times*, 25 April 2021.

O'Driscoll, Dennis, *Stepping Stones: Interviews with Seamus Heaney* (London: Faber & Faber, 2008).

O'Driscoll, Robert, 'Foundations of the Literary and Musical Revival', in Cyril J. Byrne and Margaret Harry, eds, *Talamh an Éisc: Canadian and Irish Essays* (Halifax: Nimbus Publications, 1986), pp. 48–70.

Ó Gráda, Cormac, *A Rocky Road: The Irish Economy since the 1920s* (Manchester: Manchester University Press, 1997).

O'Grady, Desmond, *The Headgear of the Tribe* (Oldcastle: Gallery Press, 1979).

O'Hearn, Denis, *Inside the Celtic Tiger: The Irish Economy and the Asian Model* (London: Pluto Press, 1998).

Ohmae, Kenichi, *The Borderless World: Power and Strategy in the Interlinked Economy* (New York: Harper Business, 1999).

Ó Laoire, Lillis, 'Irish Music', in Joe Cleary, ed., *The Cambridge Companion to Modern Irish Culture* (Cambridge: Cambridge University Press, 2005).

O'Leary, Naomi, 'The myth of the citizens' assembly', *Politico* (2019) <https://www.politico.eu/article/the-myth-of-the-citizens-assembly-democracy/>

Ó Mordha, Seán, *One Fond Embrace* (London: British Broadcasting Corporation, 1991).

Ó Riada, Seán, 'Our Musical Heritage', in Thomas Kinsella and Tomás Ó Canainn, eds, *Our Musical Heritage* (Dublin: Funduireacht an Riadigh in association with Dolman Press, 1982), pp. 19–81

Ó Riain, Seán, 'The Road to Austerity', in William K. Roche, Philip J. O' Connell, and Andrea Prothero, eds, *Austerity & Recovery in Ireland: Europe's Poster Child and the Great Recession* (Oxford: Oxford University Press, 2017), pp. 23–39.

O'Rourke, Kevin, and Ó Gráda, Cormac, 'The Irish Economy during the Century after Partition', *Economic History Review*, forthcoming.

Ord, Toby, *The Precipice: Existential Risk and the Future of Humanity* (London: Bloomsbury, 2020).

O'Sullivan, Michael, *Ireland and the Global Question* (Cork: Cork University Press, 2006).

_____, 'We Need a Political System that Encourages Strategic Thinking', *The Irish Times* (14 April 2009).

O'Sullivan, Denis, *Cultural Politics and Irish Education since the 1950s* (Dublin: IPA Publications, 2005).

O'Toole, Fintan, 'A Proud Nation that We are Happy to Share', *The Irish Times* (13 November 2021).

Pilling, David, *The Growth Delusion* (London: Bloomsbury, 2018).

Pink, Daniel, *A Whole New Mind: Why Right-Brainers will Rule the Future* (New York: Riverhead Books, 2006).

Porter, Michael E., *The Competitive Advantage of Nations* (London: Macmillan, 1990).

Quinn, Lochlann, Interview with author, 22 November 2006.

Reiz, Scott, 'Tradition and Imagery: Irish Traditional Music and the Celtic Phenomenon', in Martin Stokes and Philip V. Bohlman, eds, *Celtic Music: Music at the Global Fringe* (Lanham, MD: Scarecrow Press, 2003).

Robertson Roland, *Globalisation: Social Theory and Global Culture* (Thousand Oaks, CA: Sage, 1992).

Roche, William K., O'Connell, Philip J., and Prothero, Andrea, 'Introduction: "Poster Child" or "Beautiful Freak?"', in William K. Roche, Philip J. O' Connell, and Andrea Prothero, *Austerity & Recovery in Ireland: Europe's Poster Child and the Great Recession* (Oxford: Oxford University Press, 2017), pp. 1–22.

Rosenberg, Carolyn A., *Let Our Gaze Blaze: The Recent Poetry of Thomas Kinsella*, unpublished doctoral dissertation: Kent State University Graduate College, 1980.

Ruane, Frances, 'Resonances from Economic Development for Current Economic Policy-Making', Paper given at IPA Conference: *Economic Development 50 Years On*. Dublin Castle, November 2008.

Russell, Bertrand, *A History of Western Philosophy* (Oxfordshire: Routledge Classics, 2004).

Schubert, Carlos Buhigas and Martens, Hans, *The Nordic Model: A Recipe for European Success? Europan Policy Centre Working Paper* 20, 2005.
Scruton, Roger, *Modern Culture* (London: Continuum Books, 1998).
Shapiro, Robert, *Futurecast: 2020: A Global Vision of Tomorrow* (London: Profile Books, 2008).
Smith, Anthony D., *Nations and Nationalism in a Global Era* (Cambridge: Polity Press, 1995).
———, *Historiographical Debates about Ethnicity and Nationalism* (Cambridge: Polity Press, 2000).
Smith, Michael, 'Interview with Thomas Kinsella', *Poetry Ireland Review* 75 (2002), pp. 108–119, <http://www.jstor.org/stable/25580094>, accessed 11 November 2021.
Smyth, Gerry, *Noisy Island: A Short History of Irish Popular Music* (Cork: Cork University Press, 2005).
Stokes, Martin, ed., *Ethnicity, Identity and Music* (Oxford: Berg Publishers, 1997).
Steger, Manfred B., *Globalisation: A Very Short Introduction* (Oxford: Oxford University Press, 2013).
Stevens, Anthony, *Jung: A Very Short Introduction* (Oxford: Oxford University Press, 1994).
Stiglitz, Joseph, *Power, People and Profit: Progressive Capitalism for an Age of Discontent* (London: Penguin, 2019).
Sweeney, Paul, *The Celtic Tiger: Ireland's Continuing Economic Miracle.* 2nd edn (Oxford: Oak Tree Press, 1999).
Tansey, Paul, *Ireland at Work* (Oxford: Oak Tree Press, 1998).
TASC Report, *Inequality in Ireland Today* (Dublin: TASC publications, 2018).
Terry Eagleton, 'A Row of Shaws', *London Review of Books* (21 June 2018).
Tomlinson, John, *Globalisation and Culture* (Cambridge: Polity Press, 1999).
Tonnies, Ferdinand, *Community and Association,* Trans. C. P. Loomis. (London: Routledge & Keegan Paul, 1957).
Tubridy, Derval, *Thomas Kinsella: The Peppercanister Poems* (Dublin: University College Dublin Press, 2001).
Tunstall, Jeremy, *Media are American* (Columbia: Columbia University Press, 1977).
Vallely, Fintan, 'The Apollos of Shamrockery: Traditional Music in the Modern Age', in Martin Stokes and Philip V. Bohlman, eds, *Celtic Music: Music at the Global Fringe* (Lanham, MD: Scarecrow Press, 2003), pp. 201–218.
Victory, Gerald, 'Ó Riada on Radio', in Bernard Harris and Grattan Freyer, eds, *The Achievement of Seán Ó Riada* (Ballina: The Irish Humanities Centre and Keohanes Ltd Ballina, 1981), pp. 42–63.
Walsh, Brendan, 'Economic Growth and Development: 1945–70', in Joseph J. Lee, ed., *Ireland 1945–70* (Dublin: Gill & Macmillan, 1979).

Watson, George J., *Irish Identity and the Irish Literary Revival* (Washington, DC: The Catholic University Press of America, 1979).
Wheatley, David, '"All is emptiness and I must spin": Thomas Kinsella and the Poetry of Romance and Decay', *Irish Studies Review* (August 2008), pp. 329–333.
Whitaker, Thomas Kenneth, *Interests* (Dublin: IPA Publications, 1983).
_____, 'We Have come a Long Way, We Still Have a Long Way to Go', *Irish Times* (8 December 2001), p. 10.
_____, *Protectionism or Free Trade: The Final Battle* (Dublin: IPA Publications, 2006a).
_____, *Retrospect 2006–1916* (Dublin: IPA Publications, 2006b).
_____, Interview with the author, 28 May 2007.
White, Harry, *The Keeper's Recital: Music and Cultural History in Ireland 1770–1970* (Cork: Cork University Press, 1998).
_____, *The Progress of Music in Ireland* (Dublin: Four Courts Press, 2005).
Wilkinson, Richard, and Pickett, Kate, *The Spirit Level: Why More Equal Societies Almost Always do Better* (London: Allen Lane, 2009).
Wills, Clair, *That Neutral Isle: A Critical History of Ireland during the Second World War* (London: Faber & Faber, 2007).
Wolf, Martin, *Why Globalisation Works* (New Haven: Nota Bene, 2005).
_____, 'Re-think the Purpose of Capitalism', *Financial Times* (12 December 2018).
_____, 'Reviewing the The Narrow Corridor by Darren Acemogla and James A. Robinson', *Financial Times* (28 September 2019).
Woolf, Viriginia, *Mr Bennett & Mrs Brown* (London: Hogarth Press, 1924).
Zeldin, Theodore, *An Intimate History of Humanity* (New York: Vintage, 1998).
Zuboff, Shoshana, *The Age of Surveillance Capitalism: The Fight for a Human Future at the New Frontier of Power* (New York: Profile Books, 2019).

Covers and Cover stories

Cover story, *Newsweek* (20 April 2001).
Cover story, *The Economist* (14 October 2004).
Cover story, *Financial Times* (28 June 2019).
Front cover, *The Guardian Newspaper* (9 August 2021).
'How Ireland Get Its Way: An Unlikely Diplomatic Superpower', *The Economist* (18 July 2020).
'New Liberal Manifesto', *Economist* magazine (15 September 2018).

'Report of the Taskforce on Active Citizenship' *The Wheel: Building Stronger Communities* (2007), <https://www.wheel.ie/sites/default/files/media/file-uploads/2018-08/Report%20of%20the%20Taskforce%20on%20Active%20Citizenship.pdf>, accessed 10 November 2021.

'Sustainability 2030', *Copenhagen Institute for Future Studies* (CIFS) (2021).

TASC Report, *Inequality in Ireland Today* (Dublin: TASC publications, 2018).

'Top of the Morning: Review of *Luck and the Irish* by R. F. Foster', *Economist Magazine* (18 October 2007).

Index

Compiled by Julitta Clancy

Abbey Theatre, Dublin 73–74, 77, 87, 178, 218
abortion referendum (2018) 138, 205
Académie Francaise 181
accordion 74–75
active citizenship 7, 28, 208, 220, 222, 223
    see also civic republicanism; *meitheal*
active imagination 111
Active Individual Consumption (AIC) 133
Act of Union 17
Acton, Charles 78–79, 80, 81
Adare, Co. Limerick 72
Administration 22, 23–24, 50
Aer Lingus 35, 36, 38
Afghanistan 66
Africa 167
agriculture 150, 207
Ahern, Bertie 45, 222
airport industrial zones 31
air travel 34
algorithms 194
Altan 5, 85
alt-right 199
Amazon 194, 199
America 165, 166, 174
    see also United States
American Business Schools 35
American Management Association 36
American poets 5, 99–101
American Revolution 166
Amsterdam 204
Andrews, C.S. (Todd) 32
Andrews, Elmer 15

Anglo-Irish ascendancy 69
Anglo-Irish Free Trade Agreement (1965) 52, 149
Anholt, Simon 143, 212
An Óige 41
Anthropocene Age 194
anti-consumerism 152, 154–55, 157–58, 232
anti-materialism 18–19, 20, 61, 150, 152
anti-modernity 31, 106, 206
Antrim 166
Apocalypse 194–95, 196
Apple 199
Applebaum, Anne, *Twilight of Democracy* 186, 224
Áras an Uachtaráin 43
Arendt, Hannah 221
Aristotle 221
artificial intelligence (AI) 196, 197
Asia 58, 59, 184, 185
Association of Irish Sociologists 154–55
Auden, W.H. 100, 194
austerity 7, 56, 136, 151, 185, 201–04, 232
Australia 200
Austria 32
Aylesbury Road, Dublin 76

Bach, Johann Sebastian 102
Baggot Street, Dublin 41, 73, 89, 101
balance of payments 12, 125
Ballinafid, Co. Westmeath 92
Ballivor, Co. Meath 35–36
Ballyferriter, Co. Kerry 70
banking *see* financial services
Bank of China 165

Bank of England 199
Bank of Ireland 38
Banville, John 13, 194
Barclays 192
Barnes, Colm 38
Barrington, Donal 23, 24, 25–26, 27–28
Barrington, Tom 23
Basin Lane, Dublin 92, 113
Basin Street Upper, Dublin 92
Bauman, Zygmunt 154, 211
Beck, Ulrich 154, 160
Beckett, Samuel 165
Behaviour & Attitudes survey 126, 139, 140
Belfast 152
Belfield 28
Belguim 183
Beowulf 106
Berkeley, George 165
Berlin Wall 44
Berman, Marshall, *All that Is Solid Melts into Air* 159
Best of Times, The? (ESRI) 155–56
Bethge, Hans 101, 102
Better Life Index (OECD) 142, 233
Bhreathnach-Lynch, Síghle 19
Biden, Joe 198
Big Houses, burning of 116
biotechnology 197
Birch, David 227
births outside marriage 140
Black, Cathal 59
Black and Tans 116
Bloody Sunday (Derry, 1972) 181
Bodley, Seoirse 79
Bono 85, 86–87
Book of Invasions 117, 165
Book of Invasions: A Celtic Symphony (Horslips) 86
Bord Bia 215
Bord Fáilte 31, 215

Bord Iascaigh Mhara (BIM) 215
Bord na Móna 32, 215
Bord Telecom 34
Bothy Band 85
Bow Lane, Dublin 92, 113
Bradley, Finbarr 37, 236n
Bradley, Finbarr and Kennelly, James, *Capitalising on Culture, Competing on Difference* 166, 180, 225–27, 229, 233
Brandeis, Louis 199
Bretton Woods agreement 162, 198
Brexit 56, 136, 159, 164, 185
Britain 18, 52, 63, 94, 106, 125, 166, 172, 179, 221
British civil service 50, 51
British economic strategy 16–17
British imperialism 99
broadcast media 34
Broderick, Vincent 74
Brogan, Sonny 74
Bronze Age 166
Brown, Terence 20
Browne, Mr (teacher) 96
Bruff, Co. Limerick 71
Burke, Edmund 165
Business RoundTable 190
business sector 11, 35, 39, 152, 227–29
business studies 25, 34–39

Cadburys 190
Calasso, Roberto, *The Unnameable Present* 194
Cambridge 35
Cantilloon 165
capitalism 7, 15, 150, 162, 177, 185, 189–91, 201
    reimagining 192–93, 199, 212
Carcarnet 113
Carlow 32
Carlyle, Thomas 94

Index

Carney, Mark 199
Carney, Miss 96
Carolingian Europe 165
Casadh an tSugáin (song) 70
Casey, Michael 227
Casserly, 'The Boss' 92
Casserly family 92
Castells, Manuel, *The Information Age: Economy, Society and Culture* 163
Catholic Church 18, 19, 24, 28, 58, 94, 95, 99, 139, 165, 167, 217
   see also Vatican II
   decline in authority of 53, 130, 217
   Latin mass, replacement of 77
   'Mother and Child' controversy 24
Catholic education 95
Catholic Ireland 167, 177
Catholics 15, 29, 58, 69, 87
céilidh bands 70, 72
Celtic Revival 1, 18, 20, 31, 32, 106–7, 121, 150, 180, 207, 210, 215, 225
   economic developments 3
Celtic Rock 86
Celtic spirituality 31
Celtic Tiger 132, 152, 153, 156, 201
Cement Roadstone Holdings (CRH) 39, 152
censorship 28, 34, 99
Central Bank 133, 203, 218, 227
Central Statistics Office (CSO) 6, 126
Centre for the study of Diasporas (Lowy Institute, Sydney) 167
Ceoltóirí Chualann 5, 73–76, 84
Cerny, Philip 171
Cessair (legendary figure) 117, 119
Chapelizod, Dublin 91
Chaucer, Geoffrey 106
Chetwood, Wiliam 64
Chevron, Philip 86
Chieftains 74, 84

China 7, 58, 143, 165, 184, 196
Chinese poetry 101
Chopin, Frédéric 66, 82, 84
Christian Brothers 45, 63, 72, 96–98, 150, 217, 225
Christian democracy 202
Christianity 18, 19, 197
CIÉ Engineering Works, Inchicore 92, 93
Citizens' Assemblies 204
civic republicanism 8, 216, 220–21, 222–24, 235
civil service 31, 35, 40, 45, 47, 48, 50, 59, 90, 95, 99, 214
Civil War 26, 99
Claidheamh Soluis, An 226
Clancy Brothers and Tommy Makem 66
Clandillon, Seamus 70
Clare (county) 45
Clarks 192
classical music 22, 67, 70, 79, 80, 82, 219
Cleary, Joe 15, 87, 88, 153–54
Cleethorpes 34–35
climate change 136, 151, 185, 193–94, 194–95, 197, 198, 200
   facing up to 229–30
Clinton, Bill 165
Clonskeagh, Dublin 52
Cold War 169
collectivism 145
Colley, George 21
Collier, Paul, *The Future of Capitalism: Facing the New Anxieties* 191–92
Collison brothers 228
Columbanus 165
Commission on Emigration 11–12
Common Agricultural Policy 135
communism, fall of 186
community spirit 7, 155, 208, 215
   see also *meitheal*
competition 191, 215–16

Conference Board of America 36
Connemara 151
conscious capitalism 190
Consolidated Convention (2012) 205
Constitution of Ireland 46, 205
consumerism 152, 154, 157–58, 177, 232
consumption studies 158
convenience food market 32–33
co-operative movement 215
Córas Tráchtála Teoranta (CTT) 31
Cork 72, 78, 79, 219
Corkery, Daniel, *Synge and Anglo-Irish Literature* 103
corporation tax 213–15
corporations 189–90, 192, 193
correction houses 29
corruption 214
cosmopolitan liberalism 99
Costello, John A. 61
Costello, Lt Colonel M.J. 32
Coughlan, Anthony 149
COVID-19 pandemic 2, 7, 56, 145, 164, 180, 185, 193, 206, 216, 232
Cowen, Tyler 175–76
Cranshaw 102
Crosson, Seán 78
Crotty, Raymond 149–50
CTT (Córas Tráchtála Teo) 31, 215
Cuala Press 109
Cúil Aodha, Co. Cork 77
Culliton report (1994) 152
cultural capital 236
cultural nationalism 15, 16
culture 6–7, 8, 41, 57, 173
    and economic performance 57–61
    globalisation and 173–79
    Kinsella's retrieval of 106–7
    music and 63–71
    tradition and heritage 208, 225–26, 229, 235
    see also *dinnseanchas*

Cunningham, Tony 37
Cusack, Michael 215

Dáil Éireann 49, 180
Dallas (TV show) 176
Dargan, Michael 35–36, 38
Dark Ages 221
Darwin, Charles, *The Voyage of the Beagle* 102
Davis, Thomas 64–65
Dawe, Gerald 109
De Buitléir, Eamonn 73–74
decadence 195–96
De Fréine, Sean, *The Great Silence* 104
De Jubainville, H. D'Arbois, *The Irish Mythological Cycle and Celtic Mythology* 117
Delany, Ronnie 15–16
democracy 8, 57, 199–200, 205, 221, 224, 226
    doubts about 185–93
democratic deficit 8
Democrats (USA) 187
demographic statistics 127–30
Denmark 135, 136, 171
De Paor, Liam 20
Department of Finance 2, 13, 40, 48, 49, 90, 218
Department of Industry and Commerce 51
dependency syndrome 205–6
deregulation 57, 58, 163, 171, 190
Derrig, Tom 65
Derry 181
De Tocqueville, Alexis 221
    Democracy in America 57
De Valera, Éamon 14, 15, 19, 20, 21, 47, 60–61
development agencies 30
Devlin, Barry 86
Diderot, Denis, *Encyclopedia* 102

digitalisation 163, 164, 168, 183, 193, 194
dinnseanchas 7, 8, 208, 224–26, 230, 231, 234–36
diversity 175, 189
divorce referendum (2019) 138
Dolmen Miscellany of New Irish Writing 21–22
Dolmen Press 4, 21, 89, 107, 181
Domas 36
Donegal Gaeltacht 217
Dorgan, Seán 157
Douglas, Ian R. 168
Douthat, Ross, *The Decadent Society* 195–97
dream interpretation 111
Drogheda, Co. Louth 45, 217
Drumshanbo, Co. Leitrim 228
Duanaire: 1600–1900: Poems of the Dispossessed, An 104, 107, 108, 181, 218
Dublin 47, 72–73, 76, 77, 86, 87, 89, 150, 155, 168, 219
    Kinsella's childhood in 91, 92, 93, 113
Dublin Corporation 181
Dublin Opinion 220
Dunne, Joseph 221
Dunquin, Co. Kerry 70, 71, 73, 83
Dutch people 67–68
Dylan, Bob 66

Eagleton, Terry 210
Earlsfort Terrace, Dublin 41
East Asia 132, 152
Easterlin, Richard, *Does Economic Growth Improve the Human Lot?* 233
Easter Rising (1916) 76, 96, 116, 150
    centenary commemoration 180, 205
Eastern Europe 56, 186
Economic and Social Research Institute, *The Best of Times?* 155–56

economic boom 55, 56, 132, 153, 156, 157, 212–13
    see also Celtic Tiger
economic change, culture and 57–61
economic crisis (1956) 1, 12–13, 17, 23–24, 90, 220
Economic Development (1958) 4, 20, 21, 23, 29, 44, 53, 60, 61
economic growth 3, 6, 16–17, 52, 145, 232–34
    culture and 16, 57–58
    'de-growth' 233
    national sovereignty and 16–17
    'normal' growth, return to 232
    religion and 57–58
    since 1950s 53
    first recovery period (1958–1969) 53–54
    setback period (1970–1986) 54
    second recovery period (1987–2007) 54–57
    as sole societal goal 184, 236
    statistics 132–33
economic history, phases in 53–57
economic independence 29
economic planning
    Whitaker's contribution 5, 48, 49–52
economic policy 16–17, 47
    see also protectionism
    Whitaker's new thinking on 47–49
economic rationality 184
economic recession 136
    see also Great Recession (2008)
economic self-sufficiency 47
economic transformation 126, 128, 131–33
    see also transformation of Irish society
Economist, The 55, 132, 142, 149, 190, 210
Edge, The (U2) 87
education 28, 56, 131, 144, 153, 225–26, 231, 232, 234–35
    business studies 25, 34–39

Irish studies 235
  politics and society 235
Education Corps 212
eircom 34
Éire-Ireland 104
electronic herd 163
Eliot, T. S. 102
Elizabethan Age 46
emigrants' remittances 125
emigration 1, 11–12, 13, 17–18, 35, 90, 92, 121, 125, 128, 130–31, 133, 144, 166–67, 220
energy 195
Engels, Friedrich 94
England 13, 34–35, 69, 106, 192
English poetry 104
Enlightenment 111–12, 161, 230
Enterprise Ireland 213
entrepreneurial culture 31, 39, 153, 173, 227–28
environment 6–7, 185, 190, 193, 198, 200
  see also climate change
equality 156
  see also inequality
Erin brand 32–33
Eriugena, John Scotus 102, 165, 166
Eucharistic Congress (1932) 94
eudaemonia 221
Eurobarometer surveys 126, 136, 164
Euro currency 136, 203
Europe 15, 28, 30, 37, 44, 55, 57, 72, 78, 80, 99, 101–2, 105, 106, 126, 134, 135, 136, 141, 145, 149, 161, 165, 175, 180, 202, 203, 214, 219, 228
  alt-right movement 199
  economic meltdown 197
  Hibernicisation of 166
  musical tradition *see* classical music
European Central Bank (ECB) 202
European Community (EEC/EC) 27, 52, 59, 135, 149, 210

European Free Trade Association 52
European Monetary Union (EMU) 136
European Productivity Agency 37
European Union (EU) 132, 144, 145, 199, 202, 204, 210
  corporation tax 213
  Irish attitudes 135–38, 145, 210
  Irish referendums 135, 136, 213
  trust in, by member states 138
Eyskens, Mark 183–85, 234–35

Fabian Society 26
Facebook 191, 194, 200
Faeth Fiadha: The Breastplate of St Patrick 107
Fáilte Ireland 66
'Faith of our Fathers' (hymn) 223
Fallon, Brian 14–15, 39–40
Famine 47, 166
Fanning, Bryan 23–24
Fanning, Ronan 61
Far East 31
Faustian development 159
Fay, Martin 74
Fennell, Desmond 150–51
Ferriter, Diarmaid 14, 25
Fianna Fáil 47, 54, 61
financial crash *see* Great Recession (2008)
financialisation 184, 192, 201
financial property speculation 201
financial scandals 171
financial services 55–56, 127
  see also deregulation
Financial Times 162, 185, 190, 200–01, 213, 233
Finland 82, 135, 141, 143, 225–26
Finn, Tomás 26, 28, 29
Fintan (legendary figure) 117
fiosracht 7, 8, 208, 209–15
First Programme for Economic Expansion (1958–63) 49, 53, 60, 90, 149

Index

First Recovery Period (1958–1969) 53–54
first revival *see* Celtic Revival
FitzGerald, Garret 23, 27, 30, 48, 52, 59, 208
Fitzsimons, Andrew 98, 118
fixed direct investment 132, 135
see also overseas investment
Flaherty, Jerry 70–71, 73, 74
Flight of the Earls (1607) 166
Florida, Richard 164–65
folk music 67
Football Association of Ireland (FAI) 24
foreign investment *see* overseas investment
Foresight Factory 141
Foster, R.F. 210–11
France 56, 125, 136, 165, 193, 204, 213, 221
economic planning 5, 23
free markets 58, 134, 161, 191, 199
free trade 51, 52, 60, 99
Freyer, Grattan 72
Friedman, Thomas 160–61, 163, 168, 171, 173, 183, 192, 211, 212, 226
Friel, Brian
Dancing at Lughnasa 70
Philadelphia, Here I Come! 22
Friends of Medieval Dublin 181
Future-Foresight 126

Gaelic Athletic Association (GAA) 150, 177, 178, 215
Gaelic Ireland 31, 65, 87
Gaelic language *see* Irish language
Gaelic League 65, 177, 226
Gaelic literary tradition 103, 106, 107, 219
see also Irish literature
Gaelic musical tradition *see* Irish music
Gaelic Revival *see* Celtic Revival
Gaelscoileanna 178
Gaeltacht 77, 217, 219
Gageby, Douglas 38

Gaia 230
Gaiety Theatre, Dublin 4, 5
Galloping Green, Dublin 74
Gallus 165
Garvey, Tom 31
Garvin, Tom 24, 25, 96, 208
Gdansk 203
GDP 4, 54, 132, 155, 178, 233, 234
Geertz, Clifford 57
Geldof, Bob 85
Gemeinschaft 158
General Elections 54, 209
Geoghegan, Peter, *Democracy for Sale* 187
German language 102
German music 102
German poetry 219
Germanic tribes 166
Germany 56, 125, 136
Gesellschaft 158
Gini Coefficient 134
Giraldus Cambrensis 63, 64
Glanbia 39, 152, 215
Glaoch, An 96
Glen Dimplex 39
Glenabbey 38
Glenageary, Co. Dublin 89
Glenstal Abbey, Co. Limerick 77
Global Enterprise Monitor 227–28
globalisation 3, 6–7, 56, 122, 127, 143, 151, 159, 160–61, 187, 193, 201, 203, 211–12
and culture 173–79
and Ireland 164–68
and the nation state 168–73
origins and growth 161–64
GNP 142, 155, 179, 232
Goethe, Johann Wolfgang von 102
Faust 102, 159
golden straightjacket 163
Goldsmith, Oliver 102
Goodby, John 103

Good Country Index 143
Good Friday Agreement 1998 27–28, 46, 136
Google 194, 199
Graeco-Roman culture 77, 78, 79, 158
Grattan's parliament 17
Gray, John 197–98, 234, 235
Great Crash (1929) 47, 162
Great Recession (2008) 7, 151, 152, 157, 162, 171, 186, 198, 208, 232
    fall-out from 159–60, 164, 183, 185, 187, 200–01
    Ireland's crisis and recovery 56, 136, 149, 201–204, 212, 213, 223
Great Yarmouth 35
Greece 134, 203, 219
Greek language 166
Greeks 235
    see also Graeco-Roman culture
Greencore plc 34
Greenmount & Boyne, Drogheda 45
Greenpeace 229
Gresham Hotel, Dublin 36
Grieg, Edvard 82
Guardian 229
Guinness 38, 92, 93, 201
Gunpowder Gin 228

Haffenden, John 91
Haley, Bill 85–86
happiness 142–43, 155
Harari, Yuval Noah 194
Hardiman, Tom 38
Harman, Sidney 228–29
harp 74
harpsichord 74
Harrington, James 221
Harris, Bernard 72
Harvard 101, 193, 228
Haughey, Charles 21
Hayek, F.A., *The Road to Serfdom* 23

Hayes' Commercial Hotel, Thurles 215
healthcare 144, 153, 231
Heaney, Seamus 21–22, 118
    'The Given Note' 83
    'In Memoriam' 83
Heath, Joseph 157–58
Henderson, Rebecca, *Reimagining Capitalism for a World on Fire* 193
Hereford 34
Hermes (mythological figure) 158
Hestia (mythological figure) 158
Hirst, Paul 169
history 63, 98, 209, 235
    influence on Kinsella's poetry 115–16
    local history and tradition 7
    see also dinnseanchas
    revisionism 115, 150
Hobsbawm, Eric 169
Holland 67–68, 199
Hollywood (USA) 78
Holmes, Stephen 186
Holyhead 90
Hong Kong 152
Honohan, Iseult 220n, 221
Honohan, Patrick 133, 203–04
Horslips 5, 85, 86
horticulture 32
Houellebecq, Michel, *Submission* 193
housing 125, 144
Human Development Index 145, 233
Human Poverty Index 153
Hume, David 63–64
Hutchinson, Pearse 21
Hutton, Will 199
Huxley, Aldous 196
Hyde, Douglas 65

IDA *see* Industrial Development Authority
identity *see* Irish identity

identity politics 186
Ignatieff, Michael 174
Iliad 4, 107
imbas forosnai ritual 111
IMI *see* Irish Management Institute
immigration 121, 125, 130, 143, 153, 179
Inchicore, Dublin 91, 92, 95
independence 29, 54, 59
    struggle for 12, 15, 16, 47, 95, 97, 177
India 58, 165
individualism 145, 152, 153, 215–16, 216–17, 221
individuation 107, 108, 109–12, 112–16, 120–22
industrial development 17, 31, 32
Industrial Development Authority (IDA) 31, 32, 39, 56, 215
Industrial Export Processing Zone 31
industrial peace 55
industrial protectionism *see* protectionism
Industrial Revolution 161, 194
industrial schools 29
inequality 6, 7, 127, 133–35, 144, 153, 156, 157, 180, 185, 190, 191, 192, 203–04, 222
    concerns about 230–31
information revolution 183, 184
information technology 163
Inglis, Tom 177
Instagram 191
Institute of Public Administration (IPA) 23, 44, 157
Intel 32
intellectual curiosity 7, 208, 209, 232, 236
    see also fiosracht
intellectual malaise 15
Intergovernmental Panel on Climate Change 229
International Monetary Fund (IMF) 162, 202

internet 164
Ipsos Global Trends 143
Irish Agricultural Co-operative Agency Society 215
Irish coffee 31
Irish colleges in Europe 165
Irish culture 63
Irish Diaspora 167
Irish Farm Centre 38
Irish Free State 19, 65, 70, 180
Irish history *see* history
Irish identity 6, 18, 19, 46, 65, 69, 103, 139, 141, 145, 179
Irish image 210–12
Irish Intercontinental Hotel, Ballsbridge 37–38
Irish language 2, 18, 41, 46–47, 65, 177, 178, 225, 226
    Kinsella's interest in 91, 95, 97, 98, 104
    translations of Old Irish literature 107–8, 120–21
    see also Táin, The
    Whitaker's commitment to 45, 46, 91, 217–18
Irish literary journals 23
Irish literature 4, 21–22, 45, 98, 104
    'dual tradition' 104–5, 106
    Kinsella's recovery of 1, 103, 104, 107, 120–21
    poetry 4, 46–47, 104
    see also Kinsella, Thomas
Irish Management Institute (IMI) 35, 36–37, 38, 217
Irish missionaries 167, 215
Irish music 4, 5, 22, 64, 69–71, 74, 76, 106, 178–79, 212
    groups and bands 1, 70, 72, 84–87
    see also Ceoltóirí Chualann
    Kinsella, influences on 4, 101–2
    popular music 85
    rock 'n' roll 85–87

sean nós singing 67, 70–71, 73
special place of, in Irish culture 63–71
transformation of traditional music
    4, 71–80, 178, 219
see also Ó Riada, Seán
Irish myth and legend
    Kinsella's interest in 90–91, 95,
        117, 120
    translations 107–8
    see also *Táin, The*
Irish pride 141–42, 144
Irish pub 167, 178
Irish Republic 46, 52
Irish Revival *see* Celtic Revival
Irish Ropes 38
Irish Sea 166
Irish Sociological Chronicles 154
Irish Statesman 167
Irish Studies 235
Irish Sugar Company 32
Irish theatre 22
Irish Times 38, 143, 150, 216
Irish World Music Centre (UL) 87
Irwin Street, Dublin 92, 113
Italy 68, 165, 221

Jackson, Guy 38
Jackson, Thomas 109
Jacobi, Jolande, *The Psychology of C.J. Jung* 112
jazz 5, 72, 75, 80, 84, 88
Jesuits 23
job insecurity 201
Johnston, Dillon 101
Joyce, James 91, 102, 131, 165, 166, 219
Julianstown, Co. Meath 201
Jung, Carl 101, 113, 117, 120, 212
    influence on Kinsella 105, 107, 108–12
    theory of individuation 108, 109–12

Kalevala (Finnish epic) 225

Kavanagh, Patrick 41, 99
    Lough Derg 15
Kay, John 162
Kazantzakis, Nikos 101
Kearney, Richard 78, 107–8
Kelly, Ronan 68
Kennedy, John F. 21, 176, 214
Kennelly, James 180, 225–26, 229, 235
Kenny, Enda 209
Kenny, Ivor 37, 49
Kent State University 91
Keohane, Kieran 156
Kerry Gaeltacht 77
Kerry Group 39, 152, 215
Kerrygold 215
Keynes, John Maynard 47, 197
Kiberd, Declan 83, 181, 211
Kierkegaard, Søren 185
Killeen, Michael 31, 32
Kilmainham, Dublin 91
Kilroy, Paddy 23, 26
King, Philip 75–76, 83, 85
Kinnelly, James J. 166
Kinsale, battle of (1601) 218
Kinsella family 70, 73, 91–94
Kinsella, John Paul (Thomas's father) 92–94, 113, 115
Kinsella, Stephen 202–04
Kinsella, Thomas 3, 5, 8, 16, 21, 24, 38, 40–41, 57, 63, 68, 69, 75, 76, 79, 86, 88, 89–122, 125, 159, 165, 167, 174, 179, 180–82, 205, 207, 209, 214, 217, 219, 221, 225, 226, 235
    career: civil service 2, 90, 91, 99
    fulltime writer 91, 107
    publishing 4–5
    childhood and family 91–94, 112–15
        father 92–94, 113, 115
        mother 113–14
        poems on 112–15, 116, 120
    civic service 219, 223

education 40, 94–98, 114
individuation, search for 107, 112–16, 120–22
influences on 92–116
  family and teachers 92, 94–98, 113
  history 115–16
  Jung 5, 105, 107, 108–16
  music 4, 101–2
  overseas writers 5, 99–101, 103
legacy of: 'metaphysical' 105, 108–12
  'physical' 105, 106–9
literary objectives 103–5
myth and legend, interest in 90–91, 95, 117–19, 120
Ó Riada, friendship with 2, 41, 70–73, 80, 88
Peppercanister volumes *see* Peppercanister Press
poems and anthologies 40, 78, 92, 96, 98, 100, 112–15
  see also '1956' 13, 90; '38 Phoenix St' 113; *Another September* 100; 'Baggot Street Deserta' 89; 'Big House' 116; 'Bow Lane' 113; 'Butcher's Dozen' 102; C.G. Jung's 'First years' 109; *Collected Poems* 113; 'Death Bed' 102; *Death of a Queen* 89; 'Dispossessed, The' 102; *Downstream* 100; *Dual Tradition, The* 105; *Duanaire, An* (anthology) *see An Duanaire*; *Dublin Documentary, A* 91; 'Dura Mater' 113–14; 'Entire Fabric, The' 102; 'Finistere' 118; 'High Road, The' 113; 'His Father's Hands' 116; 'Irwin St' 113; 'Lady of Quality, A' 100; 'Land of Loss' 102; 'Liffey Hill, The' 113; 'Littlebody' 102; *Messenger, The* 93–94; 'Moralities' 102; *New Oxford Book of Irish Verse*; *New Poems 1973* 92; 'Nightwalker' 97–98, 102, 103; *Nightwalker and other Poems* 100, 101, 109; *Notes from the Land of the Dead* 100, 109, 117–18, 120; 'Oldest Place, The' 119; *One* 117, 120; 'Open Court' 102; *Other Poems* 101; Peppercanister volumes *see* Peppercanister Press; Phoenix Park' 102; 'Phoenix St' 113; *Poems* 40, 89; *Poems and Translations* 107; 'Shoals Returning, The' (elegy) 71; 'St Paul's Rocks: 16th February 1832' 102; *Selected Life, A* 83; 'Survivor' 117–18; 'Tao and Unfitness at Inistiogue on the River Nore' 116; *Technical Supplement, A* 102; *Wormwood* 119
prose writings 104–5
  Davis, Mangan, Ferguson? Tradition and the Irish Writer 104
  'The Divided Mind' 106
second revival, contribution to 1, 4–5, 88, 89–91, 107, 120–21
and third revival 208, 209
translations of Old Irish literature 1, 4–5, 106, 107–8, 120–21, 225
  see also Duanaire, An; *Táin, The*
Whitaker, relationship with 2, 90, 91
Kirby, Peadar 153, 156
knowledge society 184
Koch family 187–88
Korea 165
Korea (film) 59
Kraster, Ivan 186
Kruger Kavanagh's pub, Dunquin 70

Laffan, Brigid 204

Late Late Show 21
Latin America 167
Latin language 166
Latin Mass 77
Latvia 125
Layard, Richard, *Happiness: Lessons for a New Science* 155
Le Brocquy, Louis 5, 107
Leadbeater, Charlie 232
League of Nations 210
Lebor Gabála Érenn 117, 165
Lee, Joe 13, 20, 39, 207–08, 227
Leerssen, Joep 63
Left Book Club 94
Lemass, Seán 20, 21, 22, 45, 53, 126
liberalism 186
  see also neo-liberalism
Liberties, Dublin 91, 114
life expectancy 128–29, 144, 232
Liffey river 92, 178
Light that Failed, The: A Reckoning (Kraster and Holmes) 186
Lilla, Mark, *The Once and Future Liberal: After Identity Politics* 186
Limerick 13, 72
  see also University of Limerick
Lisbon Treaty, referendum on (2008) 135, 136, 213
Lithuania 125
living standards, rise in 125, 130
local history and tradition see *dinnseanchas*
Lockhart, Jim 86
London 13, 26, 29, 35, 55–56, 80, 87, 126, 208, 213
London School of Economics (LSE) 35
Lovelock, James 230
Lowell, Robert 5, 101
  Life Studies 101
  Mills of the Kavanaughs 101
Lowy Institute, Sydney 167

Lynch, Patrick 23
Lyons, F.S.L. 97

Maalouf, Amin 209–10
McAleese, Mary 155
McCarthy, Pete 211–12
McCarthy, James Charles Brendan (J.C.B.) 51, 52
McCormick, M.J. 37
McElligott, J.J. 48
McGahern, John 21
  'Korea' 59
McGilligan, Patrick 12
McGowan, Kieran 31, 76
Machiavelli, Niccolò 221
McKinsey's 164
McLoone, Martin 236
McMahon, Bryan, *Song of the Anvil* 73
McQuaid, John Charles 19, 24, 28, 95, 138
Macron, Emmanuel 205
Mahler, Gustav 101, 102
  Das Lied von der Erde 101
Mahon, Derek 196
Makem, Tommy 66
management education 36–37, 38
Manchester 92
Mann, Thomas 101, 102
  Joseph and his Brothers 102
Marcellus 165
Marcus, Louis 219
market values 215–16
Mars 197
Marxists 169
materialism 18, 152, 154
Mathews, P.J. 3, 20, 31–32, 180, 226
Mayer, Colin 192
Maynooth University 153
Mays, Michael 211–12
MBA (Master of Business Administration) 37
media 28, 34

see also social media
meitheal 7, 8, 208, 215–21
Melbourne Olympics (1956) 15–16
Mercer, Robert 187
Merriman, Brian 102
Messenger, The (Kinsella) 93–94
Messenger, The (magazine) 93
microchip manufacture 32
Middle Ages 159, 161
Middle East 58, 175
Midgley, Mary 230
migration 128, 130, 167, 193–94, 197
  see also emigration; immigration
Milesians 118, 119
Mill, J.S., *Principles of Political Economy* 233
Miller, Kerby 17–18, 20, 58, 166
Miller, Liam 4, 40, 89, 90–91
Mise Éire (film) 83
  soundtrack 4, 22, 76
Model School, Inchicore 95–96, 114
modernity 6, 29, 106, 158, 159, 160, 175
Molloy, Matt 85
Moloney, Paddy 74
Montague, John 21, 76, 83
  Rough Field, The 83–84
  Slow Dance, A 84
Montale, Eugenio 101
Moore, Brian 21
Moore, Thomas 68–69, 87
Moore's Melodies 68, 69, 81, 87
moral values 140
Morrison, George 73, 76
Morrison, Ian 38
Morrison, Sir George Ivan (Van Morrison) 85
Mounk, Yascha, *The People Versus Democracy* 186–87
Mount Pelerin meeting (1946) 183, 199
Mullen, Larry 87
multi-culturalism 175

multi-ethnic identities 187
multi-nationals 54, 149–50
Murphy, Richard 21
Murphy, Tom, *Whistle in the Dark* 22
'Murphys, The' (dining club) 37–38, 39, 217
music 2, 4, 79–80, 219
  see also classical music; Irish music; jazz; Ó Riada, Seán
music business 67, 68
music groups 5, 84–87
Muslims 58, 194
myths and legends *see* Irish myth and legend

NAMA 34
'Nation Once Again, A' (song) 225
National Accounts 125
National Council for Curriculum Development 235
national identity *see* Irish identity
'national question' 45–46
national sovereignty 16–17, 61
National University of Ireland 218
nationalised industries 30
nationalism 16–17, 29, 61, 96, 97, 98, 168, 169, 170
  see also cultural nationalism
  globalisation and 168–73
  music and 65, 69
nation-branding 171, 212
nation-building 35, 106, 217
Negroponte, Nicholas 168
neo-liberalism 151, 154, 158, 160, 162, 183, 184, 202, 230
  failure of 185, 186, 189, 199, 216
  Ireland's drift towards 172–73, 215–16
neo-paganism 197
Netherlands, the 143
New Age movement 151

New Oxford Book of Irish Verse 104–5,
    181, 219
Newry, Co. Down 45
Newsweek 131
new technology 34
New York 66, 104, 157
New York Times 135, 160, 163, 194, 211
New Zealand 142
Nice Treaty, referendum on (2001)
    135, 136
Ní Dhomhnaill, Nuala 224–25, 231
Nietzsche, Friedrich 185
Noah (biblical figure) 117, 120
Nobel Prize 233
Nordic countries 171–72
North Africa 56
North America 166
Northern Ireland 27–28, 28, 45, 46, 205
Northern poets 109
Norway 82, 135, 145
nostalgia 143, 155
Nye, Joseph 142

Oblate Fathers 94
O'Brien, Dan 145
O'Brien, John A., *The Vanishing Irish* 1
O'Callaghan, Margaret 99
Ó Canainn, Tomás 72
O'Carolan, Turlough 87
Ó Cearbhaill, Tadhg 38
O'Connell, Michael 153, 177, 217
O'Connell's Schools, Dublin 95, 96–98
O'Connor, Sinead 85
O'Driscoll, Dennis 21
O'Driscoll report (2005) 152
O'Driscoll, Tim 31
OECD 142, 153, 227, 233
Ó Gráda, Cormac 48, 53, 133, 145
O'Grady, Desmond 14
O'Hearn, Dennis 152
Ohmae, Kenichi 164

oil crises (1970s) 54, 162
Oireachtas reform 28
O'Keefe, Paddy 38
O'Loughlin, Michael 204
Olympic Games 16
O'Malley, Donogh 21
Ó Mordha, Sean 105
One Fond Embrace (RTÉ) 89, 105
O'Neill, Terence 45
Ó Rathaille 181
Ord, Toby, *The Precipice: Existential Risk
    and the Future of Humanity* 198
O'Regan, Brendan 31
Ó Riada sa Gaiety 4, 5
Ó Riada, Seán 3, 16, 22, 24, 40, 41, 57, 72,
    89, 98, 101, 102, 103, 125, 159, 167,
    179, 208, 214, 218–19, 222, 226
    career 2, 5, 72–73, 218
    childhood and education 71, 72
    civic service 218, 219, 223
    classical music 79, 80, 83, 88
    compositions 5, 79, 83
        Glenstal Abbey Mass 77
        Mise Éire, soundtrack for 4, 22, 76
        Nomos 2 81
    death of 80, 205
    jazz, involvement with 5, 72,
        75, 80, 88
    as John Reidy 41, 70, 72, 88
    Kinsella, friendship with 2, 41, 70–71,
        72–73, 83, 88
    legacy and influences 5, 75–76,
        77, 80–88
    groups and bands 84–87
    objective and ambition 74, 216–17
    Our Musical Heritage (radio
        talks) 77–78
    second revival, contribution to 1, 4,
        63, 71–87, 88
    and third revival 208

Index

transformation of Irish music 1, 63, 71–80, 178
   founding of Ceoltóirí Chualann 73–76
Ó Riain, Seán 202
O'Rourke, Kevin 133, 145
orphanages 29
Ó Súilleabháin, Mícheál 87
O'Sullivan, Denis 25
O'Sullivan, Michael 172, 208, 213
O'Toole, Fintan 143
Ó Tuama, Seán 218
overseas investment 6, 31, 39, 49, 52, 53, 55, 56, 60, 127, 135–36, 152, 164, 172, 234
   critics of 149, 150, 152
Oxford 35
Oxford Business School 190

Paisley, Ian 45
Pale, The 77, 78
pantheism 197
Paris 73, 87, 165
Parsons bookshop, Dublin 41
partition 45
Pasteur, Louis 56
Peace Corps 214
Peace of Westphalia (1648) 161
peat production 32
Peppercanister Press 83, 90, 96, 102, 105, 109, 111, 166, 181
   Her Vertical Smile 102
   Messenger, The 93
   Out of Ireland 83, 166
   St Catherine's Clock 105, 109
   Songs of the Psyche 96, 111
   Vertical Man 83, 102
philosophy 185, 214, 230, 235
   see also civic republicanism
Phoenix Park, Dublin 92
Phoenix Street, Dublin 92, 113

Pickett, Kate 133, 231
Pierce's Foundry, Wexford 13
Pilling, David, *The Growth Delusion* 233–34
Pink, Daniel 228–29
Planxty 84
Plato's Cave 34
Plunkett, Horace 215
Plunkett, James 38
poets and poetry 2, 4, 40, 46–47, 64, 89–90, 104, 109, 229
   see also Kinsella, Thomas
   American poets 99–101
Pogues 86
Poland 66, 82, 125
polarisation 187
political independence *see* independence
Politico (website) 205
Popper, Karl 183
population 6, 127–28, 179
Porter, Michael, *The Competitive Advantage of Nations* 67–68, 228
Portland Group, *Soft Power Index* 142
Portugal 136, 203
Post Office 93
Potter, Andrew 157–58
Potts, Sean 74
Potts, Tommie 87
Pound, Ezra 5, 99, 100, 101, 181
   Cantos 100
pragmatism 204, 205
Prague 165
pride in country 141, 144
privatisation 34, 58
Proclamation of 1916 180
promotional agencies 31, 32
protectionism 16, 17, 47–48, 50, 51, 99
   abandonment of 44, 45, 52, 53, 60
Protestants 18, 57–58, 69, 116
Putin, Vladimir 185

Quaker enterprises 192
quality of life 142–43, 157

Radio Luxemburg 70
Ráidió Éireann 70, 72, 73, 77–78
'Ranch,' The, Inchicore 92
Ranelagh, Dublin 76
Rathlin Island 166
Reagan, Ronald 162, 183
Rebel Sell (Heath and Potter) 157–58
Rebellion of 1798 116
recession *see* Great recession (2008)
redundancies 13
Reformation 57
Reidy family 72
Reidy, John *see* Ó Riada, Seán
religious affiliation 177
religious faith 57–58, 138–39
religious idealism 197–98
Renaissance 78, 161, 219, 221
Renan, Ernest, *Vie de Jesus* 102
Republicans (USA) 187
reputation 210–11, 213, 214
ressentiment 185, 199
Ricardo, David 47, 161, 162
Rice, Edmund Ignatius 96, 98
Rigby-Jones, Michael 38
Riverdance 5, 85
Roadstone 38, 39
robotics 197
Roche, Donal 38
Roethke, Theodore 101
Róisín Dubh (song) 76
Romans 63, 64, 166, 196
romantic Ireland 210, 211
Rome 165
Rooney, Sally 195
Roosevelt, Franklin D. 200
Rosenberg, Carolyn, *Let Our Gaze Blaze: The Recent Poetry of Thomas Kinsella* 91, 96, 112, 115

Rosslare Harbour 13
Rostrevor, Co. Down 44
Rousseau, Jean-Jacques 221
Rowntree 192
RTÉ 2, 89, 105, 150, 216
Ruane, Frances 4
rural electrification 59
Ruskin, John 94, 233
Russell, Bertrand 166
  History of Western Philosophy 214
Russell, George 167
Russia 185
Rutte, Mark 199
Ryan Commission 29
Ryanair 152

Salamanca 165
same-sex marriage 205
Saorstát Éireann *see* Irish Free State
Sartre, Jean-Paul, *Being and Nothingness* 72
Scotland 32
Scotus *see* Eriugena, John Scotus
Scruton, Roger 157
second Irish revival 1, 3, 121, 126, 144, 207, 209, 217
  business education 25, 34–39
  defining characteristic 179
  demographic, sociological and cultural changes 126–43
  genesis and ideology 21–25
  Kinsella's contribution 88, 89–91, 107, 120–21
  Ó Riada's contribution 1, 4, 63, 71–87, 88
  self-help organisations 215
  semi-state bodies 25, 30–34
  transformation created by *see* transformation of Irish society
  Tuairim, role of 25–30
  Whitaker's contribution 1, 21, 43–62

second recovery period
  (1987–2007) 54–57
Second Vatican Council *see* Vatican II
Second World War 72, 79, 92, 162,
  169, 221
self-confidence 1, 2, 4, 27, 41, 121–22, 126,
  145, 178, 179, 201, 226, 228
self-help organisations 215
self-sufficiency *see* protectionism
semi-state bodies 25, 30–34, 35, 39, 215
Sen, Amartya 135, 233
Senate, Irish 218
Setback Period (1970–1986) 54
Shakespeare, William 78, 94
Shamrock brand 32
Shannon Development Corporation 31
Shannon river 59
Shapiro, Robert 165
shareholder engagement 187–88, 199
shareholder value 192
Shelbourne Hotel, Dublin 75, 85
Sibelius, Jean 82
Silicon Valley 191, 197, 228
Singapore 152
Single European market 55
'Sinn Féin Myth' 29
Smith, Adam, *The Wealth of*
  Nations 161–62
Smith, Anthony D. 170
Smurfit, Jefferson 52
Smurfits 39
Smyth, Gerry 84
social media 187, 191, 194, 200
social partnership 55
Social Progress Index 135
socialism 93–94, 222
societal change, culture and 58–59
societal future, doubts about 193–99
soft power 142
Sons of Usnech, The 107
Sophocles 79

South America 56, 161
South-East Asia 185
South Korea 58, 152
Spain 56, 203
Spirit Level, The (Wilkinson and
  Pickett) 231
spirituality 31, 211, 212, 213
stagnation 12, 162, 195, 196, 197
State-sponsored bodies *see*
  semi-state bodies
statistical analysis 126–43, 210
Statistical and Social Inquiry Society 48
Steger, Manfred 161
Stiglitz, Joseph 135
  People, Power and Profit: Progressive
  Capitalism for an Age of
  Discontent 190
Stone Age 166
Stormont 45
Strauss, Richard, *Der Rosenkavalier* 88
Stripe 228
Studies 22, 23
sugar industry 33, 34
surveillance capitalism 194, 200
sustainability 200, 236
Sweetman, Gerald 12
Swift, Jonathan 102
Switzerland 143, 165
Sydney 205

Táin, The (Horslips album) 86
Táin, The (Kinsella's translation) 4–5, 90,
  91, 101, 103, 105, 107, 108, 120, 181
Táin Bó Cuailgne 225
Taiwan 31, 152
Tandy, Napper 201
Tansey, Paul 128
Tansey, Seamus 66
TASC (Action on Social Change) 134
Taskforce on Active Citizenship 222–23
Taylor, Charles 221

tech companies 7, 197, 199, 200, 228
technological solutions 197, 198, 232
Teilifís Éireann 53, 176
telecommunications 56
Telesis report (1982) 152
Temple University 112
Thatcher, Margaret 162, 183
theatre 22, 79, 87
Theatre Royal 85
Theil, Peter 191
third Irish revival 28, 207–36
third-level education 34–35, 37, 38, 131, 144
Thirty-Three Triads 107
Thomas Davis Lectures 106
Thomas Street, Dublin 113
Thompson, Grahame 169
Thornley, David 29
Thurles, Co. Tipperary 215
Tinahely, Co. Wicklow 92
Tipperary 228
Toland, John 165
Tomlinson, John 175, 176
Tonnies, Ferdinand 158–59
Topographia Hibernica (Giraldus Cambrensis) 64
tourism 31, 65
Tourism Ireland 215
traditional music *see* Irish music
transformation of Irish society (late 1950s-2020s) 125–26, 144–45, 149, 216
   critics and sceptics 149–58
   demographic change 127–30
   economic performance 131–33
   education 131
   EU membership 135–38
   inequality 133–35
   moral values 140
   quality of life 142–43
   religious observance 138–40
   sense of pride 141–42
   statistical analysis 126–43
Trimble, Gary 27
Trinity College Dublin 28, 87, 116, 149
Troika 136, 202
Trump, Donald 159, 163, 186
Tuairim 24, 25–30, 217
Tubridy, Derval 111
Tyndal, John 165
Tyrconnell Street, Dublin 92

U2 5, 86–87
Uber 198
Ulster 83
unemployment 12
Unilever 32, 200
Unionism 28
united Ireland 27–28, 45–46
United Kingdom 47, 50, 132, 135, 151, 162, 164, 175, 183, 191, 192, 200, 202, 210, 229
   see also Britain
United Kingdom Supreme Court 200
United Nations 142, 145, 170, 210
United Nations Security Council 210
United States 5, 7, 13, 32, 36, 37, 55, 56, 69, 70, 100, 135, 151, 162, 164, 165, 167, 172, 175, 183, 186, 199, 200, 202, 213, 214, 221, 226, 227
   Business RoundTable 192
   capitalism in crisis 191
   corporation tax proposal 213
   cultural domination 174, 176
   economic growth 55, 57
   Federalist Papers 221
   inequality 191
   influences on Kinsella 99–101
   investment in Ireland 135–36, 152
   Kennedy presidency 21, 176, 213
   political system 187
   popular music 66

Index 269

United States Congress 200
Uniting Ireland (Barrington) 27–28
universities 37
   see also third-level education
University College Cork (UCC) 41, 76,
    87, 218
   Ó Riada and 72, 77, 218
University College Dublin (UCD)
    23, 26, 28
   Business Studies/Commerce
      Departments 37
   Kinsella and 40, 41, 102
   students' residence 41
University of Limerick 87, 202
University of London 45

van Hayek, Frederick 183, 184
Vatican II 21, 77, 176–77
Verdi, Giuseppe 78
Victory, Gerald 79
Villon, Françoise 102

Wales 32
Walkinstown 92
Walsh, Eleanor 41
War of Independence 21, 98–99
Washington Consensus 162, 172
Watson, George 106–7
weather 18, 193
Weber, Max 18
   Protestant Ethic and the Spirit of
    Capitalism, The 57
West Cork 78, 79, 217
Western Ocean String Quartet 85
Wexford 116
WhatsApp 189
Wheatly, David 181
Whelan, Bill 85
Whitaker Memorandum 50
Whitaker, Thomas K. (Ken) 2, 3, 16, 22,
    23, 24, 38, 41, 63, 74, 75, 79, 89,
    98, 99, 103, 126, 129, 149, 159, 167,
    176, 179, 205, 208, 214, 216, 217–
    18, 220, 222, 226
   career 44
   Department of Finance 2, 40, 45,
      48, 49, 59
   retirement 218
   subsequent appointments 218
   civic service 44–47, 218, 219, 223
   economic history, study of 53–57
   economic planning 5, 48, 49–52
      see also *Economic Development*
       (1958); *First Programme for*
       Economic Expansion
   economic policy, new thinking
      on 47–49
   education 40, 45
   family background 44–45
   interests and influences 5, 45–46
      Irish language 45, 46, 91, 217–18
      literature and music 46–47
   and Kinsella, relationship with 90, 91
   and Northern Ireland 45–46
   publications
      Financing by Credit
       Creation 48–49
      Interests 44
      The Irish Economy 1957 50
      Retrospect 2006–1916 44
   reputation today 43–44
   second revival, contribution to 1, 21,
      43–62, 125, 216
   and third revival 208
   and Tuairim 26
White Claw brand 168
White, Harry 68–69, 81–82
White House 21
Wicklow hills 41
Widgery Tribunal 181
Wilde, Oscar 165, 222
Wilkinson, Richard 133, 231

Williams, Raymond 57
Williams, William Carlos 5, 99, 100, 101
Wilson, Woodrow 200
Windmill Lane Recording Studios 87, 178
Wolf, Martin 169–70, 190
Why Globalisation Works 162–63
women, status of 129–30, 131, 144, 180
Wood Quay, Dublin 181, 219
Woolf, Virginia 183
World Bank 50, 162
World Happiness Index (UN) 142

Y2K 196
Yale University 153
Yeats, William Butler 18, 19, 100, 104, 131, 209, 210–11, 213
Young Ireland 64
Young Irelanders 26
Yugoslavia 24

Zuboff, Shoshana, *The Age of Surveillance Capitalism* 194

Reimagining Ireland

Series Editor: Dr Eamon Maher, Technological University Dublin

The concepts of Ireland and 'Irishness' are in constant flux in the wake of an ever-increasing reappraisal of the notion of cultural and national specificity in a world assailed from all angles by the forces of globalisation and uniformity. Reimagining Ireland interrogates Ireland's past and present and suggests possibilities for the future by looking at Ireland's literature, culture and history and subjecting them to the most up-to-date critical appraisals associated with sociology, literary theory, historiography, political science and theology.

Some of the pertinent issues include, but are not confined to, Irish writing in English and Irish, Nationalism, Unionism, the Northern 'Troubles', the Peace Process, economic development in Ireland, the impact and decline of the Celtic Tiger, Irish spirituality, the rise and fall of organised religion, the visual arts, popular cultures, sport, Irish music and dance, emigration and the Irish diaspora, immigration and multiculturalism, marginalisation, globalisation, modernity/postmodernity and postcolonialism. The series publishes monographs, comparative studies, interdisciplinary projects, conference proceedings and edited books. Proposals should be sent either to Dr Eamon Maher at eamon.maher@ittdublin.ie or to ireland@peterlang.com.

Vol. 1   Eugene O'Brien: 'Kicking Bishop Brennan up the Arse': Negotiating Texts and Contexts in Contemporary Irish Studies
ISBN 978-3-03911-539-6. 219 pages. 2009.

Vol. 2   James P.Byrne, Padraig Kirwan and Michael O'Sullivan (eds): Affecting Irishness: Negotiating Cultural Identity Within and Beyond the Nation
ISBN 978-3-03911-830-4. 334 pages. 2009.

Vol. 3   Irene Lucchitti: The Islandman: The Hidden Life of Tomás O'Crohan
ISBN 978-3-03911-837-3. 232 pages. 2009.

Vol. 4   Paddy Lyons and Alison O'Malley-Younger (eds): No Country for Old Men: Fresh Perspectives on Irish Literature
ISBN 978-3-03911-841-0. 289 pages. 2009.

Vol. 5	Eamon Maher (ed.): Cultural Perspectives on Globalisation and Ireland ISBN 978-3-03911-851-9. 256 pages. 2009.
Vol. 6	Lynn Brunet: 'A Course of Severe and Arduous Trials': Bacon, Beckett and Spurious Freemasonry in Early Twentieth-Century Ireland ISBN 978-3-03911-854-0. 218 pages. 2009.
Vol. 7	Claire Lynch: Irish Autobiography: Stories of Self in the Narrative of a Nation ISBN 978-3-03911-856-4. 234 pages. 2009.
Vol. 8	Victoria O'Brien: A History of Irish Ballet from 1927 to 1963 ISBN 978-3-03911-873-1. 208 pages. 2011.
Vol. 9	Irene Gilsenan Nordin and Elin Holmsten (eds): Liminal Borderlands in Irish Literature and Culture ISBN 978-3-03911-859-5. 208 pages. 2009.
Vol. 10	Claire Nally: Envisioning Ireland: W. B. Yeats's Occult Nationalism ISBN 978-3-03911-882-3. 320 pages. 2010.
Vol. 11	Raita Merivirta: The Gun and Irish Politics: Examining National History in Neil Jordan's *Michael Collins* ISBN 978-3-03911-888-5. 202 pages. 2009.
Vol. 12	John Strachan and Alison O'Malley-Younger (eds): Ireland: Revolution and Evolution ISBN 978-3-03911-881-6. 248 pages. 2010.
Vol. 13	Barbara Hughes: Between Literature and History: The Diaries and Memoirs of Mary Leadbeater and Dorothea Herbert ISBN 978-3-03911-889-2. 255 pages. 2010.
Vol. 14	Edwina Keown and Carol Taaffe (eds): Irish Modernism: Origins, Contexts, Publics ISBN 978-3-03911-894-6. 256 pages. 2010.
Vol. 15	John Walsh: Contests and Contexts: The Irish Language and Ireland's Socio-Economic Development ISBN 978-3-03911-914-1. 492 pages. 2011.

Vol. 16	Zélie Asava: The Black Irish Onscreen: Representing Black and Mixed-Race Identities on Irish Film and Television ISBN 978-3-0343-0839-7. 213 pages. 2013.
Vol. 17	Susan Cahill and Eóin Flannery (eds): This Side of Brightness: Essays on the Fiction of Colum McCann ISBN 978-3-03911-935-6. 189 pages. 2012.
Vol. 18	Brian Arkins: The Thought of W. B. Yeats ISBN 978-3-03911-939-4. 204 pages. 2010.
Vol. 19	Maureen O'Connor: The Female and the Species: The Animal in Irish Women's Writing ISBN 978-3-03911-959-2. 203 pages. 2010.
Vol. 20	Rhona Trench: Bloody Living: The Loss of Selfhood in the Plays of Marina Carr ISBN 978-3-03911-964-6. 327 pages. 2010.
Vol. 21	Jeannine Woods: Visions of Empire and Other Imaginings: Cinema, Ireland and India, 1910–1962 ISBN 978-3-03911-974-5. 230 pages. 2011.
Vol. 22	Neil O'Boyle: New Vocabularies, Old Ideas: Culture, Irishness and the Advertising Industry ISBN 978-3-03911-978-3. 233 pages. 2011.
Vol. 23	Dermot McCarthy: John McGahern and the Art of Memory ISBN 978-3-0343-0100-8. 344 pages. 2010.
Vol. 24	Francesca Benatti, Sean Ryder and Justin Tonra (eds): Thomas Moore: Texts, Contexts, Hypertexts ISBN 978-3-0343-0900-4. 220 pages. 2013.
Vol. 25	Sarah O'Connor: No Man's Land: Irish Women and the Cultural Present ISBN 978-3-0343-0111-4. 230 pages. 2011.
Vol. 26	Caroline Magennis: Sons of Ulster: Masculinities in the Contemporary Northern Irish Novel ISBN 978-3-0343-0110-7. 192 pages. 2010.

Vol. 27 Dawn Duncan: Irish Myth, Lore and Legend on Film
ISBN 978-3-0343-0140-4. 181 pages. 2013.

Vol. 28 Eamon Maher and Catherine Maignant (eds): Franco-Irish Connections in Space and Time: Peregrinations and Ruminations
ISBN 978-3-0343-0870-0. 295 pages. 2012.

Vol. 29 Holly Maples: Culture War: Conflict, Commemoration and the Contemporary Abbey Theatre
ISBN 978-3-0343-0137-4. 294 pages. 2011.

Vol. 30 Maureen O'Connor (ed.): Back to the Future of Irish Studies: Festschrift for Tadhg Foley
ISBN 978-3-0343-0141-1. 359 pages. 2010.

Vol. 31 Eva Urban: Community Politics and the Peace Process in Contemporary Northern Irish Drama
ISBN 978-3-0343-0143-5. 303 pages. 2011.

Vol. 32 Mairéad Conneely: Between Two Shores/*Idir Dhá Chladach*: Writing the Aran Islands, 1890–1980
ISBN 978-3-0343-0144-2. 299 pages. 2011.

Vol. 33 Gerald Morgan and Gavin Hughes (eds): Southern Ireland and the Liberation of France: New Perspectives
ISBN 978-3-0343-0190-9. 250 pages. 2011.

Vol. 34 Anne MacCarthy: Definitions of Irishness in the 'Library of Ireland' Literary Anthologies
ISBN 978-3-0343-0194-7. 271 pages. 2012.

Vol. 35 Irene Lucchitti: Peig Sayers: In Her Own Write
ISBN 978-3-0343-0253-1. Forthcoming.

Vol. 36 Eamon Maher and Eugene O'Brien (eds): Breaking the Mould: Literary Representations of Irish Catholicism
ISBN 978-3-0343-0232-6. 249 pages. 2011.

Vol. 37 Mícheál Ó hAodha and John O'Callaghan (eds): Narratives of the Occluded Irish Diaspora: Subversive Voices
ISBN 978-3-0343-0248-7. 227 pages. 2012.

Vol. 38	Willy Maley and Alison O'Malley-Younger (eds): Celtic Connections: Irish–Scottish Relations and the Politics of Culture ISBN 978-3-0343-0214-2. 247 pages. 2013.
Vol. 39	Sabine Egger and John McDonagh (eds): Polish–Irish Encounters in the Old and New Europe ISBN 978-3-0343-0253-1. 322 pages. 2011.
Vol. 40	Elke D'hoker, Raphaël Ingelbien and Hedwig Schwall (eds): Irish Women Writers: New Critical Perspectives ISBN 978-3-0343-0249-4. 318 pages. 2011.
Vol. 41	Peter James Harris: From Stage to Page: Critical Reception of Irish Plays in the London Theatre, 1925–1996 ISBN 978-3-0343-0266-1. 311 pages. 2011.
Vol. 42	Hedda Friberg-Harnesk, Gerald Porter and Joakim Wrethed (eds): Beyond Ireland: Encounters Across Cultures ISBN 978-3-0343-0270-8. 342 pages. 2011.
Vol. 43	Irene Gilsenan Nordin and Carmen Zamorano Llena (eds): Urban and Rural Landscapes in Modern Ireland: Language, Literature and Culture ISBN 978-3-0343-0279-1. 238 pages. 2012.
Vol. 44	Kathleen Costello-Sullivan: Mother/Country: Politics of the Personal in the Fiction of Colm Tóibín ISBN 978-3-0343-0753-6. 247 pages. 2012.
Vol. 45	Lesley Lelourec and Gráinne O'Keeffe-Vigneron (eds): Ireland and Victims: Confronting the Past, Forging the Future ISBN 978-3-0343-0792-5. 331 pages. 2012.
Vol. 46	Gerald Dawe, Darryl Jones and Nora Pelizzari (eds): Beautiful Strangers: Ireland and the World of the 1950s ISBN 978-3-0343-0801-4. 207 pages. 2013.
Vol. 47	Yvonne O'Keeffe and Claudia Reese (eds): New Voices, Inherited Lines: Literary and Cultural Representations of the Irish Family ISBN 978-3-0343-0799-4. 238 pages. 2013.

Vol. 48	Justin Carville (ed.): Visualizing Dublin: Visual Culture, Modernity and the Representation of Urban Space ISBN 978-3-0343-0802-1. 326 pages. 2014.
Vol. 49	Gerald Power and Ondřej Pilný (eds): Ireland and the Czech Lands: Contacts and Comparisons in History and Culture ISBN 978-3-0343-1701-6. 243 pages. 2014.
Vol. 50	Eoghan Smith: John Banville: Art and Authenticity ISBN 978-3-0343-0852-6. 199 pages. 2014.
Vol. 51	María Elena Jaime de Pablos and Mary Pierse (eds): George Moore and the Quirks of Human Nature ISBN 978-3-0343-1752-8. 283 pages. 2014.
Vol. 52	Aidan O'Malley and Eve Patten (eds): Ireland, West to East: Irish Cultural Connections with Central and Eastern Europe ISBN 978-3-0343-0913-4. 307 pages. 2014.
Vol. 53	Ruben Moi, Brynhildur Boyce and Charles I. Armstrong (eds): The Crossings of Art in Ireland ISBN 978-3-0343-0983-7. 319 pages. 2014.
Vol. 54	Sylvie Mikowski (ed.): Ireland and Popular Culture ISBN 978-3-0343-1717-7. 257 pages. 2014.
Vol. 55	Benjamin Keatinge and Mary Pierse (eds): France and Ireland in the Public Imagination ISBN 978-3-0343-1747-4. 279 pages. 2014.
Vol. 56	Raymond Mullen, Adam Bargroff and Jennifer Mullen (eds): John McGahern: Critical Essays ISBN 978-3-0343-1755-9. 253 pages. 2014.
Vol. 57	Máirtín Mac Con Iomaire and Eamon Maher (eds): 'Tickling the Palate': Gastronomy in Irish Literature and Culture ISBN 978-3-0343-1769-6. 253 pages. 2014.
Vol. 58	Heidi Hansson and James H. Murphy (eds): Fictions of the Irish Land War ISBN 978-3-0343-0999-8. 237 pages. 2014.

Vol. 59   Fiona McCann: A Poetics of Dissensus: Confronting Violence in
               Contemporary Prose Writing from the North of Ireland
               ISBN 978-3-0343-0979-0. 238 pages. 2014.

Vol. 60   Marguérite Corporaal, Christopher Cusack, Lindsay Janssen and
               Ruud van den Beuken (eds): Global Legacies of the Great Irish
               Famine: Transnational and Interdisciplinary Perspectives
               ISBN 978-3-0343-0903-5. 357 pages. 2014.

Vol. 61   Katarzyna Ojrzyn'ska: 'Dancing As If Language No Longer
               Existed': Dance in Contemporary Irish Drama
               ISBN 978-3-0343-1813-6. 318 pages. 2015.

Vol. 62   Whitney Standlee: 'Power to Observe': Irish Women Novelists in
               Britain, 1890–1916
               ISBN 978-3-0343-1837-2. 288 pages. 2015.

Vol. 63   Elke D'hoker and Stephanie Eggermont (eds): The Irish Short
               Story: Traditions and Trends
               ISBN 978-3-0343-1753-5. 330 pages. 2015.

Vol. 64   Radvan Markus: Echoes of the Rebellion: The Year 1798 in Twentieth-
               Century Irish Fiction and Drama
               ISBN 978-3-0343-1832-7. 248 pages. 2015.

Vol. 65   B. Mairéad Pratschke: Visions of Ireland: Gael Linn's *Amharc Éireann*
               Film Series, 1956–1964
               ISBN 978-3-0343-1872-3. 301 pages. 2015.

Vol. 66   Una Hunt and Mary Pierse (eds): France and Ireland: Notes and
               Narratives
               ISBN 978-3-0343-1914-0. 272 pages. 2015.

Vol. 67   John Lynch and Katherina Dodou (eds): The Leaving of
               Ireland: Migration and Belonging in Irish Literature and Film
               ISBN 978-3-0343-1896-9. 313 pages. 2015.

Vol. 68   Anne Goarzin (ed.): New Critical Perspectives on Franco-Irish
               Relations
               ISBN 978-3-0343-1781-8. 271 pages. 2015.

Vol. 69	Michel Brunet, Fabienne Gaspari and Mary Pierse (eds): George Moore's Paris and His Ongoing French Connections ISBN 978-3-0343-1973-7. 279 pages. 2015.
Vol. 70	Carine Berbéri and Martine Pelletier (eds): Ireland: Authority and Crisis ISBN 978-3-0343-1939-3. 296 pages. 2015.
Vol. 71	David Doolin: Transnational Revolutionaries: The Fenian Invasion of Canada, 1866 ISBN 978-3-0343-1922-5. 348 pages. 2016.
Vol. 72	Terry Phillips: Irish Literature and the First World War: Culture, Identity and Memory ISBN 978-3-0343-1969-0. 297 pages. 2015.
Vol. 73	Carmen Zamorano Llena and Billy Gray (eds): Authority and Wisdom in the New Ireland: Studies in Literature and Culture ISBN 978-3-0343-1833-4. 263 pages. 2016.
Vol. 74	Flore Coulouma (ed.): New Perspectives on Irish TV Series: Identity and Nostalgia on the Small Screen ISBN 978-3-0343-1977-5. 222 pages. 2016.
Vol. 75	Fergal Lenehan: Stereotypes, Ideology and Foreign Correspondents: German Media Representations of Ireland, 1946–2010 ISBN 978-3-0343-2222-5. 306 pages. 2016.
Vol. 76	Jarlath Killeen and Valeria Cavalli (eds): 'Inspiring a Mysterious Terror': 200 Years of Joseph Sheridan Le Fanu ISBN 978-3-0343-2223-2. 260 pages. 2016.
Vol. 77	Anne Karhio: 'Slight Return': Paul Muldoon's Poetics of Place ISBN 978-3-0343-1986-7. 272 pages. 2017.
Vol. 78	Margaret Eaton: Frank Confessions: Performance in the Life-Writings of Frank McCourt ISBN 978-1-906165-61-1. 294 pages. 2017.

Vol. 79   Marguérite Corporaal, Christopher Cusack and Ruud van den Beuken (eds): Irish Studies and the Dynamics of Memory: Transitions and Transformations
ISBN 978-3-0343-2236-2. 360 pages. 2017.

Vol. 80   Conor Caldwell and Eamon Byers (eds): New Crops, Old Fields: Reimagining Irish Folklore
ISBN 978-3-0343-1912-6. 200 pages. 2017.

Vol. 81   Sinéad Wall: Irish Diasporic Narratives in Argentina: A Reconsideration of Home, Identity and Belonging
ISBN 978-1-906165-66-6. 282 pages. 2017.

Vol. 82   Ute Anna Mittermaier: Images of Spain in Irish Literature, 1922–1975
ISBN 978-3-0343-1993-5. 386 pages. 2017.

Vol. 83   Lauren Clark: Consuming Irish Children: Advertising and the Art of Independence, 1860–1921
ISBN 978-3-0343-1989-8. 288 pages. 2017.

Vol. 84   Lisa FitzGerald: Re-Place: Irish Theatre Environments
ISBN 978-1-78707-359-3. 222 pages. 2017.

Vol. 85   Joseph Greenwood: 'Hear My Song': Irish Theatre and Popular Song in the 1950s and 1960s
ISBN 978-3-0343-1915-7. 320 pages. 2017.

Vol. 86   Nils Beese: Writing Slums: Dublin, Dirt and Literature
ISBN 978-1-78707-959-5. 250 pages. 2018.

Vol. 87   Barry Houlihan (ed.): Navigating Ireland's Theatre Archive: Theory, Practice, Performance
ISBN 978-1-78707-372-2. 306 pages. 2019.

Vol. 88   María Elena Jaime de Pablos (ed.): Giving Shape to the Moment: The Art of Mary O'Donnell: Poet, Novelist and Short Story Writer
ISBN 978-1-78874-403-4. 228 pages. 2018.

Vol. 89	Marguérite Corporaal and Peter Gray (eds): The Great Irish Famine and Social Class: Conflicts, Responsibilities, Representations ISBN 978-1-78874-166-8. 330 pages. 2019.
Vol. 90	Patrick Speight: Irish-Argentine Identity in an Age of Political Challenge and Change, 1875–1983 ISBN 978-1-78874-417-1. 360 pages. 2020.
Vol. 91	Fionna Barber, Heidi Hansson, and Sara Dybris McQuaid (eds): Ireland and the North ISBN 978-1-78874-289-4. 338 pages. 2019.
Vol. 92	Ruth Sheehy: The Life and Work of Richard King: Religion, Nationalism and Modernism ISBN 978-1-78707-246-6. 482 pages. 2019.
Vol. 93	Brian Lucey, Eamon Maher and Eugene O'Brien (eds): Recalling the Celtic Tiger ISBN 978-1-78997-286-3. 386 pages. 2019.
Vol. 94	Melania Terrazas Gallego (ed.): Trauma and Identity in Contemporary Irish Culture ISBN 978-1-78997-557-4. 302 pages. 2020.
Vol. 95	Patricia Medcalf: Advertising the Black Stuff in Ireland 1959–1999: Increments of Change ISBN 978-1-78997-345-7. 218 pages. 2020.
Vol. 96	Anne Goarzin and Maria Parsons (eds): New Cartographies, Nomadic Methologies: Contemporary Arts, Culture and Politics in Ireland ISBN 978-1-78874-651-9. 204 pages. 2020.
Vol. 97	Hiroko Ikeda and Kazuo Yokouchi (eds): Irish Literature in the British Context and Beyond: New Perspectives from Kyoto ISBN 978-1-78997-566-6. 250 pages. 2020.
Vol. 98	Catherine Nealy Judd: Travel Narratives of the Irish Famine: Politics, Tourism, and Scandal, 1845–1853 ISBN 978-1-80079-084-1. 468 pages. 2020.

Vol. 99　Lesley Lelourec and Gráinne O'Keeffe-Vigneron (eds): Northern Ireland after the Good Friday Agreement: Building a Shared Future from a Troubled Past?
ISBN 978-1-78997-746-2. 262 pages. 2021.

Vol. 100　Eamon Maher and Eugene O'Brien (eds): Reimagining Irish Studies for the Twenty-First Century
ISBN 978-1-80079-191-6. 384 pages. 2021.

Vol. 101　Nathalie Sebbane: Memorialising the Magdalene Laundries: From Story to History
ISBN 978-1-78707-589-4. 334 pages. 2021.

Vol 102　Roz Goldie: A Dangerous Pursuit: The Anti-Sectarian Work of Counteract
ISBN 978-1-80079-187-9. 268 pages. 2021.

Vol. 103　Ann Wilson: The Picture Postcard: A New Window into Edwardian Ireland
ISBN 978-1-78874-079-1. 282 pages. 2021.

Vol. 104　Anna Charczun: Irish Lesbian Writing Across Time: A New Framework for Rethinking Love Between Women
ISBN 978-1-78997-864-3. 320 pages. 2022.

Vol. 105　Olivier Coquelin, Brigitte Bastiat and Frank Healy (eds): Northern Ireland: Challenges of Peace and Reconciliation Since the Good Friday Agreement
ISBN 978-1-78997-817-9. 298 pages. 2022.

Vol. 106　Jo Murphy-Lawless and Laury Oaks (eds): The Salley Gardens: Women, Sex, and Motherhood in Ireland
ISBN 978-1-80079-417-7. 338 pages. 2022.

Vol. 107　Mercedes del Campo: Voices from the Margins: Gender and the Everyday in Women's Pre- and Post-Agreement Troubles Short Fiction
ISBN 978-1-78874-330-3. 324 pages. 2022.

Vol. 108　Sean McGraw and Jonathan Tiernan: The Politics of Irish Primary Education: Reform in an Era of Secularisation
ISBN 978-1-80079-709-3. 532 pages. 2022.

Vol. 109   Gerald Dawe: Northern Windows/Southern Stars: Selected Early
          Essays 1983–1994
          ISBN 978-1-80079-652-2. 180 pages. 2022.

Vol. 110   John Fanning: The Mandarin, the Musician and the Mage:
          T. K. Whitaker, Seán Ó Riada, Thomas Kinsella and the Lessons of
          Ireland's Mid-Twentieth-Century Revival
          ISBN 978-1-80079-599-0. 296 pages. 2022.

Lightning Source UK Ltd.
Milton Keynes UK
UKHW021252261022
411126UK00001B/1

ERRATA

CORRECTIONS TO INDEX

FLOWER	PRINTED PAGE NUMBER	CORRECT PAGE NUMBER
American Brooklime	142	143
Aster, Hairy Golden	162	172
Brooklime, American	142	143
Buttercup, Shore	212	213
Campion, Bladder	272	273
Campion, Menzies	270	271
Campion, Parry's	271	272
Campion, White	269	270
Columbine, Sitka	210	212
Columbine, Western	210	212
Cusick's Speedwell	146	144
Fleabane, Showy	88	90
Fleabane, Subalpine	90	88
Forget-me-not, Mountain	98	97
Forget-me-not, Small-leaved	99	98
Leafy Lousewort	33	353
Mountain Forget-me-not	98	97
Nightcap, Granny's	212	211
Northern Bedstraw	142	342
Pepper and Salt	233	245
Primrose, Mealy	62	63
Primrose, Yellow Evening	204	205
Rhus radicans	240	242
Satinflower	40	41
Sierra Sanicle	150	152
Slipper, Golden	186	207
Speedwell, American	142	143
Speedwell, Cusick's	143	144
White Meadowsweet	345	341

OTHER CORRECTIONS

Grant information, p. 4: Miss B.E. Adams; Dr. D. Jones
Acknowledgments, p. 6: l. 3, Emerita
p. 14, 2 ll. from bottom: families
Glossary: Pistil—style and stigma
        Penanth—should be Perianth